Jefferson and the Arts: an Extended View

Jefferson and the Arts: an Extended View

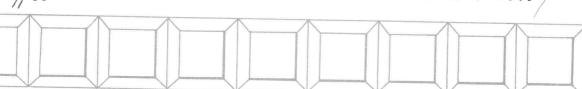

Edited and with introductions by William Howard Adams.

The Life Portraits of Thomas Jefferson
ALFRED L. BUSH

Jefferson as Art Collector
HAROLD E. DICKSON

Jefferson and Adams' English Garden Tour
EDWARD DUMBAULD

Jefferson: The Making of an Architect
FREDERICK DOVETON NICHOLS

Thomas Jefferson and the Planning of the National Capitol
PAUL F. NORTON

A Peep into Elysium
GEORGE GREEN SHACKELFORD

Jefferson and French Eighteenth-Century Furniture
SIR FRANCIS WATSON

NATIONAL GALLERY OF ART, WASHINGTON:1976.

Library of Congress Cataloging in Publication Data
Main entry under title:
Jefferson and the Arts: an Extended View
Each essay has special t.p.
Includes bibliographical references.
Contents: Bush, A. L. The life portraits of Thomas Jefferson.—Dickson, H. E. Jefferson as art collector.—Dumbauld, E. Jefferson and Adams' English garden tour.—Nichols, F. D. Jefferson, the making of an architect. [etc.]
Supt. of Docs. no: SI 8.2:J35/3
1. Jefferson, Thomas, Pres. U.S., 1743-1826—Addresses, essays, lectures. I. United States. National Gallery of Art.
E332.2.T46   973.4'6'0924   76-608152

Frontispiece: *Thomas Jefferson,* Benjamin Henry Latrobe (?), Maryland Historical Society

Contents

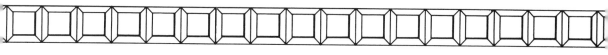

Introduction

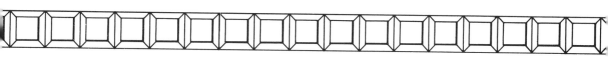

The vitality of Jefferson's life and the scope of his vision and intellectual curiosity have produced a rising tide of books. Still, his role as artist, connoisseur and patron of the arts is by no means an exhausted subject, for even a complete catalogue raisonné of his architectural drawings has yet to appear.

Early in the preparation of the National Gallery of Art's The Eye of Thomas Jefferson, it became clear that the limitations imposed by the works of art that were selected for exhibition left out the rich details that were beyond the scope of our efforts. For instance, important aspects of Jefferson's European education, through his travel and his sightseeing, could only be hinted at through contemporary drawings and engravings. The complicated and revealing relationship between him and Latrobe in the building of the national Capitol could not be placed in its full narrative context. His often confused and haphazard efforts in putting together one of the first art collections in an almost artless country is a subject too important for an appendix to a catalogue.

Among the many possibilities which were suggested for the present collection, there was the important monograph of Jefferson's life portraiture by Alfred Bush that had sadly passed out of print. Surely the occasion of a birthday party could produce the means to bring it back, revised and refurbished, since only a few of the portraits would be actually documented in the context of the National Gallery's exhibition.

My original intent was to issue each of these special essays and the catalogue of life portraits as separate pamphlets at the time of the exhibition.

However, though the decision was made to bind the essays as one, I still felt *that each of the essays is unique enough to deserve its own prefatory note—to preserve the sense of individuality within a unifying whole—a wholly Jeffersonian concept. To each who has contributed to this volume, let me here express my profound gratitude.*

WILLIAM HOWARD ADAMS

The Life Portraits of Thomas Jefferson

ALFRED L. BUSH

The Life Portraits of Thomas Jefferson

*Those nine life portraits that are known only through subsequent
reproductions are designated here by italics.*

Introduction

EVERY APRIL THE UNIVERSITY OF VIRGINIA AND THE THOMAS JEFFERSON
Memorial Foundation join in the observance of Thomas Jefferson's birthday.
The year 1962 will especially be remembered because of the exhibition of
life portraits of Thomas Jefferson held at the University of Virginia Museum
of Fine Arts from April 12 through 26, which was the most remarkable
assemblage of such likenesses thus far achieved.

The first attempt to bring Jefferson portraits together occurred in Philadelphia in 1889, during the celebration of the centennial of President Washington's inauguration; this led to Charles Henry Hart's study of Jefferson
portraiture. In honor of the dedication of the Jefferson Memorial in Washington, which took place upon his two hundredth birthday, April 13, 1943,
the National Gallery of Art opened an exhibition that included fourteen
portraits of Jefferson by ten artists. Based upon these, Fiske Kimball prepared his study, "The Life Portraits of Jefferson and Their Replicas," published in *Proceedings of the American Philosophical Society* the following
year.

In succeeding years Jeffersonian studies advanced through the documentation assembled at Princeton by Julian P. Boyd for his monumental edition of
The Papers of Thomas Jefferson. The 1962 Charlottesville exhibition
dramatically evidenced this progress. Through the generosity of many institutions and individuals, all but four of the extant life portraits of Thomas
Jefferson were brought together for a fortnight, providing an extraordinary
opportunity for on-the-spot comparative study of works of art ordinarily
widely scattered. The idea of the exhibition came from James A. Bear, Jr.,
then curator (now resident director) of the Thomas Jefferson Memorial
Foundation, who carried out the arrangements for assembling the likenesses.

Alfred L. Bush, then assistant editor of *The Papers of Thomas Jefferson,* prepared the catalogue, here reprinted and revised.

This catalogue described no less than twenty-six portraits, done from life by twenty-three artists between 1786 and 1825. The earliest portrait by Mather Brown was painted in London while Jefferson was minister to France; it is an elegant and appealing portrait of a man in his forties. The latest portrait is the life mask by John Henri Isaac Browere, showing the venerable octogenarian less than a year before his death. Although no youthful likenesses are known, the catalogue comprises an extraordinary record of Jefferson's appearance, during his public career and retirement, by Houdon, John Trumbull, Charles Willson Peale, Rembrandt Peale, Gilbert Stuart, Févret de Saint-Mémin, and Thomas Sully, as well as other practitioners of lesser skill. Some share a degree of sublimity; others are downright ridiculous. The admirably intentioned likeness of Jefferson wearing a laurel wreath (fig. 9) suggests that Tadeusz Kosciuszko was an abler soldier than portraitist. Similarly Amos Doolittle's effort (fig. 15) is stronger on good intentions than ability.

Two works clearly dominated the 1962 exhibition: the marble bust of 1789 by Houdon and the first oil portrait of 1800 by Rembrandt Peale. The former had long been known; the latter had only recently been discovered. Houdon had exhibited a plaster of the bust in the Salon of 1789. In 1804 Louis Boilly executed several paintings of Houdon at work in his studio where the cast of the Jefferson bust can clearly be seen on a shelf. Plaster versions of good quality from the sculptor's hand had been in the American Philosophical Society since 1811 and in the New-York Historical Society since 1839. The Saravezza marble bust, inscribed "houdon f 1789," which was shown at Charlottesville, had been conspicuously exhibited at the Museum of Fine Arts, Boston, since 1934. Although the Rembrandt Peale portrait of 1800 had long been known through nineteenth-century engravings, lithographs, and oil copies, the original for which Jefferson sat was long thought to be lost. Hart and Kimball had searched for it without success.

Studies undertaken in 1959 by Julian P. Boyd and his editorial staff of *The Papers of Thomas Jefferson* led to the conclusion that the 1800 Rembrandt Peale portrait had not been lost, but had simply been lurking, unappreciated, since 1893 in the Peabody Institute of the city of Baltimore. When the picture was examined and cleaned, the original surface was found to be so intact that virtually no in-painting was required.

Through the kindness of its owners, the restored Peale portrait was brought to Monticello to be exhibited at a dinner given on April 11, 1960, by the Thomas Jefferson Memorial Foundation. The dinner was held in honor of the Honorable Adlai E. Stevenson, the speaker at the University of Virginia's Founder's Day ceremonies, and of nine Jefferson Fellows at the university. Mrs. Helen Duprey Bullock, then editor for the National Trust for Historic Preservation, a Jefferson scholar who applies rigorous archival standards to cookery, planned a meal with dishes and wines that were once familiar at Monticello. It was the first dinner of Jeffersonian inspiration to be served in the Monticello dining room since the departure of the family in 1829. It proved so happy an occasion that the Thomas Jefferson Memorial Foundation has held a similar gathering on each subsequent birthday to honor the university's Founder's Day speaker. The 1960 evening remains unique, however, because of the temporary presence of the Peale portrait, which was unveiled by Mr. Boyd after dinner.

The portrait was then shown from April 12 to May 13, 1960, at the University of Virginia Museum of Fine Arts in an exhibition "The Monticello Family" that the foundation had assembled. It returned again from Baltimore to Charlottesville for the 1962 exhibition, and later in that year it was acquired by the Fine Arts Committee of the White House with funds provided for that purpose by Mr. and Mrs. Paul Mellon.

As *The Life Portraits of Thomas Jefferson* has long been out of print, the Thomas Jefferson Memorial Foundation welcomed the proposal to reprint it with revisions as one of the National Gallery of Art's publications connected with its Bicentennial exhibition, *The Eye of Thomas Jefferson,* where nine of the life portraits are to be shown. In the introduction to the National Gallery exhibition the visitor sees the Houdon bust of 1789, and the full-length portrait by Thomas Sully. The latter, painted in 1822 for the United States Military Academy, West Point, grew out of a painting that Sully had done from life at Monticello the previous year. In the part of the exhibition entitled Our Revolution is John Trumbull's *Declaration of Independence,* in which the document's author appears in the company of his political colleagues. In the Progress of the Human Mind, one finds the Saint-Mémin crayon portrait of Jefferson, done in November 1804 while Lewis and Clark were at his behest wintering in the Mandan villages of North Dakota. In Europe: The Vaunted Scene appears the engraving that Gilles-Louis Chrétien engraved in Paris in April 1789 from the lost physiognotrace drawing of Jefferson by Edmé Quenedey, while in Jefferson, Tourist are included the oil by Mather Brown, done during a visit to London, and the miniature that John Trumbull painted for Maria Cosway. The latter, which was only discovered in 1952, is for the first time seen outside the Italian convent founded by Maria Cosway at Lodi. Finally in The Jeffersonian Creation there are two portraits: the pencil sketch of 1799, from the papers of Benjamin Henry

Latrobe, and the so-called Edgehill portrait, painted in Gilbert Stuart's Washington studio in the late spring of 1805.

WALTER MUIR WHITEHILL

This profile is based on the 1809 stipple engraving by David Edwin which was engraved from a drawing by William Russell Birch which was, in turn, drawn from the original of Gilbert Stuart's medallion profile of Jefferson. After Birch made his "correct drawing" of Stuart's medallion profile in October of 1805, he "thought of engraving it ... but found {he} could not equal Mr. Edwin in it, got him to do it, took off a few impressions and sent {them to Jefferson} intending to rebite the plate to make it more lasting but spoilt the plate in attempt to rebite." These "few impressions," regarded by Jefferson as "an elegant speciment of Mr. Edwin's talent," bear the inscription "Jefferson. G. Stuart pinx W. Birch delin. D. Edwin sc. 1809 Copy Right secured according to law," and were engraved, according to Birch who assured Jefferson that his "purpose is to give them away for "no other purpose then that a proper Likeness ... may be circulated." When Jefferson presented one of them to his friend Horatio Gates Spafford in 1815, he described it as "a profile, engraved by Edwin from the original drawn by Stewart, and deemed the best which has been taken of me."

Foreword

MORE DISCRIMINATING AND DISTINGUISHED BEHOLDERS WERE NOT TO BE found than those who looked up from the misspelled catalogue entry under Houdon's name into the plaster visage of Jefferson in the late summer of 1789 in Paris and viewed the American envoy's first portrait to be honored with public exhibition. It was an imposing debut. Depicted by the greatest portraitist of his time, surrounded by the landscapes of Hubert Robert and the classical allegories of David and scrutinized by an intelligent public, Jefferson, with Houdon, emerged from the honors of the Royal Salon to continue their pursuit of the elevated objectives implicit within this remarkable portrait.

Perhaps because their creations were often received under less imposing circumstances and appreciated for less inherent reasons, Jefferson's subsequent portraitists in America were impelled to devote their talents to immortalizing "America's Distinguished Characters" in paint and pastel and plaster. A Gallery of American Worthies became the mandatory enterprise of the more ambitious of America's artists; and the inclusion of a *Jefferson,* imperative. And while the assemblies of the portraits of distinguished Americans too frequently reflected not so much the artist's recognition of his public responsibility as it did the promotion of his private interest, the imposing accomplishments of his subjects seldom allowed the portraitist to forget his obligation to history.

Appropriately the task of creating Jefferson's final portrait fell to an artist who subordinated a desire for the public's immediate acclaim to an uncompromising regard for historical authenticity. It was Browere who recorded Jefferson's countenance for the last time before Jefferson "bid adieu forever to busts and even portraits" and, within a year, to life itself. Ironically

Browere's likeness began its public life by being unveiled on the very hour of Jefferson's death, during the celebration of the semicentennial of the Declaration of Independence. But as Jefferson and his portraitists passed into the realms of history, the full magnitude of their historic accomplishments was itself obscured. It was not, in fact, to be generally brought into focus until the commemoration of later anniversaries placed it at a proper distance and brought it pointedly to the public's attention. In the celebration for the centennial of the Declaration of Independence and, most especially, the centennial of the inauguration of Washington, America's imagination was turned to its own past, and its eyes to the portraits of that past's most significant participants. In 1889 during the vast exhibition generated by the second of these centennials, Jefferson's portraits were gathered for the first time to receive the attention of the public and the exploratory study of scholars. Within a decade Charles Henry Hart made public the earliest ordering of the canon of Jefferson portraiture.

But it was an even later anniversary celebration — the bicentennial of Jefferson's birth — that was to catch the attention of a scholar and Jefferson admirer whose knowledge of Jefferson and whose capability in the analysis of iconographic materials enabled him to use that exhibition as the starting point for a study of such care and authority that all subsequent students of Jefferson's likenesses must remain massively in his debt. It was the exceptional good fortune of Jefferson iconography to have had Fiske Kimball build, from the elements set out by Charles Henry Hart, a foundation from which all further study could proceed solidly.

The 1943 exhibition, held at the National Gallery during the bicentennial of Jefferson's birth, assembled fourteen portraits representing ten distinct likenesses of Jefferson. The 1962 exhibition under the sponsorship of the Thomas Jefferson Memorial Foundation at the University of Virginia Museum of Fine Arts included twenty-four separate life likenesses of Jefferson.

On the following pages the essential information on each of Jefferson's life portraits is listed systematically with seven descriptive elements isolated to make reference and comparison convenient. The focus of the description in every instance is the life portrait, whether now extant or lost.

The dimensions of the portraits described here follow Stauffer in being expressed in inches and sixteenths of an inch. Thus 20.3 x 10.12 inches signifies 20 3/16 x 10¾ inches. When the original of the portraits reproduced on these pages is smaller than the format of this catalogue, it is reproduced at exact size.

The references noted at the end of the entry for each portrait cite only those sources which document the preceding statements and are most pertinent to the specific portrait. It should be assumed that the further sources for each artist listed in George C. Groce and David H. Wallace, *The New-York Historical Society's Dictionary of Artists in America,* New Haven, 1957, were also consulted and are frequently relied upon for the context of these entries. Another source of information on each of these likenesses which I have not always cited but have invariably consulted and found useful is the files of the Frick Art Reference Library. The prints that are noted individually here are identified, when possible, by their numerical designation in David M. Stauffer, *American Engravers Upon Copper and Steel,* New York, 1907. A few European prints are noted by their number in Stanislaus V. Henkels, *The* [Carson] . . . *Collection of Engraved Portraits of Thomas Jefferson . . . ,* Philadelphia, n.d. The following four works are cited so frequently that short titles have been employed:

Bowen: Clarence W. Bowen, ed., *The History of the Centennial Celebration of the Inauguration of George Washington* (New York, 1892).

Hart: Charles Henry Hart, "The Life Portraits of Thomas Jefferson," *McClure's Magazine, 11,* no. 1 (May 1898), 47-55.

Kimball: Fiske Kimball, "The Life Portraits of Jefferson and Their Replicas," *Proceedings of The American Philosophical Society,* 88 (1944), 497-534.

Boyd: Julian P. Boyd, ed., *The Papers of Thomas Jefferson* (Princeton, 1950-)

While every effort has been made to make this catalogue a definitive one, it is emphatically hoped that this claim will soon prove unwarranted, for few prospects are more pleasant to the student of Jefferson than the discovery of further portraits deserving a place among the company of Jefferson's life likenesses. One of the foremost objectives of this publication has been the stimulation of an informed interest in Jefferson's portraits that might make possible the recognition of further life likenesses as yet unidentified in public or private collections.

It is hoped that this gathering of Jefferson's portraits will suggest in a cumulative and memorable way what was the invariable objective of each of their creators: an authentic and penetrating portrayal of the man in whose presence each of these likenesses was created.

The Adams replica of the lost life portrait of Jefferson painted in London in 1786 by Mather Brown.
Mr. Charles Francis Adams of Dover, Massachusetts

The Life Portraits of Thomas Jefferson

ALFRED L. BUSH

1. The Portrait by Mather Brown

Whereabouts unknown

MEDIUM: John Adams' commission for a duplicate of this lost painting and Trumbull's difficulty in distinguishing correctly between the Adams replica and the life portrait indicate that not only in content, but also in medium, the original painting was duplicated in the extant replica: that it was an oil on canvas, measuring approximately 36 x 28 inches.

AUTHORSHIP: Presumably the life portrait bore an inscription identical to that still legible on the face of the Adams replica: *M Brown pt 1786.* This inscription, the artist's receipt on the reverse of the replica, Jefferson's entry in his accounts for payment to Brown for the portrait, and the report in the *New-York Packet* of October 19, 1786, of the portrait's presence in Brown's studio, are only four of many contemporary documents which indisputably establish Brown's authorship of this likeness. Trumbull doubted that the painting destined for Jefferson, which he saw in Brown's painting rooms in the spring of 1788, was the life portrait, but the artist's agreement "that the original should be" Jefferson's, and the difference in the size of payments made by Adams and Jefferson, indicate that the latter did receive the original canvas.

CHRONOLOGY: The missing life portrait was painted at Mather Brown's London studio in Cavendish Square sometime between Jefferson's arrival in London on March 11, 1786, and his departure on the 26th of the following month. The final sitting, in fact, may well have taken place the day before Jefferson set out for France when he made his payment of ten pounds to

Brown for the painting. The portrait depicts Jefferson at forty-three as America's minister plenipotentiary at the court of Versailles, "the engaging and intelligent favorite of the Paris salons." Brown, though in his sixth year of painting in England and among the more fashionable of London's portraitists, was himself a young American of only twenty-four years of age.

HISTORY: Painted on Jefferson's commission, the portrait remained in Brown's studio for more than two years awaiting the completion of the portrait of Adams which was to accompany it. Trumbull saw the painting in the artist's rooms in the spring of 1788 and at Jefferson's request supervised its shipment to Paris late that summer. Carefully packed with other paintings purchased by Jefferson, it left London on August 16, 1788, and Jefferson acknowledged receiving the "pictures in good condition" on September 10. Nothing of the portrait's subsequent history is known.

CONDITION: The life portrait is thought to have been destroyed in Jefferson's lifetime. Kimball suggested that it may have been part of the baggage that was looted and thrown into the James River when Jefferson retired from the presidency or that it was among the possessions which Jefferson had given to his granddaughter, Ellen Wayles Coolidge, which were subsequently lost at sea.

ICONOGRAPHIC IMPORTANCE: The opinion which Trumbull wrote Jefferson in March 1788 after seeing Brown's portraits of both Adams and Jefferson ("Mr. Adams is like. Yours I do not think so well of.") was one that was apparently shared by a number of Jefferson's friends. William Short reported that while the "picture by Brown of Mr. Adams is an excellent likeness; that of Mr. Jefferson is supposed by every body here to be an étude. It has no feature like him." It was undoubtedly because of this inadequacy that Mather Brown's portrait came to play only a peripheral role in shaping the public image of Jefferson. Even in more recent times, with the original canvas lost and the replica in private hands, it has never been widely known. Apart from its failure as a characteristic portrayal of its subject, the portrait is admired now, as Short's description of it as an "étude" suggests it was in his time, as one of the most attractive of Brown's works. It is also the earliest of the identified portraits of Jefferson.

COPIES: The receipt pasted on the reverse of the replica commissioned by John Adams dates its completion to shortly before May 12, 1786. This is the portrait of which Abigail Adams wrote Jefferson the following month, as dignifying a part of the Adams' London residence, and which has descended through the Adams family to its present owner, Mr. Charles Francis Adams of Dover, Massachusetts. The portrait seems not to have been further reproduced until 1860 when Timothy House's engraving of it appeared as frontispiece to George Bancroft's *History of the United States.* A later print, engraved for *Appleton's Cyclopaedia of American Biography* in 1887 by A. B. Hall, copied the Adams replica more faithfully.

REFERENCES: Bowen (1892), p. 486; Hart (1898), p. 49; Kimball (1944), pp. 499–501; Boyd, 1:lvii, facing p. 3, 10:161, 11:169, 12:206, 358, 597, 647, 13:178, 199, 280, 345, 519, 597; William Kelby, *Notes on American Artists* (New York, 1922), p. 29; Massachusetts Historical Society *Proceedings,* 47 (1913), 32–34.

2. *The Portrait by John Trumbull*

Yale University Art Gallery

MEDIUM: Trumbull's life portrait of Jefferson is painted in oil directly onto the canvas of the artist's small *Declaration of Independence* which measures 21.2 x 31.2 inches.

AUTHORSHIP: The importance and fame of the small canvas of the *Declaration of Independence* is such that Trumbull's authorship of it has been a matter of common knowledge not only to his, but to subsequent generations. The existence of three miniature portraits of Jefferson by Trumbull, all obviously related to the *Declaration* likeness, however, has frequently led students to identify one of these miniatures as the life portrait from which the Jefferson in the *Declaration* canvas was painted. Even after the discovery of Trumbull's explicit statement that the life portrait was painted directly onto the "original small Declaration of Independence," Kimball still could not "resist the conclusion that the Church miniature was painted in 1786, a year before the Declaration" — thus identifying it as another, and earlier, portrait from life. But the letter of December 19, 1788, from William Short to Trumbull, which notes that the Church and Cosway miniatures are "each . . . a copy of Mr. Jefferson's picture" and suggests the painting of still another replica for Martha Jefferson, establishes all three of these miniatures as replicas of the portrait painted "from the life" into the original *Declaration of Independence.*

CHRONOLOGY: Despite Trumbull's statement that he painted his portrait of Jefferson in "the autumn of 1787" while in Paris executing portraits of the

A detail of John Trumbull's original Declaration of Independence *showing Jefferson painted from life during the winter of 1787-1788 at Jefferson's Paris residence.* Yale University Art Gallery

French officers for his depiction of the surrender at Yorktown, it was not until late December of that year that Trumbull arrived in France. The portrait, portraying Jefferson at forty-four, was painted in Jefferson's Paris residence, the Hôtel de Langeac, sometime between Trumbull's arrival in Paris on December 19, 1787, and February 16, 1788, when the painter was once again en route for London. Trumbull had written Jefferson in August of 1787 that he supposed "winter the most certain time of meeting" in Paris the French officers whose portraits were to be painted into his *Surrender at Yorktown.* Thus in these two winter months Trumbull, at but thirty-one years of age, painted not only "Mr. Jefferson in the original small Declaration of Independence," but also "Major General Ross in the small sortie from Gibraltar, and the French officers in the Surrender of Lord Cornwallis, At Yorktown" —likenesses, "all painted from the life in Mr. Jefferson's house," which Trumbull regarded "as the best of [his] small portraits."

HISTORY: The painting left Trumbull's hands in 1832 when it came into the possession of Yale College as a result of the indenture of December 19, 1831, in which Trumbull presented this and other paintings to the college in exchange for an annuity of one thousand dollars a year, on the condition that "the said paintings shall never be sold, alienated, divided or dispersed, but shall always be kept together, and exhibited." As part of the "largest and finest collection of the works of the chief recorder of the American Revolution" this portrait was hung in the small neoclassical Trumbull Gallery which opened to the public on the Yale campus on October 25, 1832. The collection was moved in 1868 to Street Hall and again in 1928 to its present quarters in the Yale University Art Gallery.

CONDITION: In the perpetual care of the curatorial staff at Yale, the painting has been preserved in excellent condition.

ICONOGRAPHIC IMPORTANCE: Not only did Trumbull hold this portrait as among "the best of [his] small portraits," but Sizer captioned it unreservedly as the "painter at his best." Working with an eye to historical fidelity, Trumbull, representing Jefferson with unpowdered hair, in the costume of the earlier decade, and towering above his associates, has given us an image of Jefferson that undoubtedly comes remarkably close to depicting him as he appeared at the time of the presentation of his great literary achievement. This conception of the presentation of the Declaration of Independence has come to be the preeminent icon not only of the birth of the nation, but also of Jefferson's imposing position in the early events of the Revolution.

COPIES: The two miniatures painted from the life portrait for Maria Cosway, who asked Jefferson just after Trumbull's return to London early in March to give the painter "leave to make a Coppy" of the portrait, and Angelica Schuyler Church (now, respectively, at the Collegio di Maria SS. Bambina, at Lodi, Italy, and the Metropolitan Museum of Art) were in their hands by July of 1788. The following September William Short, knowing of these two replicas, suggested that Trumbull "do a very clever gallant thing": *"Send a copy of the same to Miss Jefferson."* This replica, modified considerably, was received by Jefferson's daughter in Paris in the last days of 1788. Trumbull also painted replicas of the *Declaration,* and thus of Jefferson, twice. The first, with the figures the size of life, was painted in 1818 and is now in the rotunda of the capitol at Washington. The second, painted in 1832 with figures at half life size, is owned by the Wadsworth Atheneum. The earliest of the numerous prints of the *Declaration* was engraved by Asher B. Durand in 1823.

REFERENCES: Bowen (1892), p. 486; Hart (1898), p. 47; Kimball (1944), pp. 501–505; Theodore Sizer, *The Works of Colonel John Trumbull* (New Haven, 1950), pp. 35, 72–73, pl. 13; Theodore Sizer, ed., *The Autobiography of John Trumbull* (New Haven, 1953), pp. 152, 285–288; Elizabeth Cometti, "Maria Cosway's Rediscovered Miniature of Jefferson," *William and Mary Quarterly,* 3d ser., 9 (1952), 152–155; Boyd, 10:xxix–xxx, 12:358, 405, 603, 645, 14:364–365, 440; Fawn M. Brodie, *Thomas Jefferson, An Intimate History* (New York, 1974), pl. facing p. 192.

3. The Portrait by Edmé Quenedey

Whereabouts unknown

MEDIUM: Quenedey's original life-sized portrait of 1789 was undoubtedly drawn in crayon on paper, as are the few surviving examples of his original physiognotrace delineations. The portrait was begun with the tracing, by means of the physiognotrace, of Jefferson's profile. Into this outline the details of the subject's features were then drawn by the artist. Unlike Saint-Mémin, whose later physiognotrace drawings were sold as finished portraits along with the small engravings made from them, it seems that Quenedey regarded the large drawings only as a preliminary step to the final product: the engraved miniature profiles printed from the copper plate onto which Quenedey's partner, Gilles-Louis Chrétien, transferred the original drawing by means of a pantograph.

The aquatint profile of Jefferson made about 1801 by Edmé Quen-edey from the print engraved in 1789 by Gilles-Louis Chrétien or from this print's ultimate source: the now lost physiognotrace por-trait drawn from life by Edmé Quenedey in crayon on paper on April 23, 1789, in Paris. Yale University Art Gallery

AUTHORSHIP: The only surviving version of this likeness is the print en-graved from it about 1801. The inscription on the one example of this aquatint which survives with a legend indicates that the original was drawn from life by Edmé Quenedey. This identification is confirmed by the inscrip-tions on the engravings produced in 1789 by the Quenedey-Chrétien partner-ship, which invariably read (in abbreviated form): "Dessiné par Quenedy, gravé par Chrétien inventeur du physiognotrace."

CHRONOLOGY: Jefferson's account book, Gouverneur Morris' diary and Quenedey's record of ticket holders all show that Jefferson sat for the portrait in Paris at the Quenedey-Chrétien establishment in the Rue Croix des Petits Champs just east of the Palais Royal on April 23, 1789. Six days later Jefferson called for the copper plate upon which Chrétien had engraved Quenedey's delineation, and twelve prints struck from it.

HISTORY: While Jefferson purchased a dozen engravings and the plate from which they were taken, the original drawing apparently remained in the artist's hands, although it is uncertain whether it was purposely preserved by him. It has been plausibly suggested that the drawing may still have been in the artist's possession at the time of Jefferson's election to the presidency and that it was from this that Quenedey then re-engraved the portrait, perhaps with the intention of commercial distribution. It is also possible that this version of the portrait may have been engraved by Quenedey not from the original drawing but from a proof, retained for the artist's collection, of the 1789 Chrétien engraving of the likeness. Not only does there seem to be no record of the large original drawing, other than its delineation, but even more surprisingly, nothing is known of the history of the small copper plate or the twelve examples of the 1789 engraving other than their purchase by Jefferson from the artist.

CONDITION: Since virtually none of Quenedey's large physiognotrace drawings are extant and since he apparently considered them merely a preliminary step in the execution of the engraved miniatures, it seems unlikely that his crayon original of Jefferson has survived.

ICONOGRAPHIC IMPORTANCE: The fact that examples of the engravings of this portrait are not mentioned as enclosures in any of Jefferson's letters to friends in America in the months immediately after their execution and that none are known to survive among the effects of Jefferson's friends in France, suggests that Jefferson was more interested in the mechanical aspects of the physiognotrace than he was pleased with the likeness which resulted from his first contact with it. Very probably because this is the first portrait of an American taken by means of this invention and because it records with exactness the outline of Jefferson's profile, our attention is drawn to this portrait rather than because it may represent a portrayal of insight. Since even the engravings struck about 1801 survive in such rare instances, the portrait, doubtless, had but a limited circulation.

COPIES: Neither the copper plate, engraved by Chrétien, nor any of the twelve prints (almost certainly showing the profile against a circular background) which Jefferson purchased has ever been found. Only three examples of the aquatint, engraved by Quenedey most probably about 1801 (depicting the profile against an irregular oval background), have been located. The Bibliothèque nationale possesses one with, and one without, an inscription; another example of the latter, a proof before letters, is owned by the Yale University Art Gallery.

REFERENCES: Kimball (1944), p. 497; René Hennequin, *Les Portraits au Physionotrace* (Troyes, 1932), pp. 59–60; Howard C. Rice, Jr., "A 'New' Likeness of Thomas Jefferson," *William and Mary Quarterly,* 3rd ser., 6, no. 1 (Jan. 1949), [84–]89; Boyd, 14:xlii-xliv, facing p. 361.

4. *The Portrait by Jean-Antoine Houdon*

Museum of Fine Arts, Boston

MEDIUM: Cut from Saravezza marble, the bust measures 21.4 inches high.

AUTHORSHIP: The marble is inscribed under the left shoulder *houdon f 1789.* The fame of Houdon's likeness, the signatures on the original examples of it, and the unrivaled competence of its sculptor, eliminate any doubt as to its authorship. Since there is no record of a terra cotta of this bust, the original clay maquette modeled by Houdon from life was most probably discarded in the process of making the mold from which at least three plaster examples were cast and finished by Houdon. Two of these, the Williamson example at the New-York Historical Society and the Rittenhouse example at the American Philosophical Society — both publically exhibited for more than a century in their respective institutions — are unquestionably from the hand of Houdon himself and are direct casts from the mold of the original portrait. But a plaster bust was regarded by the sculptor as only a temporary and intermediate stage in the production of a final portrait in some permanent substance such as bronze or marble. Fortunately such a final form of Houdon's *Jefferson,* which Giacometti assumed must have been executed though it was not documented as having been begun or completed and no such marble had surfaced by 1929, came to light about the time of the publication of his authoritative study of Houdon's works. Because of the emergence of this marble from obscurity "at just the same period" that there appeared on the art market a number of other Houdon portraits of American subjects, "some with signatures or dates obviously erroneous, and some of them under

29

The marble bust of Jefferson sculpted in Houdon's studio from an intermediary plaster
example of the portrait modeled from life by Jean-Antoine Houdon sometime before July of 1789 in Paris.
Museum of Fine Arts, Boston

circumstances very difficult to explain," and because "sculptors" considered it uncharacteristic of the work of Houdon's studio, Kimball questioned the genuineness of this marble. Statements of its authenticity by both Giacometti and Souffrice, the identification of the stone as Saravezza marble (that preferred and most used by Houdon), laboratory evidence that the bust is indeed an old one, the positive results of a comparison of this marble with other busts indisputably from Houdon's studio, and an unbroken and verifiable provenance tracing it, if not to Houdon's studio, into hands contemporary with it, seems, however, abundant reason to give this marble a place among the life portraits.

CHRONOLOGY: On July 3, 1789, Jefferson not only acknowledged the receipt of portrait busts from Houdon, but also recorded the payment of 1000 livres to the sculptor for these busts. The purchase included, besides the portraits of other worthies, one or perhaps two or three examples of the *Jefferson*. By the end of the following month another plaster of the bust was on public exhibition at the Salon in 1789. These circumstances indicate that the clay likeness had been completed by the middle of that year, but it can only be assumed that the marble portrait was actually executed not long before Jefferson's purchase of the plaster examples of it. Although the inscribed date on the marble could record only the year of the sitting and not necessarily that of the execution, it suggests that the marble was completed sometime between the Salon of 1789 and the end of the year.

HISTORY: The absence of any record of a payment for the marble in Jefferson's accounts indicates that the tradition that the marble was originally a gift from Jefferson to Destutt de Tracy is not correct. But as Kimball pointed out, after the summer Salon in which the plaster *Jefferson* was exhibited, de Tracy or any of Jefferson's French admirers could have had a marble executed at any time from Houdon's studio. It is recorded that the Boston marble was owned by the comtesse Sarah de Destutt, the daughter-in-law of de Tracy, and that it passed in 1839 into the possession of the related family of Leclercq de Chateauvieux at Melun. A civil paper of 1868 records that the bust was inherited by Ferdinand Leclercq, who sold it in 1928. The bust thereafter passed into the hands of the Marie Sterner Gallery in New York, from which it was purchased in 1934 by the Museum of Fine Arts, Boston.

CONDITION: Except for some few chips broken from the clothing at the front base of the bust, the marble is in superb condition. Its sharply cut lines suggest the full power of Houdon's portrait in a way in which the plasters, by the nature of the medium, cannot.

ICONOGRAPHIC IMPORTANCE: This superb likeness of Jefferson, by the greatest portraitist of his time, has been almost constantly displayed in its many versions in public and private collections since its original exhibition in the Salon of 1789. The high quality of the portrait and its extensive and enduring influence in shaping the public image of Jefferson has suggested, perhaps more than has any other likeness, a visual image which adequately encompasses the range of his accomplishment and the elevated nature of his objectives.

COPIES: At least four examples of the bust may date to the year of its execution. Besides the Boston marble and the plasters at the New-York Historical Society and the American Philosophical Society, the Boilly paintings of Houdon at work record that a bust of Jefferson was still in Houdon's studio as late as 1804, although nothing is known of the subsequent history of the latter nor of any examples of the Houdon kept by Jefferson himself. Two other examples came to light when, in 1963, the French Fine Arts Administration provided an export permit for a plaster acquired by Roy Chalk of Washington but only after another was donated to the French government by Edmond Courty. This bust is now in the collections of the Musées de Blérancourt. Copies in *biscuit de Sèvres* were reproduced commercially by the Manufacture de Sèvres during Houdon's lifetime, and later the bust was copied in America in various media. An engraving by Longacre of the bust was used as the frontispiece of Tucker's 1837 biography of Jefferson. The presidential portrait on the Indian peace medal of 1801 by John Reich was, as Jefferson himself reported, "taken from Houdon's bust." A century after examples of this medal were given by Lewis and Clark to many of the Indians met in the course of their expedition, the Reich medal was used as the basis of the obverse of the Jefferson dollar minted in 1903 to commemorate the centennial of the Louisiana Purchase. Thirty-five years later another medalist, Felix Schlag, also chose the Houdon for the representation of Jefferson in the first design of a United States coin to be selected in open competition: the Jefferson nickel. Since its first issue in 1938, this version of Houdon's portrait has undoubtedly become the most widely circulated of all Jefferson likenesses.

REFERENCES: Bowen (1892), p. 489; Hart (1898), p. 50; Kimball (1944), pp. 505–507; Gilbert Chinard, ed., *Houdon in America* (Washington, 1930); G. Giacometti, *La Vie et l'oeuvre de Houdon* (Paris, 1929); "Portrait Sculpture by Houdon," *Bulletin of the Museum of Fine Arts,* 32, no. 193 (Oct. 1934), 70–74; Thomas Jefferson to Martha Jefferson Randolph, Apr. 2, 1802 in the Jefferson Papers at the Massachusetts Historical Society; correspondence with Mrs. Robin Esch at the Museum of Fine Arts,

Boston; R. S. Yeoman, *A Guide Book of United States Coins* (Racine, 1950), pp. 88–89, 184; Max Terrier, "Le Buste de Thomas Jefferson par Houdon," *Les Amis du Musée de Blérancourt,* 1965, pp. 6–8; Brooke Hindle, *David Rittenhouse* (Princeton, 1964), p. 336.

5. *The Portrait by Giuseppe Ceracchi*
Destroyed

MEDIUM: The marble bust, larger than life, "representing Mr. Jefferson in the Roman costume," which Ceracchi considered the finished form of this portrait, was cut in his studio in Florence from the terra-cotta model that he had sculpted from life. If the bust were characteristic of Ceracchi's work in America, it would have been admired not only as a faithful and lively likeness, but also for its archaeological look as a "romanized" portrait produced in the full maturity of the artist's work.

AUTHORSHIP: That Ceracchi was the author of the colossal bust which stood in Jefferson's lifetime in the hall at Monticello and was destroyed in the 1851 Library of Congress fire has never been doubted. The surviving correspondence between the artist and Jefferson concerning the disposition of the marble and the fame of the bust during the half century of its existence abundantly confirm the correctness of this identification. Since the destruction of the original marble, however, various busts have been erroneously labeled as copies of the destroyed original. Perhaps the earliest of these mistaken identifications is that of Lipscomb and Bergh, who, in their 1903 edition of Jefferson's writings, captioned the mid-nineteenth-century bust by Henry Dmochowski Saunders as by "Ciracchi." In 1944 Kimball, misled by the vagueness of its provenance, identified the plaster bust then at Monticello as a copy of Ceracchi's marble. But this bust is now known to have been "made in the same mould in which was cast the fine, life-size, bronze statue . . . [by] the celebrated David [d'Angers]."

CHRONOLOGY: Jefferson received Ceracchi for the first time on March 2, 1791, in Philadelphia, when the sculptor was almost forty years of age. The terra cotta was modeled sometime shortly after that date, most probably before Jefferson left for New England in May. It is likely that Jefferson sat for Ceracchi in the sculptor's rooms in Mrs. Mary House's famous boarding establishment at Fifth and Market Streets — just a block north of the state

The pencil sketch by Thomas Jefferson Randolph of the destroyed colossal marble bust of Jefferson by Giuseppe Ceracchi which was sculpted from a terra cotta (now lost) modeled from life in Philadelphia not long after March 2, 1791. Ceracchi's portrait is depicted in this sketch supported by a broken column and ornamented pedestal which was presented to Jefferson as such a genuine and generous "remembrance of . . . friendship" that it contrasts ironically with the nature of Ceracchi's gift" which surmounts it. On an August evening in 1789 Jefferson returned to his Paris residence from Versailles to discover "a magnificent pedestal erected" in the hall in his absence. The gift of Mme de Tessé, it came eventually to stand in the hall at Monticello as the base of Ceracchi's colossal marble. After Jefferson's death, in fact, it accompanied that bust to its place in the Library of Congress, where the ensemble was described in 1834 as "a splendid work; the bust is elevated upon the frustrum of a fluted black marble column, based upon a circular pedestal, which is ornamented at the top by a continuous series of cherubs' heads, under a broad band encircling the pedestal, on which is sculptured the twelve signs of the zodiac. . . ." The pedestal bore an inscription which Robert Mills translated to read: "To the Supreme Ruler of the Universe, under whose watchful care the liberties of N. America were finally achieved and under whose tutelage the name of Thomas Jefferson will descend forever blessed to posterity." Like the portrait it supported, the pedestal was destroyed in the Library of Congress fire of 1851 (Boyd, 15:363-364).

house — where Madison also had rooms that year and where Jefferson himself had lived briefly in 1782–1783. Among the most celebrated European sculptors of the day, Ceracchi had some twenty years of professional work as a distinguished portraitist behind him when he portrayed Jefferson, who was then forty-eight.

HISTORY: The terra-cotta maquette of the Jefferson, along with other preliminary matter for Ceracchi's proposed monument to the American Revolution, was shipped to Leghorn, Italy, where it was claimed by the sculptor early in 1793. As soon as the terra cotta was in his hands, Ceracchi announced that he would set to work on the colossal marble, which, he led Jefferson to believe, he was to present to him as a gift. The marble bust arrived at Monticello in the spring of 1795, when Ceracchi himself was again in America, but the "gift" which Jefferson had reluctantly accepted as a mark of Ceracchi's "flattering" esteem was soon followed by the sculptor's bill for "one thousand five hundred Dollars." Despite the embarrassment of this deception and the fact that a final agreement on the payment to Ceracchi was not reached until 1800, Jefferson and his family admired the marble and gave it a conspicuous place in the hall at Monticello, where it was seen by William Wirt, who described it as "that exquisite and finished bust of the great patriot himself, from the master-hand of Caracci." Although it was "Jefferson's wish that his bust, executed by Ciracchi . . . would be presented" to the University of Virginia at his death, "the deeply embarrassed state in which his affairs were left" forced his executors to offer the bust for sale. When this was learned, many of the Charlottesville citizens present at the January 1827 sale of Jefferson's effects at Monticello petitioned the Virginia Assembly to purchase the bust as "the only sculptured memorial in Virginia of the Author of *The Declaration of Independence*," but their request was never acted upon. When Monticello was sold in 1831, the marble was removed to Edgehill, where it remained until purchased for the Library of Congress. There, in an honored place in the main reading room, it was destroyed in the fire of 1851.

CONDITION: Contemporary accounts of the Library of Congress fire leave no doubt that the bust was totally destroyed.

ICONOGRAPHIC IMPORTANCE: Considered by Jefferson as the *chef d'oeuvre* of all the attempts at his portrait, regarded by his family as an "excellent likeness" of Jefferson in "the prime of life" and as a "grand and commanding object," called by William Thornton a "superb bust, one of the finest I have ever beheld," there is little doubt that the loss of this marble — presumably the earliest portrait of Jefferson executed in the United States and the first

35

likeness of an American as secretary of state — leaves the most regrettable lacuna in Jefferson iconography.

COPIES: The terra-cotta maquette — the original sculpted maquette modeled from life — was seen by Thomas Hubert, a Philadelphia merchant, in the studios of the Pisanni brothers in Florence not long before January of 1803. Its present location, despite extensive searches in Florentine collections, is unknown. William Thornton was given permission in 1816 by Jefferson to copy the Ceracchi in plaster, but apparently did not take advantage of the opportunity. Daguerreotypes known to have been taken by Robert Mills after Congress refused him permission to copy the bust in plaster in 1850 have not been located. The only delineation of the bust that is now known is the crude sketch by Thomas Jefferson Randolph, now at the Alderman Library, which is drawn on the verso of his letter to the state of Louisiana which was seeking to purchase it in 1826.

REFERENCES: Bowen (1892), p. 489; Hart (1898), p. 47; Kimball (1944), pp. 510–511; James A. Bear, Jr., "The Giuseppe Ceracchi Bust of Jefferson," an unpublished typescript; the Jefferson-Ceracchi correspondence in the Jefferson Papers at the Library of Congress; correspondence with Professor Ulysse Desportes formerly of Hollins College and Miss Clara Dentler of Florence; Boyd, 15:363–364.

6. The Portrait by Charles Willson Peale

The City of Philadelphia

MEDIUM: As is characteristic of the portraits painted for exhibition in the Peale Museum, this oil on canvas, measuring 23.4 x 19 inches, was painted for framing in an oval, with the ground extending only to the limits of the unframed area.

AUTHORSHIP: Although traditionally regarded as the life portrait, the painting which hung in Independence Hall throughout most of the latter half of the nineteenth century and the first half of the twentieth was classified by Kimball in 1944, because of stylistic considerations based on an examination of both the surface and radiographs of the painting, as "an early copy, by a hand other than that" of Charles Willson Peale or his son Rembrandt. After an identical decision on the related painting now at the Huntington Art Gallery, Kimball made it clear that he felt that the life portrait was to be

The life portrait of Jefferson painted in December of 1791 by Charles Willson Peale in Philadelphia.
Independence National Historical Park

regarded as lost, and Charles Coleman Sellers in his comprehensive study of Peale's work in 1952 followed Kimball's example. That same year, however, Elizabeth Jones, then chief conservator of the Fogg Art Museum, removed from the canvas the repainting applied during the "restorations" of 1873–1874, 1896 and 1918–1919 and revealed for the first time in over half a century the original likeness. Study of this painting by Anne Clapp, who as a former conservator of the Independence Hall Collections is thoroughly familiar with at least a hundred of Peale's museum portraits, convinced her that the painting was indeed the work of Charles Willson Peale and one with all the earmarks of having been executed from life. Examination of x-rays of the canvas taken after the 1952 cleaning confirmed this conclusion. These considerations, added to the knowledge that this painting is now known to be that which hung originally in the Peale Museum, where its founder attempted to adhere to his "invariable rule . . . never to part with any original picture," restore this painting once again to its proper place among the life portraits of Jefferson.

CHRONOLOGY: The inscription on the earliest surviving engraving of this portrait dates the original painting to 1791. That it was painted in December of that year is established by the two letters written to arrange for Jefferson's sitting. These letters are undated but were copied into Peale's letterbooks following the last dated entry of that year — December 2, 1791. It may well be that Jefferson visited the Peale household for this sitting not long before December 16. It may also be that it was Peale's enthusiastic proselytizing of his belief that painting should be part of the essential education of every young American that prompted Jefferson to purchase on that date a "box of paints and pencils for Maria." The task of sitting for his fifty-year-old friend, whose interests and objectives were so congenial to his, in the fascinating hodge-podge of science and fine art in the cluster of museum buildings at Third and Lombard Street in Philadelphia, must have been a pleasant one for the forty-eight-year-old secretary of state.

HISTORY: Undoubtedly the painting took its place, immediately after its completion, among the distinguished portraits which hung in the Peale Museum. It is listed in the catalogue of 1795, just after its removal, with the rest of Peale's collection, to Philosophical Hall. Late in the summer of 1800 when the museum expanded into the upper floor of the Pennsylvania State House (Independence Hall), the painting took its place there. In 1827 the portrait was again moved, with the body of Peale's collection, to the Philadelphia Arcade. Under various proprietors the painting remained with the museum collection until its dispersal in the sale of 1854, when the *Jefferson* was purchased for the city of Philadelphia by P. E. Erben. From 1855 until 1958 the portrait was almost continuously exhibited, along with the likenesses of other distinguished American patriots, in the very room at Independence Hall in which the subjects of these paintings had passed their most momentous resolution as members of the Continental Congress. On permanent loan to the Independence National Historical Park, the portraits were removed in 1958 from Independence Hall to make possible the restoration of the building to its appearance in 1776.

CONDITION: This portrait's condition has suffered considerably during its career of public exhibition. Cleaned in 1873 or 1874 of a covering of copal varnish, the portrait seems not to have undergone major restoration until 1896, when John Wilkinson described the portrait as "nothing but a mass of flakes clinging to the canvas by an edge and a thread," and he relined and heavily repainted its surface. In 1918–1919 Pasquale Farina complained of the unskillful work of his predecessors and, apparently, not only cleaned but also repainted the portrait himself. In 1950 Russell Quandt, conservator at the Corcoran Gallery, was given permission to retouch some of the most badly darkened areas of repaint before the painting was exhibited in the Washington Sesquicentennial Exhibition. The painting's most important restoration, however, was carried out by Elizabeth Jones in May 1952, when the painting was again relined and several layers of the repaint were removed. Only those areas where the original painting was missing, were inpainted at that time.

ICONOGRAPHIC IMPORTANCE: Not only has this portrait been exhibited publicly almost continuously since its creation, but the engravings which copied it in 1795 and early in 1800 made it the first of Jefferson's likenesses to be distributed commercially through prints. Thus Charles Willson Peale's fresh and sympathetic portrayal of Jefferson has persistently shaped the public's visual conception of America's first secretary of state.

COPIES: The painting at the Huntington Art Gallery, with a provenance which traces it to John Conduit of Newark, New Jersey, and the painting owned in 1942 by Arthur Meeker are the only known copies of the likeness executed in paint. William Birch completed an engraving of this portrait in time to enter a "proof print" of it in the 1795 exhibition of the Columbianum, but no copy of it is known to have survived. On January 10, 1800, James Akin and William Harrison, Jr., issued a stipple engraving of Peale's portrait (Stauffer 17). The portrait was issued as an etching in 1895 by E. F. Faber.

REFERENCES: Bowen (1892), p. 487; Hart (1898), p. 47; Kimball

(1944), pp. 507–509; Charles Coleman Sellers, *Charles Willson Peale* (Philadelphia, 1947), 2:41; Charles Coleman Sellers, *Portraits and Miniatures by Charles Willson Peale* (Philadelphia, 1952), p. 110; reports from Anne Clapp and David H. Wallace.

7. *The Portrait by William Joseph Williams*

Whereabouts unknown

MEDIUM: The low price of this likeness and Jefferson's reference to the artist's work as a "drawing" suggest that, like Williams' surviving portrait of Washington, this was executed with pastel crayon on paper.

AUTHORSHIP: Jefferson's account book records only that he "Pd Williams for drawing [his] portrait 14D." It was Kimball who first suggested that the artist was William Joseph Williams. This attribution is almost certainly correct since Williams was the only portraitist with this surname active in this period and since it is now known that at about the time of this portrait William Joseph Williams passed through Philadelphia en route from New York to Richmond.

CHRONOLOGY: The drawing was probably executed on July 12, 1792, in Philadelphia — the date of Jefferson's payment to Williams as recorded in the account book — unless we conclude from a Williams family tradition about the comparable portrait of Washington that numerous sittings were required for the completion of the pastel. It is possible that the payment dates only the last of many sittings or, since Jefferson set out from Philadelphia the following day for Monticello, that the payment, made with a number of others, was merely among those for services rendered earlier that summer which he settled before his departure. The lost portrait, executed when Williams was thirty-three years of age, pictured Jefferson at forty-nine as secretary of state.

HISTORY: At its completion the portrait, as his payment makes clear, went into Jefferson's possession. It has never been determined whether it remained under his care in the Monticello collections or passed immediately into other hands. Nothing of its subsequent history is known.

CONDITION: The paucity of information concerning this likeness suggests its

*The portrait of George Washington by
William Joseph Williams, artist of the undiscovered
portrait of Jefferson executed in July of 1793 in
Philadelphia.* Alexandria-Washington Lodge

early destruction. But despite the ephemeral nature of pastel, it is possible that this portrait still reposes, unidentified, in some American collection.

ICONOGRAPHIC IMPORTANCE: Williams' candid portrayal of Washington suggests that his likeness of Jefferson was a frank and unflattering depiction that would be of interest to students of Jefferson. It seems certain, however, that its viewers were never numerous nor memorably appreciative, for the Williams pastel is among the most forgotten and uninfluential of Jefferson's portraits.

COPIES: No likeness is known which might have been derived from this portrait.

REFERENCES: Hart (1898), p. 48; Kimball (1944), p. 510; John Hill Morgan and Mantle Fielding, *The Life Portraits of Washington* (Philadelphia, 1931), p. 201.

8. *The Portrait by James Sharples*

The City Art Gallery, Bristol, England

MEDIUM: As with most of the Sharples likenesses, the Jefferson profile was drawn with the help of the physiognotrace on a thick soft-grained wooly-textured gray paper measuring 7 x 9 inches. The subject's features were then added to this outline in pastel crayon manufactured by Sharples himself, finely powdered and applied with a brush.

AUTHORSHIP: Previous students of Jefferson's portraiture have dismissed the Sharples portrait with the comment that no documentary evidence exists to prove that the likeness was taken from life. Yet since Jefferson was in Philadelphia at a time when many of his distinguished colleagues were sitting for portraits by Sharples, since there is no extant likeness from which this pastel could have been derived, and since the physiognotrace process presupposes a life sitting, there is every reason to believe that Sharples' likeness was created in Jefferson's presence. Of the two examples with histories tracing them to the collection in the hands of the Sharples family at the time of James Sharples' death, one in the Independence Hall collection, one at the City Art Gallery of Bristol, England, the latter has been generally ignored in preference to the better-known example of the portrait at Independence Hall. A comparison of these two profiles, however, suggests that it is the Bristol example which most deserves our attention. It appears to be not only conceived more freely, more spontaneously and in more depth, but in specific details seems to portray Jefferson more accurately. In the Independence Hall profile the hair appears to be conventionalized: vague curls suggest a wig — a characterization foreign both to Jefferson and to the Bristol portrait, which depicts Jefferson's hair as straight, falling naturally over his ear and ending in a queue which is misunderstood only in the Philadelphia pastel. In the Bristol example the eye not only seems more alert than in the Independence Hall likeness in which the eyelid is heavier, but the whole countenance is more intense and responsive than the flatter, more wooden features of the Independence Hall profile. The Bristol complexion is also convincing, not simply rouged-on as in the Philadelphia example. The costume of the Bristol portrait is suggestive and spontaneous; the profile in Philadelphia depicts the clothing in the more conventionalized and thorough detail of the copyist. In the Bristol example the jabot is only summarized and suggested as it would have to have been at a sitting in which Sharples, as was his custom, worked with great speed. In the Independence Hall example the jabot is a convention executed in the detailed manner of the copyist. The Bristol example shows a more

The Bristol example of the likeness drawn from life by James Sharples in 1797 in Philadelphia.
City Art Gallery, Bristol, England

subtle profile, while the Independence Hall example portrays the profile in what appears to be an exaggeration. Finally the provenance itself would suggest that the Bristol example is the life portrait, for it is likely that the pastels delineated from life would have remained with Sharples' widow, who carried out her husband's ambition of placing his American portraits in a permanent collection, while their competent copies would more logically be those given to her stepson Felix who remained in America. Final confirmation of this tentative identification of the Bristol pastel as the portrait drawn from life, however, must await a comparison of both examples in their original form.

CHRONOLOGY: Jefferson and James Sharples could not have come into contact with each other until March 1797, when Jefferson was in Philadelphia for eleven days for his inauguration as vice president. But it is likely that, instead of being executed during this brief and busy period, the pastel was drawn sometime between the vice president's return to the temporary capital on the eleventh of May and his departure for Monticello on the sixth of July of the same year. By early autumn Sharples and his family had left Philadelphia for New York, where they remained at least through the greater part of 1799. After making a tour of New England and the middle states in 1800, they returned to England the following year. That the portrait dates to 1797 when both Jefferson and Sharples are known to have been in Philadelphia, rather than to any conjectural visit of the Sharples to the temporary capitol while Jefferson was there early in 1800, is confirmed not only by the costume and the hair which together suggest the earlier date, but also by the reasonableness of the assumption that Jefferson would have been added to the Sharples collection of distinguished Americans at the earliest opportunity. During this first journey to America Sharples was under the responsibility of creating a reputation for himself and thus was at the height of his artistic ability. In his mid-forties at the time of this pastel, Sharples depicted Jefferson at fifty-four.

HISTORY: After James Sharples' death during a second residence in America in 1811, his young widow, Ellen, returned with many of the portraits from his collection, including his *Jefferson,* to England. The profile remained in her care there until her death in 1849, when the collection of which it was a part was bequeathed to the Royal West of England Academy in Bristol. In recent years these pastels have been on permanent loan to the City Art Gallery of Bristol.

CONDITION: Considering the fragility of portraits in pastel, this profile has survived in good condition.

ICONOGRAPHIC IMPORTANCE: Even if one accepts Hart's evaluation of the Sharples likeness as being "deficient in character and individuality," as the earliest portrait of Jefferson as vice president and as a likeness which has been publicly exhibited in its many versions in both England and America almost continuously since its completion, it has had an extensive and admiring audience.

COPIES: The profile at Independence Hall, which duplicates what is most probably the life portrait at Bristol, came into the Independence Hall collections in 1874 as a gift to the city of Philadelphia from F. M. Etting, who purchased it from Murray Harrison. Harrison had apparently acquired it from the Winder family, who received it with a much larger collection of Sharples portraits from James Sharples' son, Felix, as collateral on a loan. The pastel owned by Miss Ima Hogg of Houston, Texas, is from a hand other than that which drew the profiles in Philadelphia and Bristol, but its relationship to a drawing of Jefferson by Ellen Sharples, now also at Bristol, suggests that it is the production of one of the younger members of the Sharples family. The outline drawing of this portrait, mentioned in Mrs. Sharples' diary, has not been found.

REFERENCES: Bowen (1892), p. 487; Hart (1898), p. 47; Kimball (1944), p. 498; Katharine McCook Knox, *The Sharples* (New Haven, 1930); John Hill Morgan and Mantle Fielding, *The Life Portraits of Washington* (Philadelphia, 1931), pp. 359–398.

9. The Portrait by Tadeusz Kosciuszko

Whereabouts unknown

MEDIUM: The lost portrait, of which we have no record other than Sokolnicki's print, most probably was executed, as is Kosciuszko's comparable profile of William Bedlow, as a miniature aquarelle painted on circular paper.

AUTHORSHIP: The inscription of the aquatint makes the attribution of the original likeness to Kosciuszko unequivocal. And though Kimball felt that this portrait represented Jefferson "at an age far greater than" that of his last meeting with Kosciuszko and thus could "not have been from life," the costume and queue suggest its placement in the context of likenesses executed

Thomas Jefferson
A Philosopher a Patriote and a Friend
Dessiné par son Ami Tadée Kosciuszko.
Et Gravé par Mr. Sokolnicki.

The aquatint of Jefferson by Michel Sokolnicki in Paris before the end of 1799 from the aquarelle (now lost) which was painted from life in Philadelphia by Tadeusz Kosciuszko most probably in April 1798. Yale University Art Gallery

during Jefferson's vice presidency. In addition, Sokolnicki's aquatint of the portrait could only have been published in Paris between the time of Kosciuszko's return there in 1798 and Sokolnicki's departure to his new command in the Second Polish Legion on the Danube at the end of 1799, make a dating of the portrait to the period of Kosciuszko's Philadelphia residence not only possible but necessary. That the portrait was taken from life is further supported by the evidence of Kosciuszko's frequent opportunities to portray Jefferson during their friendship in Philadelphia and by the fact that no likeness survives that could have been the source of this profile.

CHRONOLOGY: Kosciuszko had been in Philadelphia since August, when Jefferson returned to that city in December 1797 as vice president. Whether the two men then resumed an acquaintance made in Philadelphia in the beginning years of the Revolution or, as seems more likely, met for the first time, a friendship developed between them in the early months of 1798 which led Jefferson to call the Polish patriot "the purest son of liberty of . . . all." The portrait which Kosciuszko painted of Jefferson most probably dates to April 1798, when Jefferson was so often involved in the administration of the Pole's business affairs. It is most likely that it was during these preparations for Kosciuszko's return to Europe, and certainly before Jefferson's parting with him on May 4, that the portrait, depicting Jefferson at fifty-five — only three years older than the artist — was completed as a memento of their friendship.

HISTORY: Kosciuszko must have carried the portrait directly to Paris in 1798 where it was put into the hands of Michel Sokolnicki, Kosciuszko's compatriot, friend, military aid and fellow artist, who completed the surviving aquatint copy of the portrait before the end of the following year. Nothing further is known of the original portrait's history except that in 1829 it may have been in the possession of another Polish printmaker — Antoine Oleszcynski — who, most probably in Paris, appears to have copied the likeness directly from the life portrait. The statement by Gardner that Kosciuszko's "pastel portrait" of Jefferson is "preserved among Poland's national relics" has never been verified and is presumably based on a misidentification of one of the Sokolnicki aquatints as the original likeness.

CONDITION: The original of this likeness may still survive, unidentified, in some European collection.

ICONOGRAPHIC IMPORTANCE: Judging from the competence of extant portraits by Kosciuszko, the distortions of his image of Jefferson seem more a result of exaggerations in the transcription of it into the aquatint by Sokolnicki rather than the inferiority of the original image. In July 1816 William

Thornton complained to Jefferson of the "injustice" of the portrait: "Nothing can be so bad," he wrote, "and when I saw it, I did not wonder that he lost Poland — not that it is necessary a Genl. should be a Painter, but he should be a man of such Sense as to discover that he is not a Painter." Oleszcynski's 1829 copy of the portrait was less a caricature and was used to represent Jefferson in biographical works published in France shortly after the completion of the new engraving. But the Kosciuszko image, in Europe as well as in America, seems never to have been a popular or widely circulated one.

COPIES: Michel Sokolnicki's aquatint of 1798 or 1799 survives in rare prints. The engraving by Antoine Oleszcynski is found re-engraved by Porret in the *Galerie Napoléon* and by Clerget (Carson 1112 and 1118).

REFERENCES: Bowen (1892), p. 488; Hart (1898), p. 48; Kimball (1944), p. 527; Helen Comstock, "Kosciuszko's Portrait of Thomas Jefferson," *The Connoisseur, 133,* no. 536 (Mar. 1954), 142–143; correspondence with His Excellency M. Michel Sokolnicki of Ankara, Turkey; Monica M. Gardner, *Kosciuszko, a Biography* (New York, 1920), p. 180; Merrill D. Peterson, *The Jefferson Image in the American Mind* (New York, 1960), p. 508 cites "Arthur Krock's column, *N.Y. Times* 21 June 1938."

10. The Portrait by Robert Field

The New-York Historical Society

MEDIUM: This unfinished portrait, painted in watercolor on cardboard, measures 9.8 x 13.8 inches.

AUTHORSHIP: The inscription on the lower edge of the face of this painting, in what has been identified as Field's hand, reads: "T. JEFFERSON. Painted by R. Field." The notes on the portrait's provenance, inscribed on the verso of the painting by a subsequent owner, also identify Field as the portrait's artist. Field's hand, in fact, is so evident in this watercolor that the closest student of this artist's work has stated that "there can be no doubt whatever that this exceedingly beautiful portrait is by Field, and an original from life." Yet previous students of Jefferson's life portraits, finding no documentary evidence that Jefferson sat for Field, have passed over this portrait in their ordering of the life likenesses. But the failure to find, in an extensive study of Jefferson's portraits, a likeness from which this watercolor might be

Robert Field's life portrait of Jefferson painted in Philadelphia about 1798.
New-York Historical Society

derived supports what is so forcefully suggested by the immediacy and freshness of the likeness itself: that it was executed in Jefferson's presence.

CHRONOLOGY: Although the portrait was traditionally said to have been painted soon after Jefferson's inauguration as president as a study for a large portrait which was never executed, Piers accepted it as an independent work and dated it, because of the youthfulness of the representation, "not later than 1797" since "it differs in no essentials from the artist's other water-colors except in being unfinished." That year, however, is the earliest, rather than the latest possible date of its execution, though the youthfulness of the portrayal does suggest a date early in Jefferson's vice presidency when Field and Jefferson were in Philadelphia together for the first time. That it was painted in Philadelphia rather than in Jefferson's first years as president after Field had moved to Washington is also suggested by the descent of the painting through Charles Chauncy, a Philadelphia lawyer and one of the founders of the Pennsylvania Academy of Fine Arts.

HISTORY: From the artist the painting went to his friend, Charles Chauncy, who left it to Thomas S. Mitchell. Mitchell presented it to Thomas J. Miles who had it in his possession for about sixty years. He left it to his son, Colonel Thomas Carswell Miles from whom it passed to J. Fred Pierson, who sold it to the New-York Historical Society in 1923.

CONDITION: The paper and pigment have faded considerably. The loss of color has given a startling prominence to the Chinese white on the eyes. Much of the modeling has been lost in the face as a result of prolonged exposure to light. A slight repair has been made to the left of the drapery, and the lower left corner of the painting is defaced by a clipping bearing Jefferson's franking signature and a postmark.

ICONOGRAPHIC IMPORTANCE: Never copied and seldom reproduced even in recent years, Field's portrait is the finest of the little-known portraits of Jefferson.

COPIES: Although Field's own image of Jefferson was presumably never copied, in 1807 Field was himself to engrave, in what Piers has called his "best plate," the most handsome and important of the multitude of prints derived from Gilbert Stuart's second life portrait of Jefferson.

REFERENCES: Kimball (1944), p. 498; Harry Piers, *Robert Field* (New York, 1927), pp. 186–187, facing 190, 195; *Catalogue of American Portraits in The New-York Historical Society* (New York, 1941), p. 159. The statement about this portrait attributed to Jefferson on p. 19 of Orland and Courtney Campbell, *The Lost Portraits of Thomas Jefferson* (Amherst College, 1959), does not appear in the original of the letter cited there.

11. *The Portrait by Charles Peale Polk*

The American Scenic and Historic Preservation Society

MEDIUM: The portrait is painted in oil on canvas and measures 27 x 23 inches.

AUTHORSHIP: When this painting was submitted to the exhibition of historical portraiture during the centennial celebration of Washington's inauguration, it was attributed to Charles Willson Peale by the exhibition's Committee on Art. Students objected to this attribution before the printing of Bowen's catalogue and six years later Charles Henry Hart identified Charles Peale Polk as the painter of the same portrait. While Polk's work has obvious similarities to that of his more competent uncle, Charles Willson Peale, in whose household he was reared after the death of his parents, the younger painter's style had matured by the time of this portrait into an expression individual enough to make the identification of his work possible on stylistic grounds. The fact that the costume and countenance portrayed in the portrait date to the time when Polk is known to have traveled to Monticello to paint Jefferson affirms not only Polk's authorship of the likeness, but also its place among the life portraits.

CHRONOLOGY: Polk, who spent the winter of 1799–1800 — at thirty-two years of age — painting portraits in Richmond, arrived at Monticello on November 3, 1799, bearing a letter from Madison introducing him as a "portrait Painter and a kinsman of Mr. Peale . . ." and stating that he was visiting "Monticello with a wish to be favored with a few hours of your sitting for his pencil." Polk's arrival is documented by Jefferson's notation in his Summary Journal of Letters of the receipt of this letter "by Mr. Polk" and by Jefferson's reference to the painter in his reply to Madison of November 22. The portrait most probably was begun on the day of Polk's arrival — November 3, 1799 — and was completed on November 5, according to the painter's own notice published in *The Virginia Gazette and General Advertiser* on November 18. The painting depicts Jefferson at fifty-six in one of his cherished Monticello interludes from his public responsibilities as vice president.

HISTORY: Hart recorded the tradition that the painting was painted under the commission of Major Isaac Hite of the Shenandoah Valley, Virginia, and that it descended to his grandson, Madison Hite, Jr., who, during the Civil War, deposited it in Baltimore with a number of other paintings for safe keeping, though he never recovered it. The portrait was subsequently owned by Dr. John M. Daniel, to whom it is said to have been presented as a gift for medical services by Dr. Robert O. Grayson, whose wife was a relative of the subject. Dr. Daniel's son gave the portrait to an aunt, Mrs. F. A. March of Easton, Pennsylvania. In 1911 it was purchased from the estate of Francis A. March by Alexander Smith Cochran, who housed it in Philipse Manor Hall, Yonkers. At Mr. Cochran's death in 1929 the portrait was bequeathed to the American Scenic and Historic Preservation Society.

CONDITION: After the death of Dr. Daniel, the portrait reportedly was badly damaged — Jefferson's eyes were said to have been torn out when the paint-

The portrait of Jefferson painted from life by Charles Peale Polk at Monticello in the first week of November 1799. American Scenic and Historic Preservation Society

ing was used as an archery target by young boys. But if the painting underwent considerable restoration while in the possession of F. A. March it is difficult to detect this today.

ICONOGRAPHIC IMPORTANCE: Polk's inability "to Obtain business in the line of [his] Profession," the *"extreme distress"* of his family, and his appeals to Jefferson in the early years of his presidency for "some Subordinate appointment," all suggest that Polk's portraits were regarded by his contemporaries as inferior works. His depiction of Jefferson has never been widely known.

COPIES: *The Virginia Gazette and General Advertiser* for November 18, 1799 carried Charles Peale Polk's notice that ". . . he has for sale, A few copies of General Washington, and Thomas Jefferson, Esq. from an original Portrait by myself, finished at Monticello on the 5th instant. . . ." At least two paintings duplicating this portrait, both of them probably replicas, survive. One is owned by Henry Beckinger Davenport III and is said to have been acquired by the Davenport family in Jefferson's lifetime. The other, given to the University of Virginia by William Middendorf, may have been the portrait owned in 1952 by John K. Byard.

REFERENCES: Bowen (1892), p. 487; Hart (1898), p. 48; Kimball (1944), p. 498; American Scenic and Historic Preservation Society *Bulletin, 1,* no. 3 (Sept. 1929), 5, 11; *Antiques, 62,* no. 6 (Dec. 1952), 433; Charles Peale Polk to Thomas Jefferson, February 28, 1802, and James Madison to Thomas Jefferson, November 2, 1799, respectively in the Jefferson Papers at the Library of Congress and the Library of Knox College; correspondence of Jacqueline Davison and S. C. March and Charles Henry Hart in the Frick Art Reference Library; correspondence of Mrs. Imogen C. Riely, correspondence of Braxton Davenport and John Cook Wyllie in the Alderman Library, University of Virginia.

12. The First Life Portrait by Rembrandt Peale

The White House

MEDIUM: In this oil on diagonal twill canvas, the lean use of paint more typical of Rembrandt Peale has given way, partly because of the roughness of the canvas, to a richer impasto. The paint was applied with the directness, spontaneity and boldness which characterize the best expositions of his early

The life portrait of Jefferson painted in Philadelphia early in 1800 by Rembrandt Peale.
The White House

style. The placement of the figure on the canvas, the simple background and the obvious shading are all derived directly from his father's style, in which the younger Peale worked with facility and confidence until his contact with Europe.

AUTHORSHIP: Although a knowledge of this portrait until recently was restricted to those persons in direct contact with it, they seem never to have lost sight of the fact that it was painted by Rembrandt Peale. When it was purchased in the mid-nineteenth century by Charles Eaton, it was surely with the knowledge that it was a surviving part of the dispersed collections of Rembrandt's Baltimore museum; and although the portrait bore no inscription and, apparently, no labels to indicate its author, the cataloguer of the collections of the Peabody Institute in 1900 attributed the painting to Rembrandt Peale. This attribution was unquestioned by Anna Wells Rutledge when she compiled her hand list of the institute's collection in 1946. The evidence of style, a provenance which traces the painting to the original collections in Peale's Baltimore museum, and, most especially, the identification of the original likeness' author on its earliest engravings confirm that Rembrandt Peale was its creator. That it was painted from life is established by the fact that it is the ultimate source of the numerous prints which made this the most extensively distributed image of Jefferson during his presidency, and also by Jefferson's request of March 21, 1801, that Rembrandt "make a copy of the portrait he took of [him]. . . ."

CHRONOLOGY: Painted sometime after Jefferson's arrival in Philadelphia in late December 1799 and before his departure for Monticello in the middle of May 1800, the portrait depicts the fifty-seven-year-old vice president on the threshold of the presidency of the United States. Though Rembrandt Peale himself had just turned twenty-two, he was a veteran portraitist, having painted Washington successfully five years before. The young painter was at the zenith of his native style, a style which was to undergo what was not a thoroughly happy sophistication during his study in Europe two years later. Rembrandt Peale had just returned to Philadelphia after an abortive attempt to establish an art museum in Baltimore; and since it was September before a card appeared in the newspapers informing Philadelphians of the removal of Rembrandt's studio to Mulberry Court, it may well have been at his temporary painting rooms at 110 Walnut Street that Jefferson sat for him. The portrait was most probably completed in a single sitting; two were required at most.

HISTORY: As part of Peale's original gallery of paintings at his Baltimore museum, it stayed on there with the collection under the custodianship of the painter's brother Rubens to whom the building and its contents were sold in 1822. When Rubens severed his ties to the collection, over ten years later, the painting was part of the effects of Rembrandt's original museum which survived many moves, at least two fires and a number of uninterested proprietors. The last of these was Charles Getz who in 1854 was privately selling the remnants of the painting collection which had originally hung in Peale's Baltimore museum. At the time Charles J. M. Eaton, forty-seven years old, affluent and infected with the collecting spirit, purchased the *Jefferson* and at least one other of the Peale paintings for his growing collection. The painting remained part of Eaton's vast and uncatalogued private collection until his death in 1893, when it was presented by Eaton's daughters to the Peabody Institute over which their father had presided as president. After scholarly attention was turned to Jefferson's portraits late in the nineteenth century, it was probably Charles Henry Hart who first recognized that the 1800 life portrait of Jefferson by Peale was unknown, for he circulated photographs of engravings of it in an unsuccessful attempt to locate the original. William J. Campbell admitted in the catalogue of portraits brought together for the centennial of Washington's inauguration that although this painting was among the most important of Jefferson's portraits, he had been unable to trace the original. Eleven years later Hart was forced to state that the original portrait was "known at the present day only through contemporary engravings. . . ." Lipscomb and Bergh failed to find it in their search for Jefferson portraits in 1903. John Hill Morgan concluded in 1930 that Peale's earliest life portrait of Jefferson was "known only by engravings . . ." and in 1937 H. E. Dickson's study of engravings derived from the life portrait concluded that the "portrait seems to have disappeared." The painting remained unknown to the committee which assembled the exhibition of portraits for Jefferson's bicentennial in 1943 in the National Gallery, and in the comprehensive study of Jefferson's portraits which resulted from this exhibition, Fiske Kimball searched without success for Peale's earliest portrait of Jefferson and finally had to pass over it as one of "the paintings reputed to stand back of various engravings of which we know nothing further." In 1953 when Rosenberger reproduced the life portraits in his *Jefferson Reader* the 1800 Peale portrait was still missing. It was not until 1959 that the Peabody portrait was identified as the long sought after life portrait of 1800. It was then purchased from the Peabody Institute by Paul Mellon and presented to the White House.

CONDITION: The portrait has survived in extraordinarily good condition. The creases caused by the unbeveled edge of the stretcher and a small three-corner tear in the area of Jeffrson's left cheek are the only notable damage. When the patch that had been used to repair the tear was cleared away, Elizabeth Packard of the Walters Art Gallery, who directed the cleaning and relining of the painting in 1960, discovered almost all of the original surface intact so that the restoration demanded virtually no new paint.

ICONOGRAPHIC IMPORTANCE: Among the earliest and most penetrating likenesses of Jefferson, this portrait is unrivaled in having played a more significant iconographic role during Jefferson's lifetime than any other portrait. Shortly after its completion it became the prototype of a widely distributed series of American and European engravings. The American public received through these engravings their first visual image of the man they were twice to choose as president. Peale's arresting portrait thus served as an important and convincing item of political propaganda. No portrait of Jefferson, with the exception of the one painted in 1805 by Gilbert Stuart which later eclipsed that of Peale in the public mind, seems to have been so frequently copied. This was, in fact, so thoroughly the image of Jefferson impressed upon the senses of the American people that political cartoonists copied its lineaments in order to make the Jefferson of their satires immediatly recognizable. It was the ultimate source of the French and English image of the man, who, next to Franklin, most nearly symbolized the New World in the eyes of the Old.

COPIES: Although Jefferson ordered a replica of this portrait from the painter, it was evidently never executed. The painting was first reproduced by David Edwin in a stipple engraving dated 1800 and in the following year in the same medium by Cornelius Tiebout. These two engravings, the only likenesses taken directly from the life portrait, became the sources for at least fifty further versions of this portrait which were painted, engraved and lithographed in the nineteenth century. Among the notable likenesses derived from this life portrait through these two prints is the handsome crayon drawing by Bouch dated 1801 and drawn from Tiebout's 1801 engraving. This crayon was itself copied in the engraving by August Gaspard Louis Boucher, later the Baron Desnoyers, that created the image of Jefferson which "is the type followed in France even to-day." This French engraving in turn served as the immediate source for the oil portrait by an anonymous copyist that is now owned by Francis L. Barton. The Desnoyers engraving also was copied in a line engraving by William Holl the younger in England and with further derivatives there became perhaps the most important of the British images of Jefferson. The head in the full-length painting of Jefferson by Caleb Boyle, now at Lafayette College, is also ultimately derived from Peale's life portrait of 1800 through the David Edwin engraving.

REFERENCES: The painting itself is most faithfully reproduced in the full color print published by the Princeton University Press in 1960; Bowen (1892), pp. 478–489; Hart (1898), p. 51; Kimball (1944), p. 498; Peabody Institute Gallery of Art, *List of Works of Art on Exhibition Including the Collections of John W. McCoy and Charles J. M. Eaton* (Baltimore, 1900), p. 27; Anna Wells Rutledge, *List of Works of Art in the Collection of The Peabody Institute* (Baltimore, 1949), p. 17; Wilbur H. Hunter, Jr., *Rendezvous for Taste, Peale's Baltimore Museum* (Baltimore, 1956), p. 6; Alfred L. Bush, "Rembrandt Peale's Earliest Life Portrait of Thomas Jefferson," unpublished typescript; Maxine Cheshire, "Portrait Used by Jefferson in Campaign Is Acquired," *The Washington Post;* Dec. 9, 1962; Julian P. Boyd, "Jefferson's Portrait" in Letters to the Editor, *The Washington Post,* Dec. 17, 1962, p. A18; *Joséphine Parures, Décors et Jardins* (Rueil-Malmaison, 1969), p. 10; Robert Macauley, *Transfer Designs on Anglo American Pottery,* no. 228; *The White House, an Historic Guide* (Washington, D.C., The White House Historical Association, n.d.)

13. *The Portrait by Edward Savage*

Whereabouts unknown

MEDIUM: The inscription on the surviving mezzotint copy of the lost original of this likeness, which refers to Savage as the painter of the portrait, and the fact that Savage's portraits were typically executed in oil on canvas indicate that the original of this likeness was also in this medium and may have measured, as do comparable portraits by Savage, about 30 x 25 inches.

AUTHORSHIP: The inscription on the mezzotint engraving of this portrait ascribes the original painting to Edward Savage. But without documentary evidence that Jefferson sat for Savage, previous students of Jefferson's life portraits have ignored this likeness. Yet since Savage and Jefferson were residents of Philadelphia together and were acquainted with each other, and since Savage was at the time painting portraits for his gallery of distinguished Americans, it is reasonable to believe that during the same year that Jefferson granted sittings to Polk, Rembrandt Peale and Stuart, he would also have been willing to sit to a painter ranked by his contemporaries with Copley, West and Trumbull as among the "American geniuses of the present time."

E. Savage Pinx.t p.   Philad.ª Published June 1. 180.

THOMAS JEFFERSON.

The mezzotint, most probably by David Edwin, from the portrait of Jefferson which Edward Savage painted from life in Philadelphia early in 1800. Historical Society of Pennsylvania

That no portrait has been found which could have been used as the source for this likeness further supports its position among the life portraits.

CHRONOLOGY: The date of Savage's first acquaintance with Jefferson is unrecorded, but since the painter did not settle in Philadelphia until 1795, they presumably could not have met until Jefferson's return to the temporary capital in 1797 as vice president. And since it was not until the winter of 1799–1800 that Philadelphia's portraitists, spurred by Jefferson's candidacy for the presidency, began requesting sittings, it is most probable that Savage's life portrait was painted not long before work on the mezzotint print of it, issued on the first of June 1800, was begun. Certainly in costume and countenance this *Jefferson* is similar to the other portraits dated to that year. It was about this time that Philadelphians were invited to Savage's "New Exhibition Gallery of Paintings" at 70 South Fourth Street for an exhibition of "original American Historical Paintings taken from the most interesting subjects. . . ." Thus it may have been in Savage's painting rooms at this address that Jefferson posed for the portrait which could have been part of this April exhibition. Jefferson, in fact, may well have given Savage his first commission to frame prints for the Monticello collections at the time of the sitting since on May 12, 1800, he paid Savage, presumably for such a service at a time when the mezzotint was close to completion.

HISTORY: As part of Savage's gallery, the painting most probably accompanied the artist in his move from Philadelphia to New York in 1801 to become part of the collection of the New-York Museum which Savage and a partner inaugurated there. These collections were later reassembled as the Columbian Museum in Boston, where it seems most likely that the *Jefferson* was destroyed when the museum and the greater part of its contents burned in 1803.

CONDITION: The original painting is thought to have been burned in the 1803 fire in Boston's Columbian Museum. The exceedingly rare mezzotint of it, which survives at the Historical Society of Pennsylvania, is neither an early printing of the engraving nor a well-preserved copy: the surface is generally rubbed and bears a flaw at the inner edge of Jefferson's eye.

ICONOGRAPHIC IMPORTANCE: The Savage likeness enjoyed a very brief reign. Its availability in the mezzotint version as a recent portrait of the newly elected president made its piracy by other engravers inevitable. Before the end of 1801 unauthorized versions of it appeared as frontispieces to the Newark and Boston editions of Jefferson's *Notes on the State of Virginia* and one of the volumes of James Hardie's biographical dictionary. But almost immediately the image was eclipsed by the superiority of Rembrandt Peale's

1800 likeness and the popularity of the numerous prints derived from it through Tiebout's engraving of February 1801. The rarity of the mezzotint is itself testimony of how rapidly and thoroughly the image fell out of favor.

COPIES: Despite the inscription on the 1800 mezzotint, which asserts that both the painting and the engraving are the work of Savage himself, Dickson's argument against Savage's competence as an engraver and his identification of David Edwin as the ghost engraver of the more important of Savage's American prints suggest that the latter is more probably the engraver of this mezzotint which seems to be the only copy taken directly from Savage's life portrait. Only one of the 1801 piracies of the mezzotint is signed — that used as frontispiece of the Newark edition of Jefferson's *Notes on the State of Virginia* which bears the signature of John Scoles. Neither the engraving in the Boston edition of the *Notes* nor that in James Hardie's *The New Universal Biographical Dictionary and American Remembrancer of Departed Merit . . .*, New York, 1801 (and subsequent editions), bears indication of the identity of the engraver.

REFERENCES: Bowen (1892), p. 489; Hart (1898), p. 48; Kimball (1944), p. 498; Louisa Dresser, "Edward Savage," *Art in America, 40,* no. 4 (Autumn 1952); Harold E. Dickson, "The Case Against Savage," *American Collector, 14* (Jan. 1946), 6–7, 17; DAB; Jefferson to Edward Savage, January 10, 1802, in the Jefferson Papers at the Library of Congress.

14. The First Life Portrait by Gilbert Stuart

Whereabouts unknown

MEDIUM: Jefferson's reference to this painting as Stuart's "1st canvas portrait" of him and one "of the common size" suggests that the portrait was painted in oil on canvas and measured, as do comparable portraits by Stuart dating to this period, about 28 x 24 inches.

AUTHORSHIP: Jefferson's negotiations with Henry Dearborn for the acquisition of this portrait, the entry in Jefferson's accounts for the payment to Stuart for this 1800 likeness, and the inscriptions on the Orme and Vernor-Hood engravings of the portrait published in England in 1801, all establish Stuart's authorship of a portrait of Jefferson painted from life in 1800. Fiske Kimball's authoritative ordering, in 1944, of Stuart's portraits of Jefferson

The engraving issued by Vernor and Hood in London on October 1, 1801, which is most probably the most faithful surviving representation of the lost portrait of Jefferson painted in May of 1800 in Philadelphia by Gilbert Stuart. Alderman Library of the University of Virginia

dispelled the confusion of misidentification and misdating surrounding this, the earliest of Stuart's life portraits of Jefferson, and established for the first time that the likeness is presumably preserved only in contemporary engravings.

CHRONOLOGY: Almost twenty years after the execution of this likeness Jefferson remembered that "it was in May, 1800" that Stuart painted his first life portrait of him. Since his payment is dated May 12, 1800, it was in the early weeks of that month, most probably in Stuart's Germantown studio, just outside Philadelphia, that the sitting took place. Jefferson, at fifty-seven, was portrayed on the threshold of the presidency. Stuart, recognized even then as the greatest of America's portraitists, was forty-four. Although the sittings were completed at the time of the payment, the artist had not as yet "put the last hand on it, so it was left with him."

HISTORY: Since the two prints which were engraved directly from the canvas were both engraved in England, it is possible that Stuart, without Jefferson's permission, shipped the painting to London for engraving. Though Jefferson's later negotiations concerning Stuart's portraits show that he still believed the 1800 canvas to be in Stuart's possession, Stuart's reference in 1820 to "the one" *Jefferson* then in his studio — the 1805 Edgehill likeness — indicates that by then the 1800 portrait was no longer in the painter's hands. Nothing has been found to document its subsequent history.

CONDITION: Kimball suggested, since the inferiority of the likeness as reproduced in the British engravings of it supports Stuart's claim of being dissatisfied with the likeness, "that Stuart 'rubbed it out,' as he said he did one of his life portraits of Washington." It is also possible, however, that the canvas was never returned from its suppositional journey to England for engraving.

ICONOGRAPHIC IMPORTANCE: Jefferson's comment that he thought Stuart's "1st canvas portrait . . . a good one" was probably elicited by his willingness to accept, after twenty years of negotiation, any of the portraits which Stuart had painted and sold to him, rather than a considered evaluation of the merits of the painter's earliest likeness. The surviving engravings preserve a representation which gives ample ground to Stuart's statement of dissatisfaction with the portrait. But in its engraved form the image had a far-reaching, if brief, currency. In England, in Germany, and in America (as frontispieces to two editions of Jefferson's *Notes on the State of Virginia*) the distortions of Stuart's 1800 portrait were perpetuated for a short while before being discarded in favor of Rembrandt Peale's likeness.

COPIES: This portrait was first reproduced in a print by Edward Orme published on August 1, 1801, in London. As Courtney and Orland Campbell have correctly pointed out, the hasty and inaccurate duplication of the original canvas in this print resulted from the shortcut which Orme resorted to in producing it. Instead of delineating Stuart's *Jefferson* faithfully as a wholly new engraved portrait, Orme merely adapted a copperplate of his earlier engraving of a portrait of Muzzio Clementi into this *Jefferson*. Engraving Jefferson's head over Clementi's, modifying the costume of the earlier portrait as little as necessary, Orme concocted a formidable pastiche of Stuart's head of Jefferson superimposed upon the slightly extended shoulders of Muzzio Clementi. On October first of the same year, Vernor and Hood issued their engraved version of the likeness — the only other taken directly from the

life portrait was painted not long before work on the mezzotint print of it, America early in 1802 is established by the fact that it was copied as the frontispiece to the 1802 Boston edition of Jefferson's *Notes on the State of Virginia,* which in turn was copied the following year for the frontispiece to the Trenton edition of the same work. German versions of this likeness, by Mayer, Topham and Netting, are based on the Orme engraving, while subsequent British versions are derived from the Vernor-Hood print.

REFERENCES: Bowen (1892), pp. 483–485; Hart (1898), pp. 54; Kimball (1944), pp. 512–523; Fiske Kimball, "Gilbert Stuart's Portraits of Jefferson," *Gazette des Beaux-Arts,* 6th series, *26* (1944), 95–112; Orland and Courtney Campbell, *The Lost Portraits of Thomas Jefferson* (Amherst College, 1959), p. 12 (on the claim advanced by the Campbell brothers, see the related discussion and references in this catalogue under Stuart's Edgehill portrait of Jefferson).

15. *The Portrait by A. B. Doolittle*

The Thomas Jefferson Memorial Foundation

MEDIUM: Measuring 3 x 3.8 inches, this is one of the few surviving American portraits in verre églomisé. In these "profiles on gold leaf shadowed a little by hatching," as Dunlap describes them, the likeness was engraved through a ground of gold applied to a transparent glass surface. After the image was engraved and the gold outside the area of the profile cut away, the surface of the glass was covered with a black paint. Viewed through the glass, the gold profile is contrasted sharply against this black ground.

AUTHORSHIP: The portrait bears no inscription, but is stylistically identical to the verre églomisé portrait of John Adams at the American Antiquarian Society which is inscribed: *AB Doolittle Fecit.* The rarity of the use of this medium for portraits in America, the stylistic coincidence of the *Jefferson* with the Doolittle *Adams* at Worcester, and the record of Doolittle's completion of profiles of Jefferson at Monticello, confirm both his authorship of this likeness and its place among those executed from life.

CHRONOLOGY: On December 23, 1803, Jefferson recorded a payment of fifteen dollars to Doolittle for three profiles. On January 7, 1804, Jefferson

The verre églomisé portrait of Jefferson engraved from life at Monticello by A. B. Doolittle in December 1803. Thomas Jefferson Memorial Foundation "gave Mr. Doolittle ord. on J. Barnes for 10. D. for profiles," and on February 10 he "gave Doolittle ord. on J. Barnes for 10. D. for profiles." The subjects of these seven profiles purchased from Doolittle by Jefferson are not recorded, but recognizing the commercial value of the president's portrait it is most likely that the earliest sitting at Monticello for Doolittle — late in December 1803 — was for the gold profile depicting Jefferson at sixty years of age.

HISTORY: This portrait hung in the tea room at Monticello in Jefferson's time and must have passed to Septimia Randolph Meikleham as part of her inheritance from Jefferson, her grandfather, since "an old portrait of Jefferson on glass" is reported as being in her possession in 1883. It was part of the estate inherited by Dr. Robert Graves and his sister, Mrs. Cantrell, children of Mrs. H. P. Meikleham by a former marriage and seems never to have left the Meikleham family until shortly before its acquisition by the Thomas Jefferson Memorial Foundation.

CONDITION: Despite the fragile nature of portraits in verre églomisé, the profile is remarkably preserved with only minor portions of the black ground detached from the glass.

ICONOGRAPHIC IMPORTANCE: Jefferson's accounts, Bentley's diary and a letter of thanks from Elizabeth Trist, suggest that this likeness was duplicated a number of times in the original medium, was distributed commercially by Doolittle, and was part of collections in cities as widely separated as Salem and New Orleans. And though Elizabeth Trist's insistence that her replica of the profile bore a "perfect . . . resemblance" seems more an effusive expression of gratitude to Jefferson for the gift than a candid appraisal of the accuracy of the portrait, the profile itself may have suggested something characteristic enough to elicit such a response. The likeness, presumably the first from life of Jefferson as president, was apparently known only in its original medium, and, excepting such unusual occasions as the celebration of the fourth of July 1804 when it was publicly exhibited in Salem, it was seldom viewed and remained known to a very small circle of people.

COPIES: Replicas of this verre églomisé *Jefferson* may have been carried north in the spring of 1804 by Doolittle himself. At least William Bentley, whose collection included the Doolittle verre églomisé profile of Adams, describes the decorations of the Salem Meeting House for the fourth of July 1804 as including a portrait of Jefferson "on glass in gold." It is also almost certain that the likeness which Jefferson sent as a gift to Elizabeth Trist that same year was a further example of this portrait. Receiving the glass profile from Isaac Briggs, who could transport it carefully from Washington with the fragile instruments he was carrying for the exploration of the Mississippi Territory, Elizabeth Trist responded to Jefferson's kindness extravagantly, calling the likeness "exactly yourself in short it elated the Spirits of us all to behold so perfect a resemblance of such a valued and dear friend, to me it is an inestimable treasure. . . ."

REFERENCES: Hart (1898), p. 48; Kimball (1944), pp. 497–498; Alice Van Leer Carrick, *Shades of Our Ancestors* (Boston, 1928), pp. 72–77; Elizabeth Trist to Jefferson, November 26, 1804 in the Alderman Library, University of Virginia; *The Diary of William Bentley* (Salem, 1911), 3:96; Colin Eisler, "Verre Églomisé and Paolo di Giovanni Fei," *Journal of Glass Studies, 3* (1961), 30–37; clipping, from an unidentified newspaper of c. 1883, titled "Mrs. Septimia R. Meikleham, Jefferson's Granddaughter" in the files of The Thomas Jefferson Memorial Foundation.

16. The Portrait by Charles-Balthazar-Julien Févret de Saint-Mémin

Worcester Art Museum

MEDIUM: On coarse textured paper measuring 23.13 x 17 inches covered with a pink watercolor wash, Saint-Mémin first traced Jefferson's profile with the help of the physiognotrace. The details of the subject's features were then delineated in this outline with gray wash and black and white chalk.

AUTHORSHIP: The only inscription on the drawing as it survives is not contemporary with its execution. Not only is the likeness unmistakably the work of Saint-Mémin, however, but the prints engraved from it and purchased by Jefferson with the original drawing bear the artist's abbreviated signature. The very nature of the physiognotrace process requires that profiles drawn with this device be taken from life.

CHRONOLOGY: Jefferson's payment on November 27, 1804, for the original crayon, the copperplate engraved from this drawing, and forty-eight small engravings struck from it, was most probably made, as was customary, on the day of the sitting. Jefferson, portrayed at sixty-one, approaching the end of his first term as president and already elected for a second term, most probably sat to the thirty-four-year-old Saint-Mémin at the artist's rooms in David Shoemaker's house on F Street in Washington where the profilist's cumbersome physiognotrace device was housed.

HISTORY: Though Jefferson's daughter Maria reminded the president in February 1804 that he had "promised us your picture if ever St. Mimin went to Washington" and noted that the artist was to be there in the "middle of this month," it was not until late in the year that Saint-Mémin and Jefferson were able to collaborate. Jefferson's purchase indicates that the drawing went directly into his hands, but nothing is known of its subsequent possession by him or his family. After its initial acquisition, the ownership of the crayon is not recorded again until its possession, with other "important and authentic Jefferson relics," by the historian George Bancroft. The profile passed, in the nineteenth century, to the historian's son, John Chandler Bancroft, and was on loan at the Worcester Art Museum from 1901 until its purchase by that institution in 1954 from the estate of Wilder D. Bancroft.

CONDITION: Before 1901, when it came to Worcester, the right edge of the portrait had been repaired with the insertion of a rectangular patch, about 3.5 x 1.3 inches, taken from the upper right margin of the sheet. Within this patch the extreme portions of the bow in Jefferson's hair have been redrawn by a restorer. At the lower edge of the portrait, written in graphite over old blemishes — and thus long after the execution of the profile — is "Tho. Jefferson."

ICONOGRAPHIC IMPORTANCE: Saint-Mémin engraved a second copper plate of his *Jefferson* and was striking prints from it for commercial sale at the time of Jefferson's second inauguration. That Jefferson's contemporaries found these prints attractive is indicated by the many examples of them which have survived. It was this print, in fact, which Thomas Gimbrede used as the basis for his likeness of Jefferson in the apotheosis titled *Jefferson the Pride of America,* which he engraved just after Jefferson's retirement from the presidency and which Septimia R. Meikleham believed to be "a testimonial circulated by the friends of her grandfather to show their appreciation of his worth and his services to his country." Later the likeness was copied in Paris in a lithograph by Langlumé dedicated to Jefferson's friend David Warden, "ancien Consul des états Unis à Paris." Through further copies the Saint-Mémin *Jefferson* became a widely circulated and familiar image of Jefferson in France. Cherished by some of Jefferson's descendants as an especially characteristic likeness, the Saint-Mémin image was extensively distributed, in both America and France, and persistently admired.

COPIES: The original copperplate purchased by Jefferson, showing the likeness circumscribed in a circle, is now in the Princeton University Library as is an example of the engravings pulled from it. The later copperplate, bearing the likeness within an oval, is owned by the Alderman Library, Univer-

The life portrait of Jefferson by Charles-Balthazar-Julien Févret de Saint-Mémin, drawn with the help of the physiognotrace on November 27, 1804, in Washington. Worcester Art Museum

sity of Virginia. Besides the original prints taken from the oval plate early in the nineteenth century, a thousand copies of the print were restruck from it in 1956 by the University of Virginia. The Langlumé lithograph and its various derivatives survive in the Bibliothèque nationale. Thomas Gimbrede's apotheosis (Stauffer 1058) and the bas-relief by George Miller (in the plaster at the American Philosophical Society which was erroneously identified by Hart as a life portrait; in a plaster owned by Mrs. J. D. Chalfant of Wilmington, Delaware; and in bronze at Monticello and the Henry Francis DuPont Winterthur Museum) are only the most notable of the many likenesses copied from the image engraved from the oval copperplate. Albert Rosenthal copied not only the original drawing in crayon in 1905, but also produced an engraved version the same year.

REFERENCES: Bowen (1892), pp. 486–487; Hart (1898), pp. 52–53; Kimball (1944), pp. 523–524; Howard C. Rice, Jr., "Saint-Mémin's Portrait of Jefferson," *The Princeton University Library Chronicle*, 20, no. 4 (Summer 1959), pp. 182–192; L[ouisa] D[resser], "A Life Portrait of Thomas Jefferson," *Worcester Art Museum News Bulletin and Calendar, 17,* no. 3 (Dec. 1951), 9–10; *A Catalogue of Portraits and other Works of Art in the Possession of the American Philosophical Society* (Philadelphia, 1961), pp. 53–54; correspondence with Miss Louisa Dresser; a clipping, from an unidentified newspaper of c. 1883, titled "Mrs. Septimia R. Meikleham, Jefferson's Granddaughter" in the files of The Thomas Jefferson Memorial Foundation; Edwin M. Betts and James A. Bear, Jr., eds., *The Family Letters of Thomas Jefferson* (Columbia, 1966), p. 256; Fawn M. Brodie, *Thomas Jefferson, An Intimate History* (New York, 1974), p. 378.

17. The Second Life Portrait by Rembrandt Peale

The New-York Historical Society

MEDIUM: Painted in oil on canvas, the portrait measures 28 x 23.8 inches.

AUTHORSHIP: Though the painting bears no inscription, Rembrandt Peale's authorship of the portrait seems always to have been acknowledged, and the painter's father's contemporary statement that "Jefferson sat" for Rembrandt Peale for this portrait establishes its place among the life likenesses. The canvas now at the New-York Historical Society, though unquestionably from Rembrandt's hand, has at times been overlooked as portraits derived from it

The portrait of Jefferson painted from life at the president's house by Rembrandt Peale on the 23rd, 24th and 31st of January, 1805. New-York Historical Society

have been presented as the original likeness. But Kimball's confirmation of the position of this painting as the life portrait is supported not only by decisive visual considerations but also by its provenance.

CHRONOLOGY: Contemporary letters of Charles Willson Peale date exactly the three sittings required by his son for this portrait. Jefferson sat for Rembrandt Peale in the president's house on January 23, 24, and 31, 1805. The portrait was virtually completed in the first two sittings, the last sitting being used only to "retouch" the painting. Though Rembrandt was only twenty-five years of age, the portraits he had painted during the previous decade, including his first life portrait of Jefferson five years earlier, had earned him an acknowledged place among the best of America's portraitists. In the years between his first portrait of Jefferson and this likeness Rembrandt had studied briefly at the Royal Academy in London, infusing the forthrightness of his native portrait manner with the sophistications of his European counterparts. Jefferson, at sixty-one years of age, is depicted in this painting shortly after his reelection to a second term as president.

HISTORY: On March 3, 1805, the eve of Jefferson's second inauguration, this portrait was displayed at a special illumination of the Peale Museum in Philadelphia. The portrait remained with the collections of the Peale Museum, in fact, until their dispersal in the 1854 sale when it was purchased by Thomas J. Bryan. Twelve years later Mr. Bryan presented it to the New-York Historical Society.

CONDITION: In the curatorial care of the New-York Historical Society for almost a century, the portrait survives in excellent condition. The canvas was cleaned in 1938 and was relined for the first time shortly before 1962.

ICONOGRAPHIC IMPORTANCE: Charles Willson Peale expressed both his and Rembrandt's satisfaction with the portrait, and students of Rembrandt's work have often called it his finest production. Though never engraved in the nineteenth century, this superb painting — almost continuously on public exhibition since its creation — has become widely admired as one of the most penetrating and memorable of Jefferson's likenesses. It is especially instructive to compare this likeness with that by the same artist five years earlier.

COPIES: Although Rembrandt advertised, on the very day it was finished, his willingness to paint replicas of this portrait, only one is known to survive: that owned by Laurence Coolidge's widow, who subsequently became Mrs. Gilbert L. Steward. About 1858 James L. Dick painted the copy that now hangs at Monticello, and Caroline Ormes Ransom executed the copy now owned by the United States Department of State sometime before July 1881. A copy by an unidentified painter was discovered in 1927 in a Fourth Avenue bookshop in New York City and is now owned by William Marcus Greve. The copy owned by the Manufacturers Trust Company is also by an unidentified copyist.

REFERENCES: Bowen (1892), p. 487; Hart (1898), p. 51; Kimball (1944), pp. 523–525; *Catalogue of American Portraits in The New-York Historical Society* (New York, 1941), pp. 160–161.

18. The Edgehill Portrait by Gilbert Stuart

Donald B. Straus

MEDIUM: Painted in oil on mahogany or walnut panel, the portrait measures 26.4 x 21.12 inches.

AUTHORSHIP: That the Edgehill panel is the original of Stuart's 1805 bust-size image of Jefferson is assured by the painter's statement to Martha Jefferson Randolph that he had "sent the original" to Monticello; by Jefferson's explicit instructions to Stuart that he should receive the life portrait; by the fact that it was the Edgehill panel which remained unfinished in Stuart's studio for sixteen years (for Stuart characteristically refused to finish life portraits of his more distinguished subjects so they could be retained as sources for the numerous replicas which he produced for ready sale); and by the unquestionable visual evidence of the likeness itself. Kimball's ordering of the Stuart likenesses and the overwhelming objective evidence, of which the unbroken provenance tracing the portrait to Monticello is alone conclusive, establish beyond question the correctness of the identification of the Edgehill panel as Stuart's life portrait. It would be unnecessary to emphasize this were it not for the fact that a contrary claim in recent years has been advanced by Orland and Courtney Campbell, a claim in which a canvas purchased at public auction in 1937, with no known history prior to that year, bearing a portrait that is manifestly the work of a hand decidedly inferior to Stuart, is proposed as the source of the Edgehill panel. Despite the conscientiousness with which this identification has been proposed, it is a claim which must be rejected.

CHRONOLOGY: Jefferson himself stated that it was "soon after" the completion of this portrait that Stuart painted the medallion profile. With the com-

73

pletion of the latter dated with exactness to June 7, 1805, it is clear that the sitting for the Edgehill portrait took place shortly before this date, most probably at Stuart's studio at F and Seventh Streets in Washington. As he portrayed Jefferson at sixty-two for this portrait Stuart was forty-nine and, as a friend told Dolley Madison, "all the rage."

HISTORY: Despite persistent attempts by Jefferson to obtain possession of this portrait, it was not until sixteen years after the sitting that he finally acquired it. In the meantime it remained unfinished in Stuart's studio, being used by him as the prototype for the various replicas. Henry Dearborn finally procured it from the painter and shipped it to Monticello, where it arrived in August 1821. It was there that the portrait hung for the remainder of Jefferson's life, descending, after his death, to the hands of his family at Edgehill, where it hung for seventy-five years. In 1902 it was purchased by a collateral descendant of Jefferson, Burton Harrison, who took the painting to his residence in Scotland. The Babcock Galleries of New York purchased the panel from Harrison in 1927 for John B. Winant, who sold it to Percy S. Straus from whom it passed by inheritance to its present owner, Donald B. Straus of New York.

PRESENT CONDITION: While the portrait was in his possession, Burton Harrison recorded that the panel had split "down the face" and reproductions made from it shortly after it left his hands show the likeness against a dark ground. Subsequently this dark ground and a considerable amount of repainting was removed to reveal the delicate, transparently painted surface of the original.

ICONOGRAPHIC IMPORTANCE: It was late in Jefferson's second term that prints of this likeness, such as the handsome one by Robert Field, began displacing the prints of the 1800 Rembrandt Peale image in the public's popularity. The likeness was persistently reproduced during his later life in America and in France, and after Jefferson's death — especially after the Stuart likeness was adopted by the government as the official image of Jefferson for use on postage stamps and currency — it triumphed over the Peale to become unquestionably the preeminent icon of Jefferson.

COPIES: Only four replicas of this portrait are recorded. The earliest, painted for James Bowdoin between 1805 and 1807, survives in the Bowdoin College Museum of Fine Arts. What is undoubtedly the second of these replicas — that in the possession of James Madison in 1814 — now hangs in the governor's palace at Colonial Williamsburg. Two further replicas, one commissioned by John Doggett and one by George Gibbs, were painted as part of sets of the first five presidents and thus were created sometime after Mon-

*The "Edgehill" portrait of Jefferson, painted from life by Gilbert Stuart in Washington
shortly before June 7, 1805.* Donald B. Straus of New York City

roe's election in 1816. The Doggett replica, destroyed in the 1851 Library of Congress fire, is known only through Maurin's 1825 lithograph and its derivatives. The Gibbs replica was sold by Colonel Gibbs' widow to Jefferson's great grandson, Thomas Jefferson Coolidge, whose descendants still own it. While the Gibbs replica seems seldom to have been reproduced, the destroyed Doggett image has been more frequently copied than perhaps any other of Jefferson's portraits. It was this version of Stuart's 1805 bust-size image which was chosen in 1867 to represent Jefferson officially on United States stamps, currency and certificates. At least four score of paintings and prints were derived from the Edgehill panel in the nineteenth century. Some thirty copies have been counted of the Bowdoin replica — many of them derived from Robert Field's 1807 engraving, which first set Stuart's portrait before the public. Less than a dozen copies of the Madison replica are known. Matthew Harris Jouett's copy of 1816, perhaps the first of the many painted from Stuart's 1805 *Jefferson,* was itself duplicated with some frequency.

REFERENCES: Bowen (1892), pp. 483–485; Hart (1898), p. 54; Kimball (1944), pp. 512–523; Fiske Kimball, "Gilbert Stuart's Portraits of Jefferson," *Gazette des Beaux-Arts,* 6th Series, *26* (1944), 95–112; Orland and Courtney Campbell, *The Lost Portraits of Thomas Jefferson* (Amherst College, 1959).

19. The Medallion Profile by Gilbert Stuart

Fogg Art Museum, Harvard University

MEDIUM: Kimball, believing the medium of this portrait to be oil on canvas, regarded as "careless allusions" Jefferson's description of it first as "a profile in the medallion stile" executed in "water colours" and later as a "sketch of me in the medallion form . . . on paper with crayons. . . ." But in 1956 Orland Campbell after a careful examination of this likeness correctly concluded that both of Jefferson's descriptions, though seemingly in conflict, are actually accurate: that the portrait was executed in gouache — opaque watercolor — over a lightly indicated crayon drawing on hand-made laid paper. The paper is mounted on thin linen, which in turn is mounted on modern artist's canvas and varnished, making the illusion that it was painted in oil almost complete, except for the chain marks on the paper.

The "medallion profile" of Jefferson, painted from life in June 1805 in Washington by Gilbert Stuart. Fogg Art Museum, Harvard University

AUTHORSHIP: Jefferson not only recorded his payment to "Gilbert Stewart for drawing" this unsigned portrait but little more than a week later sent him "his compliments" and a gift "for the trouble he gave him in taking the head à la antique." In 1813 Jefferson explained that of the three life portraits painted of him by Stuart the "third [was] in water colors, a profile in the medallion stile." Again, in 1819, Jefferson identified the author of this likeness by reporting that he had commissioned Stuart in 1805 "to sketch [him] in the medallion form." Thus both Stuart's authorship of the medallion profile and its place among the life portraits are amply recorded.

CHRONOLOGY: Jefferson undoubtedly sat for this portrait while he was "at the painting room of Mr. Stewart (the celebrated portrait painter) . . ." on the afternoon of June 7, 1805, for on that day he recorded his payment of one hundred dollars to Stuart "for drawing" his portrait. That this payment refers to the medallion portrait is confirmed not only by the letter which followed it on June 18 thanking Stuart again for "taking the head à la antique," but also by Jefferson's later explanation that the payment, "probably the treble of what he would have asked," was given to Stuart for ". . . the sketch . . . in the medallion form." Stuart was some twelve years younger than the sixty-two-year-old president when he sat for him in Stuart's studio at F and Seventh Streets in Washington.

HISTORY: The portrait was still in the hands of the painter on June 18, 1805, when Jefferson wrote that Stuart was "free to use either" the portrait in oils executed shortly before the medallion profile or the latter itself for the engravings which Stuart had contemplated having made from one of them. "The one not proposed to be used I will be glad to receive at Mr. Stewart's convenience; the other when he shall be done with it." Stuart chose to keep the earlier portrait for engraving and must have transmitted the medallion profile to Jefferson shortly before leaving Washington at the end of June. The portrait hung in the president's house for the remaining years of Jefferson's presidency, leaving, with Jefferson in 1809, to become part of the collections at Monticello. Jefferson wrote of it in 1813 as being there in his possession and two years later he generously lent the portrait to William Thornton in Washington for copying, though it was not returned until the Madisons brought it south with them after the inauguration of Madison's successor, some twenty-seven months after it had left Jefferson's hands. Two years after Jefferson's death the portrait was part of the exhibition of Jefferson's collection in Boston. After the dispersal of this collection through the Athenaeum sale, from which the medallion profile was reserved, it passed ultimately into the possession of the descendants of Jefferson's granddaughter, Ellen Wayles Randolph Coolidge, descending to the widow of Thomas Jefferson Newbold who presented it in 1960 to the Fogg Art Museum in her husband's memory.

CONDITION: Long before it was given to Harvard University the surface of the painting had been lightly cleaned so that only traces of a yellowed varnish were still visible. Other than small areas, some of them retouched, where the paper has been rubbed through to the glue sizing beneath, the portrait is in good condition.

ICONOGRAPHIC IMPORTANCE: This is not only the portrait which Jefferson listed, with only the other likenesses by Stuart, in his reply to Delaplaine's request in 1813 to know the "approved portrait" of him, but was also that which Jefferson spoke of to Horatio Gates Spafford in February 1815 as that "deemed the best which has been taken of me." Jefferson's own admiration for the likeness, as indicated in these statements and in his willingness to have it reproduced, seems to have been shared by his family. Martha Jefferson Randolph is said to have considered this the best of the two Stuart likenesses of her father that hung at Monticello and as "the portrait . . . which best gives the shape of his magnificent head and its peculiar pose." After Jefferson's death the husband of one of Jefferson's granddaughters wanted to "buy it . . . *at any price*" and in 1871 when Jefferson's great granddaughter, Sarah N. Randolph, compiled her "Domestic Life" of Jefferson it bore the medallion profile as its frontispiece. Other of Jefferson's contemporaries agreed that it was a superior portrait. William Thornton, in fact, thought it "one of the finest [he] ever saw." William Birch pronounced it "the best thing that ever was done of" Jefferson and the Duke of Saxe Weimar concluded that of the "several portraits of Mr. Jefferson" at Monticello that "the best was that in profile by Stuart." It was, then, the portrait most admired by Jefferson, by his family, and by many of his most discriminating contemporaries.

COPIES: The earliest copy of the profile seems to have been that completed "about October 1805" by William Russell Birch, who saw the portrait in the president's house, borrowed it for two days, and made the drawing of it which he put into the hands of David Edwin as the source of Edwin's superb stipple engraving of 1809. From his own drawing, Birch again reproduced the medallion profile, this time as the "enamel portrait" which was exhibited in the "First Annual Exhibition of The Society of Artists of the United States" in Philadelphia in 1811. William Thornton's earliest copy of the profile was that "in Swiss crayons" which he placed in the Library of Congress in 1816. At least two further versions of this profile were painted by Thornton, though, like almost all of these derivative likenesses, they are now unlocated. Other notable copies were painted by Charles Bird King (now owned by Gordon Trist Burke) and Asher B. Durand. And although Thornton's original intention "to attempt to model [the medallion profile] in fine washed clay" seems never to have been carried out, Hiram Powers, much later in the century, did use the medallion portrait as the basis of the head of his full-length marble (now in the House wing of the capitol at Washington).

REFERENCES: Bowen (1892), p. 485; Hart (1898), p. 48, Kimball

(1944), pp. 512–523; George C. Mason, *Life and Works of Gilbert Stuart* (New York, 1879); Lawrence Park, *Gilbert Stuart* (New York, 1926), 1:439–443; Bernhard, Duke of Saxe-Weimar-Eisenach, *Travels through North America, During the Years 1825 and 1826* (Philadelphia, 1828), 1:199; report of Dec. 16, 1956, from Orland Campbell to James A. Bear, Jr.

20. *The Portrait by Bass Otis*

The Thomas Jefferson Memorial Foundation

MEDIUM: Painted in oil on canvas, the portrait measures 30 x 25 inches.

AUTHORSHIP: The painting was commissioned by Joseph Delaplaine "for the express purpose" of serving as the source of the engraving published in his *Repository of the Lives and Portraits of Distinguished American Characters* in 1817. Advertisements announcing this publication and the inscription on the Jefferson print included in it, ascribe the original likeness to Bass Otis. Documents among Jefferson's papers which record Otis' presence at Monticello not only confirm his authorship of this likeness, but also establish it as a portrait painted from life. Since the painting mentioned by both Bowen and Hart as the original of this likeness has all the earmarks of a copy, Kimball, though he did not "determine whether any one" of the surviving versions of this likeness "is actually a life portrait," chose the painting now at Monticello to represent this image in his study of the life portraits. Stylistically this painting is manifestly the work of Otis, the reverse of the portrait bears his studio label and his daughter's 1864 certification that the portrait "was Painted from Life by [her] Father Bass Otis . . . in 1816." But while this canvas is indisputably the work of Bass Otis, there has been doubt that it is the life portrait and thus the source of Neagle's 1817 engraving, because of the obvious differences in the costumes of the two delineations and especially because the latter, unlike the bust-size painting, portrays Jefferson at half length with his hands folded in his lap. But the smaller size, the immediacy of the painting, and the summary treatment of the costume in the Monticello canvas are all attributes to be expected in the original of a portrait painted in brief sittings at Monticello. The variations between this painting and the Neagle engraving may easily be the result of liberties taken by the engraver at the suggestion of Delaplaine to produce a print more in keeping with the other portraits published in the *Repository* series. Though

The life portrait of Jefferson by Bass Otis, painted during the first week of June 1816 at Monticello.
Thomas Jefferson Memorial Foundation

Delaplaine claimed in his prospectus that a number of the portraits in his series would be engraved from portraits procured from life "at his own expense," others would be taken "from pictures already in possession of private families or public institutions." Since it was, then, the prints that were Delaplaine's objective and not the accumulation of a gallery of original paintings and since he was financially unable to afford the cost of life portraits at times (he wrote Jefferson in February 1816 that he could not afford to send an artist to paint his portrait), it is plausible that the life portrait should have been returned to Otis after the completion of Neagle's engraving, as partial payment for the painter's part in producing the image for reproduction in Delaplaine's engraved gallery of portraits. Thus the subsequent possession of the painting by Otis, rather than by Delaplaine, for whom it was expressly painted, supports the statement of the artist's daughter that this is the portrait "Painted from life by . . . Bass Otis . . . in 1816."

CHRONOLOGY: On May 11, 1816, Delaplaine announced to Jefferson that he had "engaged one of our best portrait painters, Mr. Otis of this City . . . to set out for your Mansion on the First day of June next, for the express purpose of painting your portrait for my work." Both publisher and painter arrived at Monticello on June 3, 1816 — Otis carrying with him a letter of introduction from Dr. Caspar Wistar recommending him as "an artist of rising Character" distinguished "by his ingenuity as well as his obliging disposition." The portrait was completed shortly after their arrival, for Otis and Delaplaine's stay at Monticello was a brief one. Portraying Jefferson at seventy-three, the artist was thirty-one years old at the time of the painting.

HISTORY: Immediately after its completion the painting was carried by Otis and Delaplaine to Philadelphia, where it was seen by William Thornton late in July 1816. By October of the same year the canvas was in the hands of John Neagle, who was already at work on the engraving which Delaplaine issued early in 1817. In May of the following year it was part of the seventh annual exhibition at the Pennsylvania Academy of the Fine Arts and remained there for the academy's subsequent exhibition in July. Apparently remaining in the artist's possession until his death in 1861, it passed into the hands of his daughter, Susan Otis. In 1864 it was transferred by her to John C. Trautwine whose granddaughter, Mrs. E. M. Bolles, presented the portrait in 1930 to the Thomas Jefferson Memorial Foundation. It has hung at Monticello since that date.

CONDITION: Cleaned and relined in 1959, the portrait survives in excellent condition.

ICONOGRAPHIC IMPORTANCE: After seeing Otis' portrait, William Thornton declared that "never was such injustice done to [Jefferson] except by sign painters and General Kosciusko. . . ." Yet Neagle's engraving of 1817 was only the first of many prints which, judging from their popularity, brought this likeness to an extensive public that viewed Otis' image more charitably. Before the middle of the nineteenth century prints of this portrait had been published not only in Philadelphia, New York and Boston, but also in London and Glasgow; and when Peter Maverick's engraved version of the likeness was adopted as the official cypher of the Jefferson Insurance Company, the portrait was perpetuated endlessly on the company's official papers, making it the most widely distributed image of Jefferson in retirement.

COPIES: John Neagle's engraving, which faces page 125 in [Joseph] *Delaplaine's Repository of the Lives and Portraits of Distinguished American Characters,* Philadelphia, 1817, seems to have been the source of all subsequent prints of this likeness. It was also most probably the source of the five paintings now owned respectively by David K. E. Bruce, Elizabeth L. Godwin, William C. Bryon, the University of Virginia, and the Yale University Art Gallery. Two further paintings, both derived ultimately from the Otis portrait and now unlocated, were at various times offered as portraits of Jefferson by Charles Willson Peale and Gilbert Stuart. A more notable copy of the original painting, perhaps a replica, once owned by William J. Campbell, was presented to the Chicago Historical Society in 1923 by the Iroquois Club.

REFERENCES: Bowen (1892), p. 487; Hart (1898), p. 48; Kimball (1944), pp. 525–527; Joseph Jackson, "Bass Otis, America's First Lithographer," *The Pennsylvania Magazine of History and Biography, 37,* no. 4 (1913), 385–394; Caspar Wistar to Jefferson, May 28, 1816, in the Pierpont Morgan Library; the Jefferson-Delaplaine correspondence in the Jefferson Papers in the Library of Congress.

21. The Portrait by Giuseppe Valaperta

The New-York Historical Society

MEDIUM: Valaperta's portrait was undoubtedly modeled directly in the surviving medium: a red wax bas-relief on black glass measuring 3 x 2 inches.

AUTHORSHIP: The bas-relief bears no inscription, but its provenance in the

The wax bas-relief of Jefferson sculptured from life at Monticello shortly before September 19, 1816, by Giuseppe Valaperta. New-York Historical Society

context of a collection of four other wax profiles, each of which it matches exactly in medium, size and style, and one of which bears Valaperta's signature, establishes this Italian medalist and sculptor as its author. Previous students have doubted that this portrait was modeled from life, but Valaperta's letter of introduction, endorsed by Jefferson on September 16, 1816, and the testimony of the baron de Montlezun, who was at Montpelier when Valaperta returned from Monticello with the portrait, makes its position among Jefferson's life portraits unquestionable.

CHRONOLOGY: Jefferson received Valaperta at Monticello on September 16, 1816, and sat for him either that day or shortly thereafter, for the sculptor arrived at Montpelier on the nineteenth with his wax profile of Jefferson. At Madison's residence, according to the baron de Montlezun, Valaperta put the finishing touches to the Jefferson bas-relief with the hope of working it "afterwards in ivory." This wax portrait was produced during the Italian immigrant's first year in America and in an interlude from his employment sculpting ornaments for the national capitol. Six months after modeling this depiction of Jefferson at seventy-three years of age, Valaperta disappeared from his Washington residence, presumably a suicide.

HISTORY: With seven other profiles of eminent Americans, the Jefferson wax portrait was purchased from Valaperta's estate by his executor after the sculptor's disappearance. Passing ultimately into the hands of the Gallatin family, it was presented to the New-York Historical Society in 1880.

CONDITION: Despite the fragile nature of the medium, this profile survives in good condition.

ICONOGRAPHIC IMPORTANCE: Although rarely seen and with virtually no influence in shaping the public image of Jefferson, this bas-relief is part of a series of wax portraits said to be faithful likenesses by the subjects' contemporaries.

COPIES: The ivory profile which Valaperta hoped to execute from the life portrait seems never to have been completed and no portraits are known that have been derived from this wax profile.

REFERENCES: Kimball (1944), p. 498; John Payne Todd to Jefferson, September 14, 1816, in the Jefferson Papers at the Massachusetts Historical Society; baron de Montlezun, *Voyage fait dans les années 1816 et 1817 . . .* (Paris, 1818), 1:71–72; A. J. Wall, "Joseph Valaperta, Sculptor," *New-York Historical Society Quarterly Bulletin, 11,* no. 2 (July 1927), 53–56; Charles Fairman, *Art and Artists of the Capitol of the United States of America* (Washington, 1927), pp. 452, 31, 32; *Catalogue of American Portraits in The New-York Historical Society* (New York, 1941), p. 160; Ethel Stanwood Bolton, *American Wax Portraits* (Boston, 1929), pp. 30–31, 61.

22. *The Portrait by William John Coffee*

Whereabouts unknown

MEDIUM: "About half the size of life in plaster," this lost bust of Jefferson, if it was characteristic of other work executed by Coffee while at Monticello, would logically have been sculpted with the same delicacy of detail and diminutive scale as the artist's early work in porcelain.

AUTHORSHIP: In the postscript of his letter to John Adams of May 17, 1818, Jefferson wrote that "there is now here a Mr. Coffee, a sculptor and English-man, who has just taken my bust . . . He is a fine artist. He takes them about half the size of life in plaster." This statement and Jefferson's assurance to Madison that Coffee "gives less trouble than any artist, painter or Sculptor I have ever submitted myself to" establish Coffee's authorship of a plaster bust of Jefferson sculpted from life. Though this portrait has apparently been lost since the dispersal of the Monticello collections, at least one extant plaster, that owned by Olivia Taylor, has been erroneously identified as the Coffee likeness. This attribution, announced in 1945 by Anna Wells Rut-ledge, is now known to be an error not only because the Taylor plaster quali-fies so consistently as one derived from the portrait by Peter Cardelli (see the following portrait), but also because the size, the undraped shoulders (Coffee's busts are invariably costumed), the scale of its detail, and the character of the modeling itself, are all foreign to extant work unquestion-ably identified as that of Coffee.

CHRONOLOGY: The Coffee bust was completed while the artist was in his mid-forties either immediately before, or on April 11, 1818 — the day that Jefferson introduced the sculptor by letter to Madison as an artist "lately from England" who had come "from Richmond to take your bust and mine." While Coffee may again have been at Monticello on May 7, when Jefferson, after an absence at Poplar Forest for more than a fortnight, wrote Adams that "Mr. Coffee . . . has just taken my bust," Jefferson's payment to this sculptor on April 12 "for the originals of 3. busts to wit Mrs. Randolph's Ellen's and mine" affirms that Jefferson's reference in this letter is to the completion of the bust on the earlier date, modeled one or two days before his seventy-five birthday.

HISTORY: Though busts by this artist of other members of the Monticello family have survived, nothing is known of the history of the Coffee *Jefferson* later than its completion in April 1818.

CONDITION: It is possible that the original plaster or replicas in terra cotta may yet survive, unidentified, in private or public collections.

ICONOGRAPHIC IMPORTANCE: Jefferson felt that Coffee was "really able in his art" and recommended him to Adams as "a fine artist." Extant portraits by Coffee indicate that Jefferson's recommendations were based on more than politeness and that Coffee's *Jefferson* would have been an attractive and engaging likeness. That its influence was very limited is evident from the silence which surrounds the history of this bust. It seems unlikely that it was ever known widely outside the family circle at Monticello.

The bust of Cornelia Jefferson Randolph
by William John Coffee, sculptor of the lost portrait of
Jefferson executed from life in May 1816 at Monticello.
Thomas Jefferson Memorial Foundation

COPIES: John S. Cogdell's report, in a letter to Samuel F. B. Morse in 1821, that Coffee had promised "a head of Mr. Jefferson at the North which he would send to me for the Society [The South Carolina Academy of Fine Arts]" indicates that the sculptor still had a duplicate of his *Jefferson* three years after its execution, but it is not known whether his promise to send the portrait to Charleston was kept. Perhaps, like his "strong wish to Model on [his] own Account, a Statue whole Length two feet 6 inches High, of Mr. Jefferson" in 1825, nothing further came of it.

REFERENCES: Hart (1898), pp. 47–48; Kimball (1944), p. 532; Anna Wells Rutledge, "William John Coffee as a Portrait Painter," *Gazette des*

Beaux-Arts, 6th series, *28* (Nov. 1945), [297–]312; George C. Groce, "William John Coffee, Long-lost Sculptor," *American Collector, 15* (May 1946), 14–15, 19–20; the Coffee-Jefferson correspondence in the Jefferson Papers at the Library of Congress; photographs of signed portrait busts by Coffee now in the Derby Museum and Art Gallery, England.

23. *The Portrait by Peter Cardelli*

Destroyed

MEDIUM: A helpful description of the process used by Cardelli to produce his portrait busts is that recorded in John Quincy Adams' Diary: "The first mould is taken in soft red clay worked by the hand, the second is [a] Plaister Shell moulded over it in two halves. The Bust itself is cast in this. . . ." It was this cast which Cardelli called "the plaster original." Thus the destroyed life portrait was of the same substance as its surviving copies.

AUTHORSHIP: The original plaster may have been signed, as is the sculptor's extant bust of Trumbull, below the right shoulder: "P. Cardelli F." Though the original of this bust survived into the twentieth century, the Cardelli likeness is among the last of Jefferson's portraits to be correctly identified. When the original left Edgehill at the turn of the century, its authorship was unknown. And though Hart and Kimball were aware of the correspondence which affirms Cardelli's execution of a portrait of Jefferson sculpted from life, only Kimball attempted to identify it, though he confused the Edgehill plaster with still another bust of Jefferson — one now identified as a copy of the posthumous portrait by Sidney Morse. When, in 1945, one of the casts of the destroyed Edgehill bust was finally attributed to an artist, the identification was a mistaken one: William John Coffee (see preceding entry). That the plasters derived from the Edgehill bust are copies of the original portrait sculpted by Cardelli at Monticello is now established by the consistently positive results of the comparison of these busts with portraits unquestionably by Cardelli, which they match in size, in medium, in stylistic conception, in technique of execution, and even in such details as the absence of drapery and the squarely cut form of the base. There has often been confusion as to whether the first name of the Cardelli who sculptured Jefferson was Georgio or Pietro, but the artist's broadside subscription forms for copies of this bust appeared under the name of "Peter Cardelli."

A twentieth-century plaster cast of the original plaster bust (now destroyed) of Jefferson which was modeled from life at Monticello on May 24, 1819, by Peter Cardelli.
Thomas Jefferson Memorial Foundation

CHRONOLOGY: John Quincy Adams urged Jefferson to grant Cardelli a sitting, and when Jefferson agreed to welcome the sculptor to Monticello for the purpose, Adams provided a further letter of introduction. This letter, which Cardelli carried with him, was endorsed on May 24, 1819 — the day of Cardelli's arrival at Monticello. The bust, then, must have been modeled shortly after that date when Jefferson was seventy-six years of age. Cardelli's age is unknown, but Jefferson's sitting was only one of a series of sculpturing opportunities — including sittings with Monroe, Adams and Madison — which fell to the sculptor that year and induced him to leave his employment carving ornaments on the capitol in the optimistic hope that he could support himself by the sale of plaster casts of his busts of eminent Americans.

HISTORY: Cardelli left not only a plaster bust for Jefferson at Monticello but also either the mold from which it was produced or yet another plaster cast of it, and perhaps other busts as well. Low water delayed the shipment of these materials until late that year when, with the exception of the original plaster, they were returned to the artist's possession. After the sale of Monticello in 1830, the bust was moved to Edgehill, where it eventually became part of the property of Carolina Ramsay Randolph, the sole owner of Edgehill at the time of her death in 1902. When, at that time, the Edgehill relics from Monticello were left to three of her nieces, the Cardelli bust came into the possession of one of them, Cornelia Jefferson Taylor. Because of a broken pedestal this plaster had apparently been stored in the Edgehill attic for some time. The bust subsequently was at Lego, the residence of Cornelia Jefferson Taylor for several years. Sometime after its acquisition from Edgehill in 1903 and before 1910, a concern in New York City was engaged to produce plaster reproductions of this bust. In the process of executing these casts the original is said to have been destroyed.

ICONOGRAPHIC IMPORTANCE: The influence of the Cardelli bust in the nineteenth century was slight. Apparently Cardelli's plans for subscription were not successful, and his portrait of Jefferson was neither duplicated as frequently nor distributed as widely as the artist hoped. Though Cardelli often had difficulty in producing satisfactory representations of his subjects (John Quincy Adams, during a series of sittings, felt that Cardelli would "ultimately not get a likeness") this bust is recognizably Jefferson.

CONDITION: The original plaster is said to have been destroyed sometime between 1903 and 1910 in the process of making a cast for reproducing the bust for commercial sale. The copies of this bust, in plaster like the original, survive in good condition.

COPIES: No examples of this likeness that might have been cast as replicas and sold to subscribers in response to Cardelli's broadside have been located. The number of casts taken from the original plaster by the New York firm that reproduced it before 1910 is not known, but at least four of these survive. One is owned by the Thomas Jefferson Memorial Foundation; another by Margaret Randolph Taylor and Olivia Taylor of Charlottesville. The example at Redlands, Albemarle County, is owned by Robert Carter. Another example was owned by the late Mary Walker Randolph.

REFERENCES: Hart (1898), p. 47; Kimball (1944), p. 498; *Catalogue of Portraits and other works of art in the possession of The American Philosophical Society* (Philadelphia, 1961), pp. 1–2; Charles E. Fairman, *Art and Artists of the Capitol of the United States* (Washington, 1927), p. 46; the Cardelli correspondence at the Massachusetts Historical Society; the Cardelli-Trumbull correspondence at the Morristown National Historical Park; report of Miss Olivia Taylor; the Cardelli broadside in the Madison Papers at the Library of Congress.

24. The Portrait by Thomas Sully

The American Philosophical Society

MEDIUM: Painted in oil on canvas, the portrait measures 30 x 25 inches.

AUTHORSHIP: The public nature of this commission and the fame of the likeness that resulted from it are such that Sully's authorship of this portrait has been continually acknowledged. The artist's monogram and his notation that this portrait was painted "From Jefferson, 1821; finished 1830" — both inscribed on the reverse of the canvas at the American Philosophical Society — distinguish this half-length from its replicas as the portrait painted from life.

CHRONOLOGY: Late in January 1821 Jefferson was informed of the desire of the "Superintendent, Officers, Professors, Instructors, and Cadets of the U. States Mil. Academy" to commission Thomas Sully to paint a portrait of him to be added to those hanging in the "Academic Library" as "being alike one of the Founders, and Patrons of both" "Our Republic . . . and the Mil. Academy." Jefferson responded cordially, and though he felt that the trouble of Sully's journey would be "illy bestowed on an ottamy of 78," he nevertheless agreed to the sitting, which took place at Monticello in March 1821. According to Dunlap, the thirty-seven-year-old Sully "was an inmate of Monticello twelve days, and left the place with the greatest reluctance."

HISTORY: In 1830, on the commission of William Short, who presented the portrait to the American Philosophical Society in June of that year, the artist added the finishing touches to the portrait for which Jefferson had posed nine years before. The painting has hung for almost a century and a half in an honored position in Philosophical Hall in Philadelphia, home of the distinguished institution over which Jefferson presided as president from 1797 until 1814.

CONDITION: Soundly painted and free of the repainting of later "restorers," the portrait survives in excellent condition. A modern relining has covered the original inscription on the reverse of the painting.

ICONOGRAPHIC IMPORTANCE: As its frequent reproduction bears testimony, Sully's portrait offers us the finest image of the Jefferson of the late Monticello years. Surviving in untampered condition the portrait is an unusually reliable record of Jefferson's coloring, depicting accurately the fresh complexion and the traces of the sandy hue still in his hair and eyebrows. Not only has the life portrait moved the participants of the distinguished conclaves which gather annually in Philosophical Hall, but its extensive reproductions, in replicas, copies, engravings, and transmutations into sculpture, have given the Sully likeness a far-reaching and admiring audience. As the ultimate source of the great full-length at West Point, the portrait is also significant in its relationship to one of only two portrayals of Jefferson at full length, for his imposing stature was a memorable aspect of his presence. There is no better testimony of the effect of the West Point image on its viewers than that of James Fenimore Cooper. At West Point in April 1823 Cooper, whose "antipathies . . . to Mr. Jefferson" were well known, was induced, despite the fact that he insisted that he would rather "have gone twice as far to see the picture of almost any other man," to enter the library to view Sully's recently installed full-length of Jefferson. On his first confrontation with the painting Cooper "desired the gentlemen with [him] to wait, until [he] could go" for Mr. Charles Mathews, his guest, a distinguished British comedian and also a collector, and . . . a very respectable critic." Mathews, wrote Cooper later,

> pronounced it one of the finest portraits he had ever beheld, and that he would never have forgiven me if I had let it escape his notice. But you will smile when I tell you its effects on myself. There was a dignity, a repose, I will go further, and say a loveliness, about this painting, that I never have seen in any other portrait. . . . I saw . . . Jefferson, standing before me, not in red breeches and slovenly attire, but a gentleman, appearing in all republican simplicity, with a grace and ease on the canvas, that to me seem unrivalled. It has really shaken my opinion of Jefferson as a

The life portrait of Jefferson painted by Thomas Sully at Monticello in March 1821.
American Philosophical Society

man, if not as a politician; and when his image occurs to me now, it is in the simple robes of Sully, sans red breeches, or even without any of the repulsive accompaniments of a political 'sans culotte.'

COPIES: Recognizing that this life portrait was used as the prototype for the upper portion of both the small full-length completed by Sully on April 10, 1822 (now owned by Edward S. Moore), and the large full-length finished on May 7 of the same year (now hanging, as it did in Jefferson's time, at West Point), Kimball nevertheless suggested that the related full-length sketch by Sully owned by John Hill Morgan was a study painted from life rather than from the half-length. Another related sketch, brought to light since Kimball's study and now owned by Hugh Murray Savage, has also been suggested as a life study. However the fact that every detail of the pose and even the lighting in both of these watercolor sketches duplicates exactly what is found in the original half-length and that they possess the addition of fictitious settings can only lead to the conclusion that both were studies for the West Point full-length based on the half-length life portrait. While it seems likely that Sully, during his stay at Monticello, would have sketched Jefferson's full stature for the projected full-length, until such a sketch is found with earmarks which clearly distinguish it from the studies taken from the half-length, the suggestion that Sully sketched Jefferson from life at full length must remain an unsupported one. Among the many replicas of the original half-length, the most notable are the painting once owned by President Monroe, which is now in the possession of the Jefferson Society at the University of Virginia, that purchased by the government in 1874 which now hangs in the Senate corridor of the United States Capitol, and a canvas, once in the possession of Lafayette, which is presently unlocated. The latter was used by David d'Angers in producing his bronze full-length of Jefferson, the head of which, according to Lossing, "was modeled chiefly from an excellent portrait by Sully, in the possession of LaFayette." The David d'Angers likeness, and thus the Sully, was again used by a sculptor when Moses Ezekiel produced his bust of Jefferson. J. W. Casilear included the Sully *Jefferson* in his engraved series of presidents in 1834 and thus produced the first of many prints of the Sully likeness.

REFERENCES: Bowen (1892), pp. 485–486; Hart (1898), p. 55; Kimball (1944), pp. 527–531; Edward Biddle and Mantle Fielding, *The Life and Works of Thomas Sully* (Philadelphia, 1921), p. 191; James Franklin Beard, ed., *The Letters and Journals of James Fenimore Cooper* (Cambridge, 1960), 1:95–96; *A Catalogue of Portraits and Other Works of Art in the American Philosophical Society* (Philadelphia, 1961), pp. 54–55.

25. The Portrait by John Henri Isaac Browere

New York State Historical Association, Cooperstown, New York

MEDIUM: The method and the exact nature of the medium used by Browere in casting his life masks were closely guarded secrets never transmitted beyond his son, Albertus. Jefferson was able to record only that the process involved "successive coats of thin grout plaistered on the naked head, and kept there an hour." The liquid substance (Jefferson referred to it as such in the first draft of his description of the sitting) used by Browere for the cast was undoubtedly the same used so successfully in executing his other portraits, so it must have been conditions peculiar to the atmosphere at Monticello which allowed this liquid to dry so rapidly "that separation became difficult and even dangerous" and obliged Browere to "use freely the mallet and chisel to break it into pieces and get off a piece at a time." From this repaired mold of Jefferson's "living person," was cast, in plaster, the life portrait into which such details as the open eyes and the hair were cut directly by the artist.

AUTHORSHIP: Though unsigned, the very nature of this "life mask" and its provenance with the body of Browere's portraits have made its position among the life portraits and its authorship by Browere unquestionable.

CHRONOLOGY: In a nineteenth-century transcript of a certificate, dated October 15, 1825, which survives among Browere's papers, Jefferson certifies that "Mr. Browere has this day made a mould in Plaister composition, from my person for the purposes of making a portrait Bust and Statue for his contemplated National Gallery." The plaster cast from this mold into which Browere cut the open eyes, the hair and other details was almost certainly completed before the sculptor left Monticello, since Madison, on October 19, certified that "a Bust . . . taken by Mr. Browere from the person of Mr. Jefferson, has been submitted to our inspection and appears to be a faithful Likeness."

HISTORY: Browere's work in collecting his gallery of life masks was monumental but unappreciated in his time, and thus "on his death Bed he wished the Heads of the Principle ones to be detached, Boxed up and nothing done with them for 40 years." Complying with this request, his son, Albertus, closeted them until the centennial of the signing of the Declaration of Independence, when he set to work remounting the busts, "Putting Drapery to Some," hoping that they would be exhibited in Philadelphia during the centennial celebration and might ultimately be purchased by the government. But even in the interest in America's historic past that was generated by the

The original plaster cast from the life mask which was molded directly from the "living person"
of Jefferson on October 15, 1825, at Monticello. New York State Historical Association

centennial, neither the government nor the committee in charge of the centennial exhibitions seems to have shown interest in Browere's life masks and they lapsed once again into obscurity. It was Charles Henry Hart who rediscovered them in 1897 still in the care of the artist's descendants and who made them and their significance public knowledge. Fearing the dispersal of the collection, Hart, as had Albertus Browere before him, urged, unsuccessfully, that the government purchase it *en bloc.* Hart further suggested that the most important of the life masks be "cast in imperishable bronze." It was not until 1940, however, and then by a private individual, Stephen Clark, that the main body of the collection was purchased, duplicated in bronze and placed on permanent loan at the New York State Historical Association at Cooperstown. On Mr. Clark's death in 1960 the collection, including Browere's *Jefferson,* passed to the association as a gift with the injunction that neither the original nor the bronze replica should ever leave Cooperstown.

CONDITION: Kimball stated that the bust of Jefferson had been "more than once repaired" but a careful examination of the original plaster reveals no detectable repairs. The whole plaster is covered with a putty-colored glossy finish which most probably was applied when the busts were refurbished by Albertus Browere in 1876. This finish has flaked in a few places, but there is no evidence of any significant damage.

ICONOGRAPHIC IMPORTANCE: Madison was joined in his certification of the accuracy of Browere's likeness of Jefferson by contemporaries whose judgments of works of art were informed and candid. Samuel F. B. Morse found it a "perfect facsimile," and Rembrandt Peale, whose own two portraits of Jefferson record his penetrating knowledge of the subject's lineaments, thought Browere's portrayal "in truth a faithful and a living Likeness." It was, however, Browere's polychrome full-length version of this portrait, unveiled on the hour of Jefferson's death, which the artist said "gave an effect . . . which will not ever be forgotten . . . by the thousands" who viewed it in New York's City Hall during the celebration of the semi-centennial of the Declaration of Independence. But Browere's report of the impact of his *Jefferson* upon his contemporaries is obviously exaggerated, as his own subsequent decision to draw it into obscurity indicates. It was not until its rediscovery at the end of the nineteenth century that it was recognized as "the most faithful portrait possible, down to the minutest detail, the very living features of the breathing man, a likeness of the greatest historical significance and importance."

COPIES: In May 1826 Browere began work on a full-length portrayal of

Jefferson, based on his life mask, which was to be presented, for the duration of the celebrations on the fourth of July of that year, to the Corporation of New York "to be publickly exhibited to all who desire to view the beloved features of the friend of science and of liberty." The sculptor wrote Jefferson on June 13 that on that day he had "completed your full-length statue (nudity) and to-morrow I intend, if spared, to commence dressing it in the costume you wore at the time of your delivery of the Declaration of American Independence." Though Jefferson was too ill to respond to Browere's request for "a full and explicit account of the form and colour of his dress," the artist was able after "unremitting exertions, to finish and place it in [the City Hall banqueting room], exactly at the hour of the dissolution of Mr. Jefferson." There this full-length, colored and clothed statue represented Jefferson's "lofty and majestic figure standing erect; his mild blue and expressive eyes beaming with intelligence and good will to his fellow men. The scroll of the Declaration . . . clutched in his extended right hand. . . . His left hand resting on the hip. . . ." No trace of this statue has been found nor of any portrait which might have resulted from Browere's offer to the University of Virginia to "erect in marble or bronze a statue to the memory of its founder." The only duplication of the Browere *Jefferson* now extant is the bronze replica cast on Mr. Clark's commission in 1940.

REFERENCES: Hart (1898), p. 47; Kimball (1944), pp. 523–523; "Certificates relative to the Busts of General LaFayette Executed in Plaister By John H. I. Browere" at the New York State Historical Association; James Madison to Jefferson, June 14, 1825 in the Madison Papers at the Library of Congress; the Browere-Jefferson correspondence in the Jefferson Papers at the Library of Congress; Charles Henry Hart, "Unknown Life Masks of Great Americans," *McClure's Magazine, 9,* no. 6 (Oct. 1897), 1053–1060; Charles Henry Hart, *Browere's Life Masks of Great Americans* (New York, 1899); correspondence with Louis C. Jones.

A Note on Further Portraits

Excluded from this essay are a number of portraits, both suppositional and existing, which have been put forward at various times as part of the canon of Jefferson's life-likenesses. These include posthumous portraits, based on one or more of the identified life portraits, which clearly have no place among those likenesses created in Jefferson's presence, portraits of unidentified subjects erroneously identified as portrayals of Jefferson, and a number of rumored "portraits" whose existence has never been established. Only the most noteworthy of these are indicated briefly here.

LATROBE: Following Kimball and my own attachment to an appealing likeness, I included the drawing attributed to Benjamin Latrobe in the 1962 exhibition of Jefferson's life portraits and in the first edition of this monograph. Since that time editorial work on Latrobe's papers and our knowledge of Latrobe's hand in extant drawings have progressed in directions that make the attribution unacceptable. And without Latrobe's authorship its place among the life portraits must be relinquished until some new and substantial evidence appears.

EPPINGTON: Eva Turner Clark, in her study of *Francis Eppes, His Ancestors and Descendants* (New York, 1942, p. 253), quotes Egbert Giles Leigh, Jr. (1851–1915) as writing, "It is a matter of real distress to me that so many of the Eppington portraits and old relics are lost. Among the portraits was one of Mr. and Mrs. Jefferson, presented by Mrs. Jefferson to Mr. and Mrs. Francis Eppes." Unfortunately further record of such a gift or even of the existence of this double portrait has not been found.

DU SIMITIÈRE: In 1959 Paul Sifton suggested as a portrait of Jefferson drawn about 1776, the miniature likeness in plumbago on ivory among the

Du Simitière materials at the Historical Society of Pennsylvania (*Antiques,* 76, no. 3 [Sept. 1959], 250–251). There are such significant differences between the features of the individual represented in this Du Simitière drawing and those of Jefferson as recorded in his established portraits, however, that the miniature cannot be accepted as a depiction of Jefferson. From a study of the costume of this miniature, Frederick P. Todd, director of the museum at West Point, concluded that the personage in the ivory "is definitely in a uniform" and that it is probably that "of an English junior officer of about the period of the American Revolution."

COSWAY: It has more than once been suggested that Maria Cosway depicted Jefferson during the many opportunities she had to observe him in Paris, but the absence of any record of such a portrait and the restriction of Mrs. Cosway's references concerning Jefferson likenesses to the Trumbull miniature — the only portrait of the American which she bequeathed with her other effects to the Collegio at Lodi — strongly suggests that this replica was the only depiction of Jefferson in her hands.

PARADISE: The inventory of 1812 of the Paradise house in Williamsburg mentions a large portrait of Jefferson, but whether it was part of the Paradise household in Europe, and thus most probably a replica of Mather Brown's canvas, or was acquired after the return to the United States is unknown. It is most likely, though, that this portrait was derived from one of the likenesses described in this catalogue.

RAMAGE: The late Mrs. Breckinridge Long had in her possession at one time a miniature said to be a portrait of Jefferson by John Ramage (Frick Art Reference Library files). Until this portrait can again be located it cannot be determined whether Jefferson actually sat for Ramage when both were in New York City during Jefferson's first months as secretary of state.

"TH. J." Art Collector

HAROLD E. DICKSON

Foreword

DURING HIS LIFETIME, THE WALLS OF JEFFERSON'S BELOVED MONTI-
cello "hung thick" with art, as William Wirt described it. Both American
and European visitors were impressed by the astonishing collection in what
had become for the third president a veritable private museum.

In his first plans for Monticello and before he was to establish a family
there, it would appear that Jefferson envisioned a private gallery-library, with
the simplest living quarters attached for the owner and curator. Even with
the later changes that the house underwent, the works of art in the entrance
hall and west drawing room remained the center of his growing collection
until his death.

That the author of the Declaration of Independence would also be one of
America's first connoisseurs of the arts compounds his legacy to the Republic
two hundred years later. Professor Dixon has explored this less well-known
side of Jefferson's interests — Jefferson would have called it his "passion" —
and has documented the subject with thoroughness and skill.

Benjamin Latrobe wrote to Jefferson during his presidency that the president, by his example and enthusiasm, had "planted the fine arts in America."
Professor Dixon's essay illuminates that observation by placing Jefferson's
commitment and taste in the context of the first tentative decades of America's
cultural infancy.

WILLIAM HOWARD ADAMS

After Guido Reni. *Herodiade Bearing the Head of St. John on a Platter.*
Thomas Jefferson Memorial Foundation, Charlottesville

"TH. J." Art Collector

HAROLD E. DICKSON

EVERY STREAM MUST HAVE A BEGINNING, YET NOTHING IS ON RECORD TO indicate precisely where to look for the springhead of Thomas Jefferson's lifelong concern with the arts.

Sometime during the early pursuit of his comprehensive and systematic studies in human knowledge a place was reserved for the "fine arts." A section so termed (though devoted mainly to literature) headed the list of basic books for a library drawn up by Jefferson in 1771 for his kinsman, Robert Skipwith.[1] Included in the list were Daniel Webb's *An Inquiry into the Beauties of Painting; and into the Merits of the most celebrated Painters, Ancient and Modern* (1760) [2] and three works of "criticism" that had been influential in the formation of his own ideas: William Hogarth's *The Analysis of Beauty* (1753), Edmund Burke's *A Philosophical Inquiry into the Origin of Our Ideas of the Sublime and Beautiful* (1757), and, by Lord Kames (Henry Home), a three-volume *Elements of Criticism* (1762). Jefferson was then twenty-eight; and years before that, in the early 1760s while he was a student at the College of William and Mary or in the course of broad and rigorous readings leading to his admission to the bar in 1767, he would have come to know these and other writings of artistic relevance.

It is possible, too, to surmise that the arts were included in the wide-ranging discussions of that group of four who gathered often in the royal governor's mansion at Williamsburg and included Governor Francis Fauquier himself; George Wythe, Jefferson's revered mentor in the law; Dr. William Small, a Scotsman who taught mathematics at the college and blended humanism with his science; and the young Jefferson, who at seventeen was brought into this circle by Dr. Small.[3]

During those ripening years when all of Jefferson's physical world lay between Williamsburg and his up-country home, and when his cultural contacts were mainly with families of the tidewater aristocracy, there were all too few works of art that he could actually have seen — a fair number of portraits (not painting of a high order, however esteemed the portraits were as likenesses), perhaps a few engravings, and no sculpture.

However, his aesthetic as well as geographical horizons would have been broadened when in the spring and early summer of 1766 he traveled by way of Annapolis and Philadelphia as far as New York, returning by water to Williamsburg.[4] On this, Jefferson's first trip outside the confines of his native state, he was introduced, especially in Philadelphia, to an urban society in which cultivation of the arts had progressed to a state beyond anything that he had witnessed.

With the largest population in the colonies, approaching thirty thousand,[5] Philadelphia had become the prospering cynosure of American communities, and a number of its more affluent citizens were actively supporting the arts, collecting paintings and sculptures for their townhouses and country seats.[6] At Bush Hill, among pictures assembled by James Hamilton throughout the preceding three decades, was an admired *Saint Ignatius* by Murillo that had come from a Spanish prize vessel, and in the garden were "seven statues in fine Italian marble." Hamilton's brother-in-law William Allen, that "true Mycaenas of Philadelphia," who had sent his son and a nephew on the Grand Tour in 1759 (the young Benjamin West sailing with them to Leghorn), owned original paintings and copies of many of the Italian old masters. But among these and others the conceded "foremost among Philadelphia's collector's" was Dr. John Morgan; and it was to him that Jefferson bore a letter from Dr. George Gilmer, who introduced the visitor from the south as "my particular friend." [7]

Dr. Morgan was eight years older than Jefferson, and in knowledge of the world was vastly more experienced. He had but lately returned, "flushed with honors," from five years of medical studies abroad, during which he had been joined by his fellow townsman Samuel Powel, both of them beginning art collectors, for a year's Grand Tour. What remains of Morgan's journal reveals his thoroughgoing and perceptive attention to all the arts wherever he went.[8] In Rome he followed the "Course of Antiquities" given by James Byers, and as doctor and patron he befriended the Swiss artist Angelica Kauffmann who was later to work in England. A list of "articles collected by Dr. Morgan during his travels" attests to his employment of copyists in obtaining paintings as well as his acquisition of a considerable group of prints and drawings.[9]

It had been Jefferson's intention upon coming to Philadelphia to "make the stay necessary for innoculation" against smallpox,[10] and there is no actual record of the extent or conduct of his visit. But given his natural curiosity and a circumstantial background such as the foregoing, it can safely be assumed that at that time he heard more, saw more, and came to understand more about art collecting than in all his previous experience. If Dr. Morgan talked about his travels as he wrote about them, he would have struck his guest as an enthusiast for the fine arts. Then in all likelihood, as time permitted, the Virginian would have been received in some of the homes of those friends of Dr. Morgan who shared his interest in art.

In addition, Dr. Morgan had a bibliophile's passion for books, and his private library, "one of the most catholic in all the colonies,"[11] containing works on architecture, the fine arts, and archaeology, must have had a special attraction for Jefferson.

With all such possibilities considered, there remains one reasonable certainty — that the young Jefferson gained most of his introductory acquaintance with the arts through books.[12] Of those mentioned above, he should have found it enjoyable as well as edifying to pick up *Webb's Essay on Painting,* a small octavo volume of two hundred pages, pleasantly didactic in approach, that introduced the reader to the elements and "celebrated" masters of the art. Hogarth's *The Analysis of Beauty,* a lively "endeavour to shew what the principles are in nature, by which we are directed to call the forms of some bodies beautiful, others ugly," would have provided stimulating reading. To the anti-rationalist Edmund Burke, beauty was "no creature of our reason, since it strikes us without reference to use" — this last a concept toward which Jefferson would have been less sympathetic than toward Hogarth's "beauty of fitness." While at college, he may have been introduced by Dr. Small to the voluminous works of Lord Kames; and he may have heard more directly of the *Elements of Criticism* from Dr. Morgan, who had been at Edinburgh when the work first appeared and had come there recommended to Lord Kames' favor by Benjamin Franklin.[13]

These books had been listed by Jefferson for Robert Skipwith, and there were others that he himself had owned at this time. Older than Hogarth's treatise by thirty years was Jonathan Richardson's tripartite opus, *Essay on the Theory of Painting* (1715), *Two Discourses: I. An Essay on the Whole Art of Criticism as it relates to Painting . . .,* and *II. An Argument in behalf of the Science of a Connoisseur . . .* (1719). William Gilpin's *An Essay on Prints . . .* (1768) discussed methods of engraving, printmakers, and their works, offering also "some Cautions that may be useful in collecting." Jefferson had a "Da Vinci on painting" and also the three-volume *Delle Vite de' piu Eccellenti Pittori, Scultori et Architetti* by Giorgio Vasari published between 1548 and 1563. Fiske Kimball was sure that at this time Jefferson must have owned Horace Walpole's *Aedes Walpoliana* (1747).

The first book on sculpture which Jefferson is recorded as owning was Joseph Spence's *Polymetis: or, An Enquiry concerning the Agreement between the Works of the Roman Poets, and the Remains of the Antient Artists* . . . (1747), a volume of text and plates that would have been relished by Jefferson, with his love for the literature and arts of antiquity. There was also the folio *Segmenta nobilium signorum e statuaru* (1638), containing one hundred engraved plates by the French painter-engraver François Perrier of sculptures then extant in Rome. There is evidence that Jefferson made use of and perhaps owned Richardson's *An Account of the Statues and Bas-reliefs, Drawings and Pictures in Italy, France, etc. with Remarks* (1722), the first English guide to the art treasures of Europe.

The titles of these books in themselves show the breadth of knowledge that Jefferson was to bring to his later collecting; and their guidance was invaluable when it came to formulating his own concepts as to the role of the arts in society.[14]

As an integral part of his social philosophy, his aesthetic ideas were rooted both in antiquity and in the Age of Reason, with basic sources in the doctrines of Epicurus and of that Jeffersonian "trinity," Francis Bacon, John Locke, and Isaac Newton. To these must be added Lord Kames, whose "accurate criticism," it was early predicted, would "render him in the critical art, what Bacon, Locke, and Newton are in philosophy." [15] Stated Jefferson, "We have indeed the sense of what we call *the beautiful*, . . . that is exercised chiefly on subjects directed to the fancy, whether through the eye in visible forms . . . or to the imagination directly." [16] He believed that like the moral sense, man's aesthetic feeling is innate, yet has its separate identity: the good and the beautiful are not synonymous. However, in functioning, both must be directed toward a common goal of contributing to man's well-being, to his freedom. There was for Jefferson no art for art's sake.

In this light, then, art is to be tested and distinction drawn between the "nobler" arts, those that serve to elevate the condition of mankind, and others that only "serve to amuse" and therefore are deemed "subordinate." In the first category Jefferson placed the "practical" arts of architecture and landscape design. He believed that the arts of the second category, including painting and sculpture, could be innocently enjoyed as long as they did not assume the importance of necessities. Nevertheless, these lesser arts, he granted, could contribute to human welfare in two ways: they could provide inspirational representations of great men and morally instructive happenings, and they could "give a pleasing and innocent direction to accumulations of wealth which would otherwise be employed in the nourishment of coarse and vicious habits." [17] Not an aesthetician, Jefferson "despised the artificial canons of criticism" and, like many others in the eighteenth century, placed more emphasis on the content of a painting or sculpture than on its purely visual qualities.

The earliest evidence of Jefferson's desire to own works of art comes from about two years after he began the building of Monticello in 1769. Inscribed on a leaf of his construction notebook under the title of "Statues, Paintings etc." are two lists of masterworks of classical sculpture and late Renaissance painting, which were made undoubtedly with the intention of acquiring replicas for his house and grounds.[18] The practice of acquiring copies of masterpieces was common, and was exemplified in the copy-filled collections that Jefferson may have seen in Philadelphia. He would have read Jonathan Richardson's extended comments on copies and originals and would not have questioned the writer's dictum that "a copy of a very good picture [or statue, it could be added] is preferable to an indifferent original." [19]

Joseph Spence had stated that "among all the statues of the antients . . . there are about twenty that might be placed in the first class." [20] From this category came the thirteen sculpture selections of Jefferson's desiderata lists:

Venus of Medici, Florence

Herculese Farnese, Rome

Apollo of Belvidere, Rome

Antinous, Florence

Dancing Faunus

Messenger pulling out a thorn.

Roman slave whetting his knife

The Gladiator at Montalto

Myrmillo expiring, Rome

the Gladiator reposing himself after the engagement. (companion to the former.)

Hercules and Antaeus. in Ch[----]on's anatomy

the two wrestlers

the Rape of the Sabines (3 figures)

Fiske Kimball demonstrated that Jefferson had compiled this list with reference to the descriptions of ancient statuary by Richardson, Spence, and Perrier, and to Joseph Addison's *Remarks on the Several Parts of Italy* (1705).[21] Ardent classicist that he was, Jefferson had a strong liking for sculpture, an art traditionally allied with that of architecture. It has been pointed out that Monticello itself had its spiritual affinity with a Roman villa,[22] and in wanting to furnish his own retreat with sculpture, Jefferson might have remembered Cicero's "awaiting impatiently the statues" ordered for his academy and confessing to his friend Atticus, "This is my little weakness." [23]

There were only six subjects in Jefferson's first workbook list of desired paintings, but when in 1782 he copied it into his library catalogue, one item, a "Diana Venetrix," had been dropped and six others added, making a total of eleven:

*Belisarius from Salvator Rosa (Date obolum Belisario)

Jeptha meeting his daughter by Zocchi

St. Ignatius at Prayer by

*The Prodigal son from Salvator Rosa. 8f[eet] 3I[nches] high, 65 5½I wide

*Susanna & the two elders by Rubens. 6f high, 7f 8½I wide

*The stoning of St. Stephen from Le Soeur. 9f 8½I high, 11f 3¾I wide

*Curtius leaping into the gulph, from Mola. 6f 6¼I high, 11f 4½I wide

*Cocles defending the bridge, companion to the other

Paul preaching at Athens, from a cartoon of Ra. Urbin

The sacrifice of Iphigenia

Seleucus giving his wife Stratonice to his son

In the first painting list no artists' names had been given, and sources for that selection have not been determined. But Fiske Kimball was able to show that five of the six additions of 1782 (indicated above by asterisks), with their painters identified and dimensions given, came from the *Aedes Walpoliana,* where the sixth, a *Belisarius* belonging to Lord Townsend, is also mentioned and commended.[24] That Jefferson did have in mind the acquisition of replicas is implied in a note appended to the first list: "[Charles] Bellini tells me that historical paintings on canvas 6f. by 12f. will cost £15 if copied by a good hand." [25]

Following his resignation as governor of Virginia in 1782, having spent thirteen years in public office, Jefferson was eager to return to his still unfinished residence in the Piedmont, where the marquis de Chastellux visited him that spring and afterward wrote: "We may safely aver, that Mr. Jefferson is the first American who has consulted the fine arts to know how he should shelter himself from the weather." [26] All too soon, however, he was returned to the Continental Congress, and in 1784 he was sent abroad as minister plenipotentiary to join John Adams and the aging Franklin. Hence it turned out that his early collecting aspirations had been only trials of the wind, a prelude to actual flights of art buying in Europe.

Before leaving the country, Jefferson for the first time on record commissioned a painting. Anticipating a need for a likeness of General Washington, and "passing through that city [of Philadelphia] on my way from Annapolis to Boston to embark for Europe," he ordered the work from the London-trained Joseph Wright, who had recently painted the subject from life. Ample documentation records that Wright's *George Washington* was done when the general "attended the meeting of the Cincinnati, in Philadelphia, in May 1784"; that the artist was only allowed "time to finish the head & face, & sketch the outlines of the body"; that a payment of seventeen pounds and ten shillings was left with Joseph Hopkinson, who on the last day of May reported that the head was finished; and that the uncompleted and unframed canvas followed Jefferson to France, where the Wright figure outlines "and the drapery were afterward finished at Paris by [John] Trumbull."[27]

JEFFERSON FIRST ESTABLISHED HIMSELF IN PARIS IN OCTOBER 1784, IN the Hôtel de Landron, No. 5 Cul-de-sac Taitbout,[28] where he remained for a year. Then, with the resignation of Franklin and his own assumption of the office of minister plenipotentiary to the court of Louis XVI, he moved to more spacious quarters in the Hôtel de Langeac, a fine residence designed by Chalgrin, located in the Champs Elysées at the customs gate called Grille de Chaillot.[29] Faced with the necessity of furnishing his residences in a manner suitable to his official and social station, and rejecting as uneconomical the idea of renting equipment, Jefferson promptly engaged in shopping on a scale that was unprecedented for him. Frequent entries in his accounts record purchases of household fittings; and not unexpectedly, he began to acquire *objets d'art.*

The first of these were mentioned with the anonymity of, say, rugs or draperies, and included the following: "Two pictures of heads, 7 livres; d° half lengths, viz. an ecce homo and another, 18 livres; two small laughing busts, 21 livres; a Hercules in plaister; five paintings (heads)" — all of these bought within a fortnight after his occupation of the Hôtel de Landron. Conveniently, there had been held on October 16-19, 1784, a sale of the collection of the late M de Billy, *premier valet de garderobe du roi,* a sale that included some sixty *tableaux,* along with a miscellany of prints, marbles, porcelains, and jewelry. "A Virgin Mary weeping on the death of Jesus," supposedly by Carlo Maratti, according to Jefferson's later cataloguing, came from the de Billy collection.[30]

On the following January tenth it was recorded, "pd for a picture with six figures 24 f." Then in February, seemingly with increased discrimination, Jefferson selected five canvases from the more than three hundred offered at the sale of a collection formed in the early 1700s by M Dupille de Saint

Severin. The following items went to "l'Envoie d'Amerique": no. 36, "St. Peter Weeping for his Offence," by Guido Reni; no. 59, "Magdalene Penitent," by "Joseph de Ribera, called Spagnolet"; no. 215, "Democritus & Heraclitus, called the laughing and weeping philosophers"; no. 248, "Herodiade Bearing the Head of St. John on a Platter," by Simon Vouet; and no. 306, "The Prodigal Son," by an "unknown master." [31] Of these, the large *Herodiade,* then called a Vouet but considered to be after a Guido Reni in the Galleria Nazionale d'Arte Antica in Rome, has been returned to Monticello and reinstalled in its place over the parlor mantlepiece.

The several lists of Jefferson's own collection compiled in after years show that he continued to acquire copies after established artists of the past, somewhat as he collected books by reputable authors, as though following the maxim of Richardson that a simulation of greatness was preferable to the originality of nonentities. Again it must be remembered that this was the attitude of his time, and one generally followed by art lovers — witness the collections from which his acquisitions were made. In those first months, when he was furnishing his Parisian residence with pictures as with other accoutrements, his choice was not free but was conditioned by what the market had to offer — for one thing, a great deal of religious art. Moreover — a fact basic to any consideration of his collecting —Jefferson was not then or at any time a very wealthy person, and in comparison with the lavish expenditures of other diplomatic representatives, his own were restricted by circumstances to a relatively modest outlay. [32]

After a year in Paris it was an altogether more sophisticated Jefferson who would tell his correspondent James Madison, "You see I am an enthusiast on the subject of the arts." In the beginning the presence of Franklin and Adams, his previous acquaintance with the marquis de Chastellux, who had visited Monticello, and especially his friendship with the well-connected marquis de Lafayette had facilitated his entrée to the society of the waning Ancien Régime. Assemblies where the arts were conversational leaven had been opened to him. Friendships with artistically knowledgeable persons of both sexes — whether the comtesse de Tessé or the baron de Grimm ("the oracle of taste at Paris in sculpture, painting and the other fine arts," wrote Jefferson [33])—had multiplied. For the first time he had been able to confront original works of art which had been known to him only through copies or engravings. He had indeed come to envy the French their architecture, painting, sculpture, and music. Yet lest this seem frivolous to Madison, he felt constrained to add to his first admission, "But it is an enthusiasm of which I am not ashamed, as it's object is to improve the taste of my countrymen, to increase their reputation, to reconcile to them the respect of the world &

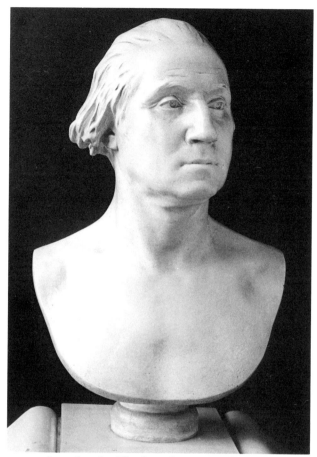

Jean-Antoine Houdon. *George Washington.*
Boston Athenaeum

procure them it's praise." [34] Within that first year, too, he had become acquainted with some artists of more than localized renown, most auspiciously, with the distinguished French sculptor Jean-Antoine Houdon.

Jefferson had been only midway on his passage to Europe, when the governor of Virginia, Benjamin Harrison, dispatched a letter asking his assistance and that of Franklin in selecting an artist — "the most masterly hand" — to execute a statue of George Washington lately ordered by the state assembly.[35] No doubt with knowledge of this project Jefferson had obtained the portrait by Joseph Wright. Governor Harrison, too, anticipating that a likeness would be required by a sculptor working abroad, had commissioned of Charles Willson Peale a full-length *Washington,* a canvas that would reach Jefferson in April 1785 and that apparently then remained with him throughout his residence in Paris.[36] Recommended by Jefferson as "the first statuary in the world," Houdon was selected, and he went in person to Mount Vernon in 1785 to model his subject from life. Completed in Paris, the Houdon work was mounted on its pedestal in 1796 in the Jefferson-designed state house at Richmond.[37]

More pertinent to the subject of Jefferson as collector was his eventual acquisition of no less than seven fine plaster portrait busts by Houdon that were to be housed at Monticello. One of these, of course, was a *Washington;* another was of Franklin, taken from the bust that Houdon had shown at the Salon of 1781; in that same Salon the artist had entered a "buste en platre couleur du terre cuite" of *John Paul Jones,* another replica of which was presented by the subject to Jefferson near the beginning of 1786; a *Lafayette* was a by-product of another commission from the Commonwealth of Virginia for two portrait busts in marble, one first intended for the marquis but given to the city of Paris, the other placed in the capitol at Richmond; there were plasters of Turgot and Voltaire; and seventh, the *Jefferson* dating from his last year in Paris. Of the latter he obtained at least three copies, one, now lost, for Monticello, and one each that belong to the American Philosophical Society and the New-York Historical Society.[38]

Evidently these busts were Jefferson's only Houdon acquisitions; but at one time, no doubt with considerations of buying, he did make note of prices for "plaisters" of three of the sculptor's other works: the *Diana* (25 guineas), *La Frileuse* (15 guineas), and the well-known *Ecorché* (12 louis).[39]

In addition to the Houdon bust of his predecessor in office, Jefferson must early have acquired an oval painting of *Benjamin Franklin* that he catalogued as "drawn for the Abbé Very [Verri] by Greuze." Actually a replica of the Joseph Duplessis "fur collar portrait" of 1778, it is thought by Charles Coleman Sellers to have been painted by Jean Valade, by whom it was sold to Jefferson.[40]

Apparently for the first time in his life Jefferson himself sat for a formal portrait, when, during his visit to England in March and April 1786, he was painted by the twenty-four-year-old American artist, Mather Brown. With the original lost, perhaps in Jefferson's lifetime, it is now known through a replica made for John Adams, then American commissioner in London.[41] The copy was made as part of an exchange of portraits, in which Jefferson particularly asked for an "original" of Adams. Hence it was that the latter, for the second time, sat for Brown just before departing from England. The *John Adams* of 1788 was pronounced "like" by Trumbull. On the table before Adams, in a kind of homage, lies a large volume labeled "Jefferson Hist. of Virginia" (i.e., the *Notes on the State of Virginia).*[42]

When in the fall of 1786 Jefferson was first hoping to induce Adams to have his portrait painted, he explained, "I wish to add it to those of other principal American characters which I have or shall have." [43] This seems to be the first documentation for a projected new plan in his collecting, that of assembling representations of individuals of distinction, who had contributed either intellectually or by deeds to the discovery and rise to independence of his country.[44] The thrust of his art activities thus would be diverted to the more "useful," hence "nobler," and in the end more American purpose of commemorating man's progress toward freedom. It was this, more than any other factor, that would put Jefferson's personal stamp on the collection of paintings, sculptures, prints, medals and curiosities that came to enrich the interior of the later Monticello.

Even then he had in mind another "character." While traveling with Adams in England, he had noted at Birmingham a portrait of Sir Walter Raleigh, the pioneering colonizer of the state of Virginia; and he subsequently asked Adams' son-in-law, William Stephens Smith, "the favor to get it for me." What he did get was of course a replica, which in his catalogue would appear as "Sr. Walter Raleigh. copy from an original by Holben," though actually Holbein had died before the subject was born. Nevertheless, Raleigh did belong in the company of those "first discoverers" who were soon to be brought into the Jefferson collection.[45]

In the summer of 1787, not long after the *Raleigh* had been received, Jefferson inquired of his friend Philip Mazzei, who had studied medicine in Florence, about possibilities of obtaining copies of the "original" likenesses, *Christopher Columbus, Fernando Cortez, Ferdinand Magellan,* and *Amerigo Vespucci,* all of which he had noted in "the list of pictures in the Gallery of the Grand Duke at Florence." [46] A copyist was engaged, one Giuseppi Calendi, and the replicas were executed in the fall of 1788 and delivered early in January. Jefferson welcomed them, considering it to be "of some public concern that our country should not be without the portraits of its first discoverers." Of the four, only the *Columbus* is known to have survived. Later on, two more likenesses "copied from the original[s] in the gallery of the Medicis for T. J." were added to the collection, one of Castruccio Castraccani, the benevolent despot of Lucca, praised by Machiavelli, the other of the Genoese admiral and statesman, Andrea Doria.[47]

The most important happening of Jefferson's English tour in the spring of 1786, insofar as his art interests were concerned, was his meeting with the Connecticut-born John Trumbull, then nearing thirty and at the apex of his development as a painter. Jefferson, wrote Trumbull, invited him "to come to Paris, to see and study the fine arts there, and to make his house my home, during my stay." This the painter did in the following summer, from early August into September.[48] With the zeal of a diligent tourist Trumbull

115

ferreted out "all that related to the arts, in Paris and its vicinity," filling a journal with observations and disclosures of an artist's discernment, which was superior to that of Jefferson. At social gatherings and on visits to studios, he came to know Houdon, Jacques-Louis David (whom he soon claimed as "a warm and affectionate friend"), and other artists of the city; and it was he who, by introducing his host to the Richard Cosways — the English miniaturist and his artistically talented wife — was instrumental in launching the so celebrated friendship between Jefferson and the lovely Maria Cosway. Jefferson himself was drawn more deeply than ever into the milieu of the arts.

Through the three years following their meeting, Trumbull was to assist Jefferson in a number of matters and perhaps from time to time to advise him about art purchases, though it is difficult, on the evidence, to accept at face value the sweeping claim made in advertising the sale of the Monticello collection in 1833, that "the selection was made with the assistance of Col. Trumbull . . . whose taste directed the selection." [49] Yet Jefferson must initially have learned a good deal from this far from modest painter, and there are data, too, to show that he took an interest in Trumbull's recently undertaken "national enterprise," a projected series of scenes about the winning of American independence.

Two of these pictures were brought in 1786 to the Hôtel de Langeac, where among others David came to see and commend them. [50] At this time, too, Jefferson made suggestions and sketched diagrams for the composition of a third, *The Declaration of Independence*. Later Trumbull was to present Jefferson with a "premier ebauche" of still another in the series, *The Surrender of Cornwallis at Yorktown*, done in 1787 as one of "various studies" but now apparently lost. [51]

Trumbull again visited the Hôtel de Langeac in the fall of 1787, bringing with him the unfinished picture of the *Declaration*, into which most of the heads were yet to be painted. Critical opinion both then and now ranks Jefferson's likeness for the *Declaration*, which Trumbull painted at that time, among "the best of [Trumbull's] small portraits." [52] When a copy of the portrait was delivered to the subject's daughter Martha late in 1788, in a shipment that included "books for your [Jefferson's] list Payne has been able to procure," there was also included what Jefferson considered "a perfect likeness" of Thomas Paine, one of the small oil portraits on wood panels that were a Trumbull specialty. Long missing and lately rediscovered, though with the eyes mischievously damaged, the little picture retains its great interest as one of the rare existing life portraits of the Revolutionary pamphleteer. [53]

John Trumbull. *The Declaration of Independence.* Engraved by J.F.E. Prud'homme.
Yale University Art Gallery, The Mabel Brady Garvan Collection

For another group of representations of famous men, this time all of them British, Jefferson enlisted Trumbull's assistance, inquiring early in 1789 as to whether "pictures of Newton Locke, Bacon, Sydney, Hampden, Shakespeare exist," and "what would it cost to have them copied by some good young hand who will do them well and is not of such established reputation as to be dear?" Trumbull arranged for the copying of canvases of the first three mentioned at a cost of three guineas each, double what was paid Jefferson's Italian copyist, and the ever-treasured likenesses of Bacon, Newton, and Locke — "the three greatest men that ever have lived," Jefferson would say — were added to the collection. Only the *Locke* is now known to exist, and has been returned to Monticello.[54]

Among Jefferson's official assignments during the latter part of his stay in Paris was that of supervising completion of the series of medals voted by

Congress to officers of the Revolution "who distinguished themselves on particular occasions."[55] The first of ten, each to be accompanied by a sword, had been ordered in 1776 for General Washington, honoring the "particular occasion" of the evacuation of Boston (to be pictured on the reverse side). But the execution of the other nine medals had been delayed, when Jefferson in 1787 was asked to see them completed. To expedite the work Jefferson distributed the commissions among three French sculptors: Pierre-Simon-Benjamin Duvivier, Augustin Dupré, and Nicolas-Marie Gatteaux. Complete sets of medals in silver or bronze, boxed in Paris, were issued for selected recipients — that ordered by Congress for George Washington is in the collection of the Massachusetts Historical Society. Washington's own gold medal, the work of Duvivier, whose design was shown at the Paris Salon of 1789, was acquired a century ago for the City of Boston and placed in the Boston Public Library.

It was while these medals were being struck in Paris that Jefferson obtained from the workmen two sets of proofs in pure tin — "white metal" — one for himself and a second for James Madison. To the latter he wrote that the proofs "are in fact more delicate than the medals themselves." Identified in his later catalogue are the ten subjects: "Generals Washington, Gates, Stewart, Wayne, de Fleury, Paul Jones, Colonels [William A.] Washington, Morgan, Howard, Greene." At Monticello Jefferson's set of proofs was displayed in the lower tier of works hung in the parlor.

Jefferson's catalogue listed other medals acquired in these years, among them a *Franklin* "of bronze by Dupré," a *Louis XVI* in tin proof, and in bronze "the entry of the King (Louis XVI) into Paris" — this forebodingly followed in the catalogue by "the Taking of the Bastille, a medal in bronze," commemorating the event that took place just ten weeks before the American envoy's final departure from France.

The diplomatic mission in Europe was for Jefferson an altogether enlightening experience, and aesthetically it was a veritable revelation. Yet his fundamental attitudes were not radically affected; and for all his proclaimed enthusiasm for the arts of the Old World, he nevertheless questioned the relevance for his young country of the luxury arts of painting and sculpture. These, he advised Americans planning to travel abroad, "are worth seeing, but not studying." On grounds of practicality, he explained, they were "too expensive for the state of wealth of our country. It would be useless, therefore, and preposterous, for us to make ourselves connoisseurs in those arts."[56]

WHEN JEFFERSON SAILED HOMEWARD IN THE FALL OF 1789, WITH TWO years of his appointment unspent, he anticipated returning soon to France.

However, upon landing in Virginia he received a communication from President Washington inviting him to serve as the new nation's first secretary of state. Accepting with reluctance this fresh call to duty, and after spending a short time at Monticello, he arrived in New York on a Sunday, March 21, 1790, met with the president after his return from church, and among other things delivered to him the congressional gold medal that had been ordered fourteen years before.

From this point onward, while he served in sequence as cabinet member, vice president, and president before finally retiring to Monticello, Jefferson's own purchases of art works became more sporadic, though they never ceased. But at the same time, with the mounting of his renown as a public figure, and later as word spread of the nature and extent of the collection at Monticello, gifts came to him in increasing numbers, many with their intrinsic value enhanced by the circumstances in which they were given.

Only a fortnight after his initial meeting with Washington, Jefferson wrote to his chargé d'affaires in Paris, William Short, "My pictures of American [characters] will be absolutely incomplete without one of Lafayette." Soon Joseph Boze, *peintre du roi,* was engaged, and Short managed with difficulty to schedule painting appointments with an always busy subject. By late fall the likeness of the marquis de Lafayette had been finished and sent overseas, together with the artist's bill for twenty louis, to cover painting, framing, and packing for shipment.[57]

Again while still in New York Jefferson placed an order for two sets of the forthcoming engravings of John Trumbull's *Battle of Bunker's Hill* and *The Death of Montgomery in the Attack on Quebec* — from the canvases that had been brought by the painter to the Hôtel de Langeac on his first visit there. Trumbull, too, had come home in the fall to promote the sales of his prints and to obtain likenesses of individuals to be represented in his historical series. Not long after this, however, he broke with Jefferson over political and religious issues and for years to come was to remain "cold and distant" toward his one-time friend.[58]

When the seat of government was moved to Philadelphia Jefferson rented and promptly began remodeling a house conveniently situated on Market Street. The household belongings, to which he had expected to return in Paris, now shipped from abroad in eighty-six cases, were arriving in October.[59] An intriguing glimpse of the installation in the Philadelphia house of some of his pictures is provided by a story told by Jefferson to Benjamin Rush about a happening at one of Jefferson's dinners:

The room being hung around with a collection of the portraits of remarkable men, among them were those of Bacon, Newton and Locke.

Andrew Hamilton asked me who they were. I told him they were my trinity of the three greatest men the world had ever produced, naming them. He paused for some time: "The greatest man," said he, "that ever lived was Julius Caesar." [60]

Jefferson came to own a portrait of James Madison painted in 1790, no doubt in Philadelphia, by the immigrant English artist Robert Edge Pine. It is tempting to surmise that he may have asked for it for his collection of "characters," as had been done in the case of Adams. But not pleased with this one, he later wrote of it as "only a bust portrait . . . & it is but an indifferent one." [61]

One "gift" that he received turned out instead to be a rather costly purchase. At the beginning of the decade the Italian sculptor Giuseppe Ceracchi had come to the United States with hopes of obtaining from Congress a commission to execute a national monument to Liberty. Failing in this, he did take back to Florence the modeled heads of a number of Americans, including Jefferson and Hamilton. And it was his curious practice, having asked a subject to accept a likeness carved in marble, to "present" one, for which the unsuspecting recipient then would be charged. This happened to Jefferson, who sat to Ceracchi probably in March 1791 for a maquette and who, upon receiving a large marble bust several years later — "a little mark of my esteem," wrote the artist — was billed for the sum of "one thousand five hundred dollars," of which five hundred ultimately was paid. [62] The portrait long stood in the entrance hall at Monticello opposite another Ceracchi marble of Andrew Hamilton. Hamilton also had been deceived by the sculptor's approach. For a bust delivered in July 1795, Hamilton, the following March, noted caustically in his accounts, "For this sum through *delicacy* paid upon ceracchi's draft for making my bust on his own importunity & as a favor to him 620." [63]

At the end of 1793 Jefferson resigned as secretary of state and retired for an interlude to Monticello, where the remodeling of his house was in full progress and where he would be "the most ardent farmer in the state." But three years and three months after leaving Philadelphia, he returned to that city for his inauguration as vice president, and eventually his two terms as president rounded out a dozen more years in the service of the nation.

Back in Philadelphia, his boardinghouse quarters would have needed little in the way of appointments; and when he moved into the president's house in Washington he used government funds to provide it with elegant new furnishings, but not with works of art. In the room-by-room inventory of the contents of the president's house drawn up at the end of his occupancy, only one painting is listed, "a full length picture of Genl. Washington — Gilt frame."[64] Nevertheless it was a time in which his private collection was generously amplified with gifts.

Among the "dangerous aliens" forced by the nefarious Alien and Sedition Law to leave the United States in 1798 was Jefferson's very good friend Thaddeus Kosciusko, the Polish patriot who had supported the Revolutionary cause. Kosciusko left with Jefferson "an original sketch" by Benjamin West of *The Parting of Hector and Andromache,* given to him by the artist in London, and a watercolor of the Swedish castle of Gripsholme done by one of his officers. Another "dangerous" acquaintance of Jefferson's forced then to leave the country was the French rationalist comte de Volney. On the last day of the century the eccentric but capable John James Barralet of Philadelphia sent Jefferson the "Volney, in pencil" that would later hang in the Monticello parlor.[65]

It was the comte de Volney who in 1801 sent Jefferson from Paris a model of "the largest of the pyramids of Egypt, called Cheope" — a reminder of Napoleon's Egyptian expedition. Jefferson observed in acknowledging the gift, "I had not supposed [the pyramids] to appear so flat." This souvenir of Egypt was placed in the hall at Monticello near what was then recorded as "a Cleopatra in marble," the gift of Governor James Bowdoin, Jr., of Massachusetts.[66] A correction added later in Jefferson's catalogue was to identify this figure, some forty inches long, as "Ariadne reclined on the rocks at Naxos." The original, long a "prime ornament" of the Belvedere in the Vatican, was then situated temporarily in the Galerie des Antiques du Musée Napoleon in Paris.

Busts of two of Europe's reigning emperors came to Jefferson as president: a marble *Napoleon Bonaparte,* and a plaster *Alexander I* of Russia. His receiving the latter in 1804 initiated a cordial exchange of correspondence between Jefferson and the Russian ruler, whom he admired, though he came to regard Napoelon as a "moral monster."[67]

The variety of the gifts he received gives an indication of the diversity of Jefferson's pursuits. From the ornithologist Alexander Wilson came two watercolors of birds of Virginia; from the rising young architect Robert Mills, several drawings of buildings. A chapter in the *Notes on the State of Virginia* had dealt with the American Indian, and Jefferson received two stone carvings, the first, in 1790, of a kneeling woman — "the best piece of workmanship I ever saw from their [the Indians'] hands" — which he presented to the American Philosophical Society, and in 1800 "two busts of Indian figures, male and female . . . dug up at a place called Palmyra in Tennisee."[68] An obscure artist, William Roberts, presented him with two canvases catalogued as "The Natural Bridge of Virginia" (a property owned by Jefferson) and

"The passage of the Potomac through the Blue Ridge," the latter a view at Harper's Ferry.[69]

Always there were prints. In time undetermined numbers of them were to fill one or more "large" portfolios at Monticello, while choice ones were framed and hung.[70] Characteristically Jefferson disliked fancy and costly frames for them, decrying "the tawdry taste prevailing for the gew-gaw gilt frames, these flaring things that injure greatly the effect of the print." [71]

Among American engravings acquired between his return from abroad and his retirement from the presidency were a *George Washington* "done by Wright who drew the picture of him that I have [in June 1790] at Paris"; a *Liberty as Goddess of Youth* published in 1796 by Edward Savage, who would shortly paint Jefferson's portrait; Birch prints of Philadelphia and Mount Vernon; and two engraved views of Niagara Falls after John Vanderlyn, who on the last day of December 1805 was "paid for the pair of prints twenty dollars," with ten dollars added for their framing.[72]

Because the life portraits of Jefferson have been the subject of extended investigation by Alfred L. Bush,[73] the several that were owned by the subject have not been treated here. It may be observed at this point, however, that fully one-half of the twenty-six known images drawn from life date from between 1791 and 1805, when Jefferson held governmental offices.

At the end of winter in 1809, his presidency over, Jefferson arrived home, having lingered in Washington for the inauguration of his successor. He was never again to travel any great distance from Monticello. The remodeling of his residence was completed, and it would be painted that summer. The place now was ready to house the Jefferson collection, canvases and miniatures, portrait busts and medals, masterworks and artifacts, all of them then presumably assigned to the permanent places in which they would be catalogued.

Of two often-cited handwritten lists of Jefferson's art treasures, one in private hands and the other in the library of the University of Virginia at Charlottesville,[74] the shorter and surely the earlier is inscribed on fourteen small pages that may have come from a notebook and is known as the Kirk-Jefferson list. In it some fifty-eight paintings are itemized, most of them with brief comments, but only a few with artists' names attached. About two-thirds are of Biblical subjects and the rest from ancient history, with the exceptions of one landscape, one still life, and four portraits — *Washington, Madison, Lafayette,* and *Franklin.* There are no sculptures, prints, or drawings here listed.[75]

Much of this list was transcribed into the second, longer one, which does implement its title, "Catalogue of Paintings Etc. at Monticello." Dating from

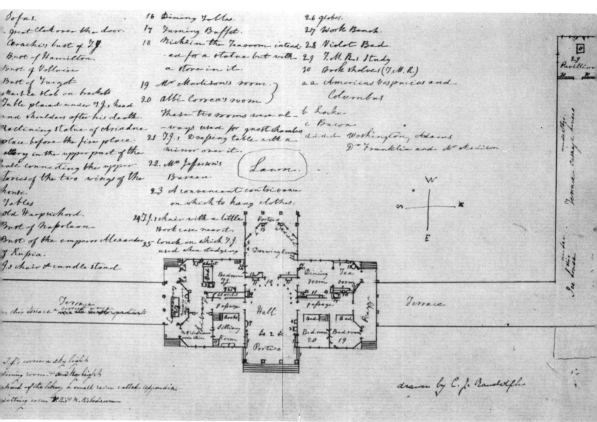

Cornelia Jefferson Randolph. *Sketch of Monticello floor plan.*
Thomas Jefferson Memorial Foundation, Charlottesville

no earlier than 1803,[76] it includes paintings, sculptures, prints, drawings, miniatures and medals, many of them described, among its 126 entries. Seventeen of these are numerically listed for the entrance hall, forty-nine for the parlor, ten for the dining room, and an unnumbered miscellany of thirty-six items for the tea room. This is neither an exhaustive nor a final listing, for it does not include those objects in the more private parts of the house and of course it contains none of the subsequent additions. Yet it provides a welcome basic outline for an assessment of the Monticello collection *in situ*. On a tour of the public rooms of Monticello taken, say, around 1810, the works might have been viewed somewhat in the following fashion:

Entering the hall from the east portico, a visitor's interest would have been quickened by the profusion and heterogeneity of its contents, a mélange of art and natural science specimens, of which the latter first caught the eye. From the walls protruded the heads of a number of animals — elk, deer, buffalo, ram and the *os frontis* of a mammoth from the fossil bones unearthened at Big Bone Lick on the Ohio by William Clark. Clark with Merriwether Lewis, had been sent by Jefferson on their famed western expedition, relics from which also were displayed here. Jefferson's list cited two paintings on buffalo pelts, "a battle between the Panis & Osages" and a "map of the Southern waters of the Missouri by a Ricora [?] chief." And it was the baron de Montlezun who noted with aversion the "two figures of man and woman sculptured by savages — very hideous." [77]

On the left side of the hall, near the door of the passage to Jefferson's study, reclined the marble Cleopatra-Ariadne, and near it was the "facsimile" of the Cheops pyramid. Eleven paintings of Biblical themes, all but two from the New Testament (there is no need here to identify more than a few of the collection's many replicas), were hung about the walls. Two of the plasters by Houdon, *Turgot* and *Voltaire,* stood on pedestals before the piers dividing the three openings of the east front; and facing one another from the two sides of the room — "opposed in death as in life," remarked Jefferson — were the marble busts of himself and Hamilton by Ceracchi. The *Jefferson,* "in the Roman costume" and larger than life, rested on "a truncated column, on a pedestal of which are represented the 12 tribes of Israel and the 12 signs of the zodiac" — an object given to Jefferson earlier in Paris and seemingly mistaken by the visiting Duke of Saxe-Weimar for "a marble stove." [78]

A pair of doors, either of which moved the other by means of an ingenious contrivance under the floor, opened into the parlor, or drawing room, a handsome interior with vistas onto the lawn through four tall windows and a glazed door in its polygonal western end. This room contained the select portion of Jefferson's collection. Of sculptures there were only the busts of Napoleon Bonaparte and Alexander I, on pedestals that flanked the door to the terrace. But paintings and prints almost completely covered the walls — William Wirt observed that these were "hung thick with the finest reproductions of the pencil." [79] As on the crowded walls that Jefferson had seen abroad in the salons and in private collections, his pictures were stratified, and their catalogue listings sectioned into upper, middle, and lower tiers.

Here portraits filled the upper tier, with prominent places around the western walls given to a distinguished company: *Columbus, Vespucci, Locke, Bacon,* and, of the Americans, *Washington, Adams, Franklin,* and *Madison* (the fine Stuart medallion of *Jefferson* may also have been among these [80]). Other portraits at this level represented Newton, Magellan, Cortes, Raleigh, and Lafayette. In the middle tier were the canvases *Castracani* and *Doria,* with the *Hoche* and *Rittenhouse* engravings. The only painted portrait in the lower tier was Trumbull's little panel *Thomas Paine,* along with Barralet's drawing of Volney and prints representing Kosciusko and Count Rumford.

Here, too, hung Jefferson's set of tin proofs of the congressional medals.

At this time George Ticknor reported seeing over the fireplace in the parlor "the Laughing and Weeping Philosophers, dividing the world between them,"[81] but the later Randolph plan shows it replaced by another of the Severin sale pictures, "Herodiade bearing the head of St. John on a platter," the canvas that hangs there now. Ticknor brushed off some fifteen remaining paintings of Christian and classical subjects in a terse sentence, "There were other pictures, and a copy of Raphael's 'Transfiguration.' "

The single still life of the collection, "a market piece on canvas," appropriately was seen in the dining room. With it there, in the upper of two tiers, were six canvases of religious subjects and two depicting "Diogenes in the market at Athens . . . copied from Rubens" and "Diogenes visited by Alexander. An Original" — by whom not specified. The lower tier was mainly comprised of pictures of places, and included the paintings of the Natural Bridge and the scene at Harper's Ferry, the two Niagara Falls engravings after Vanderlyn, prints of the famous Colebrookdale cast-iron bridge that Jefferson had seen in England, "The Diocletian Portico" from the Roman palace at Spalatro, a view of New Orleans, and an interestingly conjoined trio — an elevation and plan of Monticello drawn by Robert Mills, the Birch view of Mount Vernon, and "the President's house at Washington in water colors by King." A Jefferson descendant recalled that on either side of the arched opening into the tea room were a *Holy Family* after Raphael, "which Mr. Jefferson had copied in the Louvre," and Benjamin West's study, *Hector and Andromache,* the gift of Kosciusko.[82]

The pleasant semioctagonal tea room to the north of the dining room was in Jefferson's time a center of family life. There mounted on wall brackets were the rest of the Houdon plasters, "large as life," including the *Washington, Franklin, John Paul Jones,* and *Lafayette.* Four smaller busts, each listed as "a cast bronzed," were *Tiberius, Nero, Otho,* and *Vespasian.* In this room, smaller and less formal than the reception and dining areas, were a few engravings such as a "Date obolum Belisario" and "Moncada, a print remarkable for its execution," both presented to Jefferson by "two young Americans educated in Rome,[83] but no large paintings. There was instead a concentration of small pieces. More than a dozen miniatures, framed singly or in groups, represented prominent American friends of Jefferson; and there was the intriguing small likeness on glass — *verre églomisé* — of himself, a profile engraved from life by Amos Doolittle in 1803 that has been returned to Monticello.[84] Quite a few of the medals in tin and bronze were displayed here, including a *Franklin* (bronze) by Dupré and a Franklin-designed "infant America protected by Minerva from the lion." And recalling the days when a much younger Jefferson had been one of those who rebelled against the British lion was "a medallion in wax" of Lord Boutetourt, the next to last royal governor of Virginia.

Such was the Jefferson collection essentially as it stood when, in 1815, its owner cited a total of 120 pictures (no sculptures) as part of his taxable property.[85] The size and interest of it were increased, moreover, by some gifts and purchases made later during the last decade of his life.

Early in 1818 Jefferson subscribed, at a cost of ten dollars and twenty-five cents, to one of the milestones of American printmaking, the engraving by the young Asher B. Durand of Trumbull's *The Declaration of Independence*[86] — the picture that Jefferson had helped to compose in sessions with the artist at the Hôtel de Langeac. He was concerned about proper framing, that it be simple and not costly. And he asked Trumbull (their friendship renewed) whether "one of mere outline" might be made, "which could be sold for a dollar apiece," to enable greater numbers of Americans to own this representation of a key event and of the first mural to be placed in their not yet finished national capitol.[87]

Also in the spring of that year the English sculptor and portraitist John William Coffee, lately come to the United States, first visited Monticello. Jefferson told his neighbor Madison that Coffee had traveled from Richmond "to take your bust and mine." During this and subsequent visits Coffee executed "the busts in plaister of myself and all the grown members of our family." Three were done, including a *Martha Jefferson Randolph,* one of her daughter Ellen Wayles Randolph, and one of Jefferson, at a cost of 105 dollars; more followed, including *Thomas Jefferson Randolph, Cornelia Jefferson Randolph,* and depictions of members of "some other families of our neighborhood" — one of Madison was made for Jefferson. Coffee's modeled portraits, less than life size and notably delicate in their detailing, owed much to his early training and employment as a worker in porcelain.[88]

In February 1820, James Robinson sent a replica of William Rush's recent sculptured bust of Andrew Jackson, for which Jefferson thanked the donor, expressing esteem for Jackson, praising Rush as "an artist of whom our country has a high and just admiration" and saying that the work would be given "a place in my most honorable suite, with those of Washington, Franklin, Fayette, etc." That summer Charles Willson Peale, always a fond promoter of his children's enterprises, sent Jefferson a description and a sketch he had made of Rembrandt Peale's *The Court of Death,* a huge canvas that was to be profitably exhibited about the country. And word came from Liverpool, England, that a schooldays chum, James Maury, son of the man of the same name who had taught them both as boys, was having forwarded for "a place in your Collection at Monticello" a small porcelain bust of William Roscoe, the English historian and reformer admired by Jefferson — it would, he said, be included among his "favorite characters." [89]

In the summer of his eighty-third year, Jefferson received from Benjamin Guild of Boston a "plaister" replica of the marble bust of John Adams, lately made for the city of Boston by the visiting French sculptor J. H. Binon and placed in Faneuil Hall. Jefferson thought it "a good likeness" insofar as he could judge over the span of years since he had last seen Adams. Again in thanking the sender he wrote, "I place it with pleasure in the line in my cabinet of his predecessors and successors." [90] It was to be, in fact, the end of that "line."

Barely a month before both his and Adams' deaths on July 4, 1826, Jefferson acknowledged the gift of a medal struck to commemorate the completion of the Erie Canal. The record of his collecting thus concludes with this token of an accelerated westward development of the nation that he had watched grow from its founding on the Atlantic seaboard.

THE DISPOSAL OF THE JEFFERSON COLLECTION BEGAN NOT MANY months later with the enforced sale at auction of his debt-laden estate and belongings, held at Monticello on January 15, 1827. Some art works, mostly engravings, were sold, after which the dwindling bulk of the collection was three more times offered at public sales, first in New York, then incorporated with the second annual exhibition at the Boston Athenaeum in 1828, and a last one held in 1833 at Chester Harding's Gallery in Boston. [91] Piece by piece the collection was scattered, some things withheld by members of the Jefferson family, others acquired by individuals and institutions, often at "sacrifice" prices, and much of the remainder fading off into an oblivion from which at intervals certain works have been, and continue to be, salvaged.

When the Harding sale was being held in Boston, William Dunlap was at work in New York on the two volumes of *A History of the Rise and Progress of the Arts of Design in the United States,* to be published the following year. In his conclusion, Dunlap with evident satisfaction discussed the growth of art collecting in the nation since its founding. Many collections were mentioned, and itemized lists of the outstanding holdings of Robert Gilmor, Jr., of Baltimore and Philip Hone of New York were given. It is revealing to compare the roster of a collection such as Gilmor's with Jefferson's "Catalogue of Paintings etc. at Monticello."

The Gilmor list — running to over a hundred works, then pronounced "undoubtedly original," together with "about 130 not mentioned" — reflects the taste and industry of a gentleman of substance bent on gathering for his

127

private enjoyment the fruits of his connoisseurship. It well exemplifies one of Jefferson's two allotted functions for the non-productive arts, "to give a pleasing and innocent direction to accumulations of wealth."

Jefferson's initial and rather haphazard art buying in Paris had also been of that nature — "to give a pleasing and innocent direction" — though with no great wealth to support it. However, the collection that he brought home in 1790 already had been diverted toward other ends that would become increasingly overriding. If his purposeful concentration on representations of eminent men and things pertinent to the history of his country seems more intellectual than aesthetic, it was precisely that quality which made the growing collection more personal, more Jeffersonian, bringing it into alignment with his life interests.

It was indeed a lively and meaningful array of art objects that bedecked and practically filled to overflowing the hospitable interior of Monticello. All of it, replicas as well as the many original materials of great merit, gave indication of the owner's informed tastes and of his long having, as Edmund Randolph put it, "panted after the fine arts." Thomas Jefferson, of course, was unique among the nation's founding fathers in the range and intensity of his preoccupation with the arts. His collecting seems all the more remarkable when viewed as only one component of his protean record of achievement.

Notes

1. Thomas Jefferson, *The Papers of Thomas Jefferson,* 1, ed. Julian P. Boyd (Princeton: Princeton University Press, 1950): 78-79; hereinafter this work will be cited as *Papers.*

2. Publication dates are of first editions, not necessarily of those owned by Jefferson.

3. Karl Lehman [-Hartleben], *Thomas Jefferson, American Humanist* (New York: The Macmillan Company, 1947), pp. 39-40.

4. *Papers,* 1:20. Jefferson letters are dated at Annapolis on May 25, 1766, and at Williamsburg, after his return, on July 23, 1766.

5. Carl Bridenbaugh, *Cities in Revolt, Urban Life in America, 1743-1776* (New York: Capricorn Books, 1955), p. 217.

6. Details that follow are taken largely from Carl and Jessica Bridenbaugh, *Rebels and Gentlemen, Philadelphia in the Age of Franklin* (New York: Oxford University Press, 1955), esp. pp. 184-218.

7. *Papers,* 1:18.

8. John Morgan, *The Journal of Dr. John Morgan of Philadelphia, from the City of Rome to the City of London,* ed. Julia Morgan Harding (Philadelphia: J. B. Lippincott, 1907).

9. Morgan, *Journal,* pp. 239-243.

10. *Papers,* 1:20, Jefferson to John Page, May 25, 1766.

11. Carl and Jessica Bridenbaugh, *Rebels and Gentlemen,* p. 95. Dr. Morgan's library "went up in smoke" when his home was burned during the Revolution: Morgan, *Journal,* p. 38.

12. Works owned by Jefferson dealing with the arts are treated bibliographically in E. Millicent Sowerby, ed., *Catalogue of the Library of Thomas Jefferson,* 4 (Washington: The Library of Congress, 1952-1959): 389-399, and 5:41.

13. Carl and Jessica Bridenbaugh, *Rebels and Gentlemen,* p. 283.

14. Chief sources for the capsulized resumé that follows have been H. M. Kallen, "The Arts and Thomas Jefferson," *Ethics, 53,* no. 4 (July 1943), 260-283; Eleanor D. Berman, *Thomas Jefferson among the Arts* (New York: Philosophical Library, 1947); and Karl Lehman, *Jefferson, Humanist.*

15. Arthur E. McGuinness, *Henry Home, Lord Kames* (New York: Twayne Publishers, 1970), p. 59: quotation from *The Critical Review* of 1762.

16. Kallen, *"The Arts,"* p. 281: Jefferson to Thomas Law, 1814.

17. Berman, *Jefferson,* p. 19: Jefferson to Sully, Jan. 8, 1812.

18. Fiske Kimball, *Thomas Jefferson, Architect* (New York: Da Capo Press, 1968), fig. 79: the lists are reproduced in facsimile.

19. Jonathan Richardson, *The Works of Jonathan Richardson . . .* (London, 1773), p. 226.

20. Joseph Spence, *Polymetis . . .* (London, 1747), p. 83.

21. Fiske Kimball, "Jefferson and the Arts," *Proceedings of the American Philosophical Society, 87,* no. 3 (July 1943), 141-142.

22. Lehman, *Jefferson, Humanist,* pp. 177-188.

23. Marcus Tullius Cicero, *Letters to Atticus,* 1, trans. E. O. Winstedt (Cambridge, Mass.: Harvard University Press, 1962), p. 23.

24. Fiske Kimball, "Jefferson," p. 242.

25. See note 18. Some prints by Hogarth and Francis Hayman were also mentioned in Jefferson's original listing.

26. Fiske Kimball, "Jefferson," p. 242.

27. For a summary of the documentation see, *The Magazine Antiques, 15,* no. 5 (May 1929), 380.

28. Marie Kimball, *Jefferson, the Scene of Europe, 1784-1789* (New York: Coward-McCann, Inc., 1950), p. 10. Acknowledgment is made to this rich and reliable source for much of the material that follows.

29. Howard C. Rice, Jr., *L'Hôtel de Langeac, Jefferson's Paris Residence, 1785-1789* (Monticello and Paris: the Thomas Jefferson Memorial Foundation, 1947). An engraving of the Grille de Chaillot and a plan of the second floor of the Hôtel de Langeac are reproduced in *Papers,* 8:147.

30. Marie Kimball, *Scene of Europe,* pp. 114-115. Data and references for many individual objects cited here and later are found in the alphabetized "Monticello Archives" (hereinafter so cited), in typescript, compiled by James A. Bear, Jr., at Monticello.

31. Marie Kimball, *Scene of Europe,* pp. 114-115.

32. Upon assuming his new responsibilities Jefferson had to ask for an advance on his salary, which in any case never covered his expenses. Marie Kimball writes *(Scene of Europe,* p. 126): "In serving his country as minister to France, [Jefferson] laid the cornerstone to the debts that were eventually to ruin and leave him insolvent in his old age."

33. Marie Kimball, *Scene of Europe,* pp. 104-105.

34. *Papers,* 8:535, Jefferson to Madison, Sept. 20, 1785.

35. Marie Kimball, *Scene of Europe,* p. 55. The resolution was passed June 24, 1784.

36. Charles Coleman Sellers, "Portraits and Miniatures by Charles Willson Peale," *Transactions of the American Philosophical Society, N.S., 42,* pt. 1 (1952), 236-237: the Peale canvas is owned by the Fogg Museum of Harvard University.

37. Marie Kimball, *Scene of Europe,* pp. 55-63: a concise summarizing of Jefferson's role in obtaining the Houdon *Washington.*

38. One plaster for Monticello, since lost, and two respectively at the American Philosophical Society and the New-York Historical Society. *Papers,* 15:xxxvi-xxxix: notes on each of the Houdon busts obtained by Jefferson.

39. Marie Kimball, "Jefferson, Patron of the Arts," *The Magazine Antiques, 43,* no. 4 (Apr. 1934), 165.

40. Charles Coleman Sellers, *Benjamin Franklin in Portraiture* (New Haven and London: Yale University Press, 1962), pp. 253-254.

41. Alfred L. Bush, *The Life Portraits of Thomas Jefferson* (Charlottesville: Thomas Jefferson Memorial Foundation, 1962), pp. 14-16.

42. Andrew Oliver, *Portraits of John and Abigail Adams* (Cambridge, Mass.: Harvard University Press, 1967), pp. 46-54.

43. *Papers,* 10:479, Jefferson to William Stephens Smith, Oct. 22, 1786.

44. Jefferson's was a more widely embracing concept than Charles Willson Peale's gallery of "Portraits of distinguished characters in the revolutionary war" which he probably had seen in Philadelphia. See, Charles Coleman Sellers, *Charles Willson Peale* (New York: Charles Scribner's Sons, 1969), pp. 191-192.

45. Monticello Archives. The *Raleigh* was received by Jefferson in July 1787. It was acquired by the Thomas Jefferson Memorial Foundation in 1965.

46. *Papers,* 15:xxv, and 25:vi.

47. Monticello Archives.

48. John Trumbull, *The Autobiography of Colonel John Trumbull, Patriot-Artist, 1756-1843,* ed. Theodore Sizer (New Haven: Yale University Press, 1953), pp. 96-121. See also, Y. Bizardel, "L'experience parisienne d'une peintre americaine au XVIII siècle," *Gazette des Beaux-Arts,* s. 6, 60 (Oct. 1962), 429-442.

49. Catalogue of the sale of Jefferson's collection "at Mr. Harding's gallery" in Boston, July 19, 1833 (photostat in Monticello files).

50. Trumbull, *Autobiography,* pp. 93, 111. These "first fruits" were *The Battle of Bunker's Hill* and *The Death of General Montgomery at Quebec.*

51. Theodore Sizer, *The Works of Colonel John Trumbull, Artist of the Revolution* (New

Haven: Yale University Press, 1967), p. 100.

52. Bush, *The Life Portraits,* pp. 17-19.

53. Sizer, *Trumbull,* pp. 154-156.

54. Monticello Archives. The Jefferson papers contain references to these acquisitions dating from the early months of 1789.

55. *Papers,* 16: xxv-xli, 53-79: a detailed resumé with illustrations of the history of the medals.

56. Berman, *Jefferson,* p. 85: Jefferson's notes for Messrs. Rutledge and Shippen, June 3, 1788.

57. Monticello Archives.

58. Trumbull, *Autobiography,* pp. 173-175.

59. Marie Kimball, "Thomas Jefferson's French Furniture," *The Magazine Antiques, 15,* no. 2 (Feb. 1929), 128.

60. Sarah N. Randolph, *The Domestic Life of Thomas Jefferson* (New York: Harper and Brothers, 1871), p. 351.

61. Monticello Archives: Jefferson to William Morgan, Feb. 4, 1809.

62. Bush, *The Life Portraits,* p. 27. This work destroyed by fire in the Library of Congress in 1851.

63. Andrew Hamilton, *The Papers of Andrew Hamilton,* 18, ed. Syrett (New York: Columbia University Press, 1967): 504; also, Wayne Craven, *Sculpture in America* (New York: Thomas Y. Crowell Company, 1968), p. 54.

64. Marie G. Kimball, "The Original Furnishings of the White House," *The Magazine Antiques, 15,* no. 6 (June 1929), 486.

65. Monticello Archives.

66. Monticello Archives.

67. Randolph, *Jefferson,* pp. 311-312.

68. *Papers,* 17:xxx, 20: the single kneeling woman is illustrated. See also, Berman, *Jefferson,* pp. 106-107.

69. Monticello Archives.

70. The Monticello Archives contain numerous references to a "large" portfolio of prints.

71. Berman, *Jefferson,* p. 88: Jefferson to Trumbull, Jan. 8, 1818.

72. Monticello Archives.

73. Bush, *The Life Portraits.*

74. Thomas Jefferson, *The Jefferson Papers of the University of Virginia,* ed. Constance E. Thurlow and Francis L. Berkeley, Jr. (Charlottesville: University of Virginia Press, 1950),

p. 38: no. 2958, "Catalogue of Paintings etc. at Monticello," was published in *Antiques, 59,* no. 4 (Apr. 1951), 308, 311; no. 5291, a photostat of the original belonging to Mrs. Edwin Page Kirk, is printed in full in Marie Kimball, *Scene of Europe,* pp. 323-327. Also in private hands is a third, "brief" list, not seen by the writer, that is thought to be a preliminary draft for no. 2958.

75. Omissions from this list—for example, of the "discoverer" and "trinity" portraits—seem significant. Even a presumed *terminus ad quo* date of 1790, that of the *Madison,* cannot with certainty be accepted for the entire list when it is noted that in the original the four portraits are separable, the first three on an otherwise blank first page, and the *Franklin* added at the end in a somewhat different handwriting. If the four portraits were to be disregarded, what remained would be a list exclusively of art-paintings, such as might conceivably have been compiled by Jefferson while acquiring them in Paris.

76. The list included two works of the 1803 date, the Birch *Mount Vernon* and the Mills drawing of *Monticello.*

77. Monticello Archives.

78. Marie G. Kimball, *The Furnishings of Monticello* (Charlottesville: The Thomas Jefferson Memorial Foundation, 1946), p. 10.

79. Berman, *Jefferson,* p. 79.

80. A supposition of Courtney Campbell in "Tentative Survey of the Pictures in the Parlor at Monticello," a typescript with a diagram of the installation, in the files at Monticello.

81. Paul Wilstach, *Jefferson and Monticello* (Garden City, N.Y.: Doubleday Page and Company, 1925), p. 110.

82. Monticello Archives: quoting Martha Jefferson Trist Burke.

83. Monticello Archives. Jefferson had included in his early desiderata list the *Belisarius* by Salvatore Rosa in the collection of the Earl of Townsend, showing the beggared and blinded general receiving an "obolum." The "Moncada" may have been from a portrait of Francisco Moncada, Count of Osuna (1586-1653), who is seen as the Spanish commander in Velásquez's *Surrender of Breda.*

84. Bush, *The Life Portraits,* p. 60.

85. "The Jefferson Papers," *Collections of the Massachusetts Historical Society,* 2nd series, 1: 325. An 1815 memorandum lists his art hold-

ings as "16 portraits in oil / 1 d° crayon / 64 pictures, prints, engravings with frames, more than 12 i[nches] / 39 d° under 12 i. with gilt frames."

86. Monticello Archives.

87. Berman, *Jefferson,* pp. 88-89, and Trumbull, *Autobiography,* pp. 309-311.

88. George C. Groce, "John William Coffee, Long-lost Sculptor," *The Magazine Antiques, 15,* no. 5 (May 1946), 14-15, 19-20.

89. Monticello Archives.

90. Monticello Archives: Jefferson to Gould, Aug. 5, 1825. The plaster bust of Adams arrived at Monticello in a damaged but reparable condition.

91. Mabel Munson Swan, *The Athenaeum Gallery,* 1827-1923 (Boston: D. B. Updike, The Merrymount Press, 1940), pp. 34, 85-89. Living in Boston and responsible for the sales there was Jefferson's granddaughter, Mrs. Joseph (Ellen Wayles Randolph) Coolidge.

Jefferson and Adams' English Garden Tour

EDWARD DUMBAULD

Foreword

ANYONE WHO HAS HAD AN OCCASION TO FOLLOW JEFFERSON'S TRAIL through his long and busy life is in debt to Edward Dumbauld for his useful guide, *Thomas Jefferson American Tourist*. Aside from its special qualities of organization and information, giving us time, place, cities and sights of the president's travels, it is a delight to read.

At the suggestion of Lyman Butterfield, editor-in-chief of the Adams Papers, I was able to prevail on the judge of the United States District Court, Western District of Pennsylvania, to undertake the present assignment as a part of the National Gallery of Art's Bicentennial program. In addition to an introduction, Judge Dumbauld has brought together in these pages all of the relevant notes, diary and account book entries and references in correspondence documenting the famous tour of English gardens of the two future presidents of the United States.

Sir Nicolaus Pevsner has rightly pointed out that the English romantic landscape, revolutionary in its concept, is perhaps England's greatest contribution to the arts in the eighteenth century. Both Jefferson and Adams were attuned to these developments, and Jefferson particularly had studied the literature on the subject from an early age, when he was beginning to experiment with the virgin stretches of mountain grandeur where he planned to build his house. While each perceived the layout and architecture of the famous English gardens in his own way and with his own particular prejudice, their notes record a special understanding of nature and pleasure in man's ability to shape it to new and surprising effect.

It is indeed fair to say, for both of these architects of the American republic, that the ultimate measure of the republic's success would be in the quality of the life produced by the revolutionary experiment. Adams justified the study of war during the Revolution in order that his descendants could study the fine arts. Jefferson, for his part, thought the virtues of the new republic should be reflected in its architecture, sculpture and city plans.

In the end, the environment itself, as an extension of the body politic, would reflect the achievement or failure of the accommodations men made with nature as they tested their new machinery of government in support of "life, liberty and the pursuit of happiness." For Adams and Jefferson, to study the landscape of a foreign country and to consider its aesthetics and imposed organization in relation to American topography and to their dreams for the new nation's success was a natural extension of that earlier collaboration in Philadelphia in the summer of 1776.

WILLIAM HOWARD ADAMS

Jefferson and Adams'
English Garden Tour

EDWARD DUMBAULD

THOMAS JEFFERSON AND JOHN ADAMS WERE RESPONSIBLE, PERHAPS more than any other of the "Founding Fathers," for the adoption of the Declaration of Independence. Jefferson, though not a notable orator, was a skilled penman, whose writings were considered by Adams and other members of the Continental Congress as remarkable for their "peculiar felicity of expression." [1] To him was entrusted the task of drafting the Declaration. Adams (as well as the astute Benjamin Franklin) contributed several amendments,[2] and Adams was in Jefferson's estimation "our Colossus on the floor" of Congress, "our main pillar in debate." [3]

Within less than a decade after the Declaration of Independence these three renowned signers were reunited in a foreign capital. In 1784 Jefferson sailed for France as a diplomatic envoy appointed by Congress to act with Adams and Franklin in negotiating treaties of commerce with foreign nations. The first such treaty was concluded in 1785 with Frederick the Great of Prussia. In the same year, the aged and ailing Franklin returned to America, and Jefferson succeeded him as minister plenipotentiary to the French court, while Adams was sent to London as the first American minister to be received by his former sovereign George III. In 1786 Adams urged Jefferson to join him in London to complete the negotiation of a commercial treaty with Portugal. Agreement was reached with the Portuguese envoy, but the proposed treaty never took effect. Nor could any arrangement be effected with Tripoli to curb the depredations of Barbary pirates; nor a compact with Great Britain regarding trade with the United States. But although Jefferson's official visit to England bore no diplomatic fruit, it enabled him to obtain a first-hand acquaintance with conditions in that country. He attended dinner parties and the theater; he noted the state of architecture and the mechanical arts, patronized a London tailor, made purchases at other tempting shops (not neglecting the booksellers), and sat for the first portrait ever painted of him. The artist was Mather Brown, and a duplicate was made for Adams.

Jefferson's five-year sojourn in Europe enabled him to gratify his love of the arts [4] to an extent not possible in his native land. To his political disciple James Madison he wrote from Paris, "You see I am an enthusiast on the subject of the arts. But it is an enthusiasm of which I am not ashamed, as it's object is to improve the taste of my countrymen."

Music had long been one of his first loves. While serving in the Virginia legislature at Williamsburg, he declared to an Italian friend that "music . . . is the favorite passion of my soul, and fortune has cast my lot in a country where it is in a state of deplorable barbarism." [5] To Charles Bellini, a native of Florence and professor of modern languages at William and Mary College, he wrote from Paris, "Were I to proceed to tell you how much I enjoy their architecture, sculpture, painting, music, I should want words. It is in these arts they shine. The last of them, particularly, is an enjoinment, the deprivation of which with us cannot be calculated. I am almost ready to say that it is the only thing which from my heart I envy them, and which in spight of all the authority of the decalogue, I do covet."

Jefferson's own accomplishments as a violinist are well known. It is said that while he was courting the comely widow Martha Wayles Skelton, a rival heard him merrily playing the violin in her company and silently departed, abandoning the field to the talented musician. Better authenticated is his participation in concerts at the governor's palace in Williamsburg during the administration of Governor Francis Fauquier, as well as his fanciful project of employing Italian winegrowers to cultivate the vine in Virginia by day, while performing as a chamber-music orchestra at Monticello in the evening. [6]

Painting and sculpture [7] constituted a source of pleasure, but when formulating a catalogue of "Objects of Attention for an American" for the benefit of two young compatriots traveling in Europe, Jefferson emphasized the practical objective of acquiring knowledge which could be used at home. Hence, since the cultivation of painting and sculpture was too expensive for the state of wealth in America, "it would be useless . . . and preposterous, for us to make ourselves connoisseurs in those arts. They are worth seeing, but not studying." For the same reason Jefferson believed that "lighter mechanical arts" and manufactures should not be examined minutely, since circumstances rendered it "impossible that America should become a manufacturing country during the time of any man now living." But agriculture, as well as mechanical arts, "so far as they respect things necessary in America, and inconvenient to be transported thither ready-made" (such as forges, stone quarries, boats, bridges, and the like), were worthy of attentive study.

Architecture, too, was "worth great attention. As we double our numbers every twenty years, we must double our houses. Besides, we build of such perishable materials that one-half of our houses must be rebuilt in every space of twenty years, so that in that time houses are to be built for three-fourths of our inhabitants. It is, then, among the most important arts; and it is desirable to introduce taste into an art which shows so much." [8]

Jefferson felt gardening "peculiarly worth the attention of an American, because it is the country of all others where the noblest gardens may be made without expense. We have only to cut out the superabundant plants." [9]

The gardens of England delighted Jefferson. "The gardening in that country is the article in which it excels all the earth. I mean their pleasure-gardening. This, indeed went far beyond my ideas." A tour of English gardens, in company with Adams, was the high point of the Virginian's visit to London in 1786. Fortunately, both statesmen recorded their impressions of this pleasurable jaunt. The New Englander commented interestingly on the trip in his diary,[10] while Jefferson noted his more utilitarian observations in a compilation entitled "Memorandums made on a tour to some of the gardens in England described by Whateley in his book on gardening." [11] Moreover, the customary entries in Jefferson's Account Book listing expenses during that period furnish useful information concerning details of the journey.[12] Material from these three sources will be brought together here, arranged according to date.

Whately's accuracy impressed Jefferson:

While his descriptions in point of style are models of perfect elegance and classical correctness, they are as remarkeble for their exactness. I always walked over the gardens with his book in my hand, examined with attention the particular spots he described, found them so justly characterised by him as to be easily recognised, and saw with wonder, that his fine imagination had never been able to seduce him from the truth. My enquiries were directed chiefly to such practical things as might enable me to estimate the expence of making and maintaining a garden in that style. My journey was in the months of March and April 1786. [13]

Even before the memorable garden tour with Adams (which began on April 4, 1786 [14]), Jefferson had undertaken sightseeing expeditions in England. On March 22, 1786, expenses are recorded in his Account Book for "seeing castle at Windsor." [15] The Adamses later visited Windsor on June 21, 1786.[16]

On April 2, 1786, Jefferson visited Chiswick, Richmond, Twickenham, Hampton Court, Esher Place, Cobham, Painshill, and Weybridge. The next day he was at Woburn Farm, before returning to London. He was accompanied on this trip by his English servant John and by Colonel William Stephens Smith, who was to become the son-in-law of John and Abigail Adams on June 12, 1786. Colonel Smith was secretary of the legation at London and had been the bearer of the invitation from Adams urging Jefferson to join him in London. Smith had also been Jefferson's traveling companion from Paris to the English capital, sharing "a cabriolet to Calais" before embarking on the Channel crossing. Their joint expenses from Paris to Calais amounted to £29-14-9, and from Calais to London £19-19-6.[17]

Soon after the two diplomats returned to London on April 9 or 10, 1786, they went to visit the workshop in Blackfriars of John Viney, who manufactured wheels by bending timber into a circular shape. Benjamin Franklin had proposed the method to Viney. Jefferson's later reaction to publicity claiming originality for the Englishman's process was to retort patriotically that New Jersey farmers had long made wheels by bending saplings, and that they had probably learned to do so from a passage in the Iliad "because ours are the only farmers who can read Homer." [18] In the same locality Jefferson likewise visited the works where James Watt and Matthew Boulton developed the steam engine as a source of power for industry.[19]

After completion of the tour with Adams, Jefferson also made excursions to Enfield Chase, Moor Park, Kew, Ranelagh, and Buckingham House, which were duly described in his *Memorandums*.[20] On another jaunt, through Hyde Park to Osterley Park and Sion House, he was accompanied by the Adams family.

On April 26, 1786, after making preparations for his departure, Jefferson "set out from London for Paris." En route that day he visited the observatory and hospital at Greenwich. By way of Dartford, Rochester, Sittingbourne, and Canterbury he proceeded to Dover. On April 27, he went to see Dover Castle, and dismissed his English servant John. On the 28th he bade adieu to England. Traveling with his servant Petit, he enjoyed a speedy passage "of three hours only" and reached Paris "in 48 hours from Calais."

Jefferson was never again in England, except while delayed at Cowes on the Isle of Wight for almost two weeks in the fall of 1789 awaiting favorable winds for his return voyage to America. Being unable to find a vessel sailing directly from a French port, he was obliged to cross the English Channel before embarking on the *Clermont* for Norfolk. During the interval

Pieter Andries Rysbrack. *Chiswick Villa and the Serpentine Lake.*
Trustees of the Chatsworth Settlement, Devonshire Collection, England

he visited Newport and Carisbrook Castle, where Charles I had been confined in 1648, and an escape plan failed because the royal girth exceeded the available space in the casement window).[22] "After getting clear of the eternal fogs of Europe . . . the sun broke out upon us," the returning diplomat wrote, and "after a most pleasant & prosperous" voyage of "only 26. days from land to land" he set foot on Virginia soil. A month and a day after arriving in Norfolk Jefferson and his two daughters reached Monticello, where a joyous welcome awaited them.

After Jefferson's visit to England in 1786, he and Adams were together again in Europe in 1788, this time in the Netherlands. Adams undertook a hasty visit from London to that country in order to take leave of their High Mightinesses before his return to America.[23] Jefferson met him there to negotiate a loan from Dutch bankers which would assure funds for the continued payment of interest on American government obligations, thus maintaining the nation's credit.

Returning to England, Adams and the doughty Abigail embarked on the

Lucretia from Cowes.[24] "On the 20th of April, 1788, Mr. Adams bade farewell to the shores of the ancient world," his grandson later recorded.[25] As the ship entered Boston harbor on June 17, 1788, a volley of cannon saluted from Castle William, and Governor John Hancock dispatched the secretary of the commonwealth to greet the returning diplomat and to invite him to the Hancock mansion to receive there the compliments of his numerous friends. The party proceeded in the state barge and in the governor's carriage to the mansion. Adams was "welcomed on shore by three huzzas from several thousand persons" and "the bells in the several churches rang during the remainder of the day." At the governor's house on the 18th he was presented with a complimentary address by the legislature of Massachusetts, and made an appropriate response.[26]

From Paris Jefferson wrote, "I have received with a great deal of pleasure the account of your safe arrival and joyful reception at Boston. Mr. Cutting was so kind as to send me a copy of the address of the assembly to you and your answer, which with the other circumstances I have sent to have published in the gazette of Leyden, and in a gazette here. It will serve to shew the people of Europe that those of America are content with their servants and particularly content with you." [27]

The foregoing summary of the travels of Jefferson and the Adams family in England will now be amplified by presenting verbatim extracts from the sources mentioned above, arranged according to date.

March 22, 1786

JEFFERSON, ACCOUNT BOOK
pd seeing castle at Windsor 5/

April 2, 1786

JEFFERSON, ACCOUNT BOOK
gave servants at Chiswick (D. of Devonshire's) 4/6
gave postilion at Richmd. 3/
gave servts at Twickenham, Pope's garden, 2/
gave servts. at Hampton court 4/6 — do. At Esher place 6/
pd postillion at Cobham 24/6 — gave servts at Payns hill 7/
pd post horses at Cobham 7/6 — postilion at Weybridge 2/
borrowed of Colo. Smith 52/6

JEFFERSON, MEMORANDUMS
Cheswick, Belongs to D. of Devonshire. Garden about 6. acres. The Octagonal dome has an ill effect, both within and without; the garden shews

still too much of art; an obelisk of very ill effect. Another in the middle of a pond useless.

Hampton court. Old fashioned. Clipt yews grown wild.

Twickenham. Pope's original garden 3½ as. Sr. Wm. Stanhope added 1½ acre. This is a long narrow slope, grass and trees in the middle, walk all round. Now Sr. Wellbore Ellis's. Obelisk at bottom of Pope's garden as monument to his mother. Inscription. Ah! Edithe matrum optuma, mulierum amantissima, Vale. The house about 30 yds. from the Thames; the ground shelves gently to the water side. On the back of the house passes the street, and beyond that the garden. The grotto is under the street, and goes out level to the water. In the center of the garden a mound with a spiral walk round it. A rookery.

Esher place.[28] The house in a bottom near the river. On the other side the ground rises pretty much. The road by which we come to the house forms a dividing line in the middle of the front. On the right are heights, rising one beyond and above another, with clumps of trees. On the farthest a temple. A hollow filled up with a clump of trees, the tallest in the bottom, so that the top is quite flat. On the left the ground descends. Clumps of trees. The clumps on each hand balance finely. A most lovely mixture of concave and convex. The garden is of about 45. as. besides the park which joins. Belongs to Lady Francis Pelham.

Claremont. Ld. Clive. Nothing remarkeable.

Paynshill. Mr. Hopkins. 323. as. garden and park all in one. Well described by Whateley.[29] Grotto said to have cost 7000.L. Whately says one of the bridges is of stone.[30] But both are now of wood. The lower 60 f. high. There is too much evergreen. The Dwelling house built by Hopkins. Ill situated. He has not been there in 5. years. He lived there 4. years while building the present house. It is not finished. It's architecture is incorrect. A Doric temple beautiful.

ADAMS, DIARY

On Saturday night returned from a Tour to Portsmouth, in which We viewed Paines Hill in Surry, as We went out; and Windsor as We returned. We were absent four days. Paines Hill is the most striking Piece of Art, that I have yet seen. The Soil is an heap of Sand, and the Situation is nothing extraordinary. It is a new Creation of Mr. Hamilton. All made within 35 Years. It belongs to Mr. Hopkins, who rides by it, but never stops. The owners of these enchanting Seats are very indifferent to their Beauties. — The Country from Guilford to Portsmouth, is a barren heath, a dreary Waste.[31]

JEFFERSON, ACCOUNT BOOK

pd entert[ainmen]t, at Weybridge, & post hire £2-2
gave servts. at Woburn farm 6/6 — postilion at Twickenham 3/
pd post hire at London 18/6 — repd John for turnpickes 16/
pd turnpike 1/-advanced to John 5/

JEFFERSON, MEMORANDUMS

Woburn.[32] Belongs to Ld. Peters. Ld. Loughborough is the present tenant for 2. lives. 4. people to the farm. 4. to the pleasure garden. 4. to the kitchen garden. All are intermixed, the pleasure garden being merely a highly ornamented walk through and round the divisions of the farm and kitchen garden.

ADAMS, DIARY

Mr. Jefferson and myself, went in a Post Chaise to Woburn Farm, Caversham, Wotton, Stowe, Edghill, Stratford upon Avon, Birmingham, the Leasowes, Hagley, Stourbridge, Worcester, Woodstock, Blenheim, Oxford, High Wycomb, and back to Grosvenor Square.

JEFFERSON, ACCOUNT BOOK

pd coachman 5/ — postilion at Twickenham 2/.
pd at Woburn farm (Ld. Loughborough's) to postiln. 18/servants 3/6
Sonning hill. pd postillion 18/6
Caversham. (mr Marsac's) gave servts. 3/6
Reading. postilion 29/6 — turnpikes 13/6

JEFFERSON, MEMORANDUMS

Caversham. Sold by Ld. Cadogan to Majr. Marsac. 25. as. of garden, 400. as. of park, 6 as. of kitchen garden. A large lawn, separated by a sunk fence from the garden, appears to be part of it. A straight broad gravel walk passes before the front and parallel to it, terminated on the right by a Doric temple, and opening at the other end on a fine prospect. This straight walk has an ill effect. The lawn in front, which is pasture, well disposed with clumps of trees.

JEFFERSON, ACCOUNT BOOK

at do. entertt. 26/1 servts. 3/ horses to Thames 22/7
Thame. postillion 2/
Wotton. (Marquis of Buckingham's) servants 3/
Buckingham. guide 7/6 — postillions 55/

Wotton.[34] Now belongs to the M. of Buckingham, son of George Grenville. The lake covers 50. as. the river 5. as. the bason 15. as. the little river 2. as.=72. as of water. The lake and great river are on a level. They fall into the bason 5. f. below, and that again into the little river 5. f. lower. These waters lie in form of an L. The house is in middle of open side, forming the angle. A walk goes round the whole, 3. miles in circumference, and containing within it about 300. as. Sometimes it passes close to the water, sometimes so farr off as to leave large pasture ground between it and water. But 2. hands to keep the pleasure grounds in order. Much neglected. The water affords 2000. brace of carp a year. There is a Palladian bridge of which I think Whateley does not speak.

April 6, 1786

at do. pd entt. 22/ — horses to Banbury 23/do. for servts Buiester 10/6
at do. servts. 3/ — gave John for expences 21/books.
Stowe (Marquis of Buckingham's) servants 8/
Buckingham, pd for books 9/
Banbury. postilion 4/
Kineton.[35] postilion 3/6 — horses to Stratford upon Avon 10/
Stratford upon Avon. postilion 3/
do. seeing house where Shakespeare was born 1/
seeing his tombstone 1/ — entt. 4/2 — servts. 2/horses to Hockley 12/

Stowe.[36] Belongs to the M. of Buckingham, son of G. Grenville, and who takes it from Ld. Temple. 15. men and 18. boys employed in keeping pleasure grounds. Within the Walk are considerable portions separated by inclosures and used for pasture. The Egyptian pyramid [37] is almost entirely taken down by the late Ld. Temple to erect a building there, in commemoration of Mr. Pitt, but he died before beginning it, and nothing is done to it yet. The grotto, and two rotundas are taken away. There are 4. levels of water, receiving it one from the other. The bason contains 7. as. the lake below that 10. as. Kent's building is called the temple of Venus.[38] The inclosure is entirely by ha! ha! At each end of the front line there is a recess like the bastion of a fort. In one of these is the temple of Friendship, in the other the temple of Venus. They are seen the one from the other, the line of sight passing, not thro' the garden, but through the country parallel to the line of the garden. This has a good effect. In the approach to Stowe, you are brought a mile

The Cobham Monument, Stowe Gardens

through a straight avenue, pointing to the Corinthian arch and to the house, till you get to the Arch. Then you turn short to the right. The straight approach is very ill. The Corinthian arch has a very useless appearance,[39] inasmuch as it has no pretension to any destination. Instead of being an object from the house, it is an obstacle to a very pleasing distant prospect. The Graecian valley being clear of trees, while the hill on each side is covered with them, is much deepened to appearance.

Stratford upon Avon is interesting as it is the Scene of the Birth, Death and Sepulture of Shakespear. Three Doors from the Inn, is the House where he was born, as small and mean, as you can conceive. They shew Us an old Wooden Chair in the Chimney Corner, where He sat. We cutt off a chip according to the Custom. A Mulberry Tree that he planted has been cutt down, and is carefully preserved for Sale. The House where he died has been taken down and the Spot is now only Yard or Garden. The Curse upon him who should remove his Bones, which is written on his Grave Stone, alludes to a Pile of some Thousands of human Bones, which lie exposed in that Church. There is nothing preserved of this great Genius which is worth knowing—nothing which might inform Us what Education, what Company, what Accident turned his Mind to Letters and the Drama. His name is not even on his Grave Stone. An ill sculptured Head is sett up by his Wife, by the Side of his Grave in the Church. But paintings and Sculpture would be thrown away upon his Fame. His Wit, and Fancy, his Taste and Judgment, His Knowledge of Nature, of Life and Character, are immortal.

April 7, 1786

JEFFERSON, ACCOUNT BOOK

do. breakfast 1/6 — servts. 1/
Hockley. postilion 2/6 — horses to Birmingham 10/
Birmingham. postilln. & turnpikes 3/ — books 9/ — candlestick 15/
do. hairdresser 1/6 — servts. 1/ — entt. 13/8 — servts. 1/6
Leasowes (Shenstone's. now Horne's) servts. 5/
Stourbridge. horses from Birmingham 15/postilln. & turnpikes 4/6

ADAMS, DIARY

At Birmingham, We only walked round the Town and viewed a manufactory of Paintings upon Paper.

JEFFERSON, MEMORANDUMS

Leasowes.[40] In Shropshire. Now the property of Mr. Horne by purchase. 150. as. within the walk. The waters small. This is not even an ornamented farm. It is only a grazing farm with a path round it. Here and there a seat of board, rarely any thing better. Architecture has contributed nothing. The obelisk is of brick. Shenstone had but 300£ a year, and ruined himself by what he did to this farm. It is said that he died of the heartaches which his debts occasioned him. The part next the road is of red earth, that on the further part grey. The 1st. and 2d. cascades are beautiful. The landscape at No. 18. and prospect at 32. are fine.[41] The Walk through the wood is umbrageous and pleasing. The whole arch of prospect may be of 90°. Many of the inscriptions are lost.

April 8, 1786

JEFFERSON, ACCOUNT BOOK

do. entt. 6/6 — horses to Bromsgrove 12/6 — servts 3/

Hagley (Ld. Westcott's) servts 5/ — entt. in the village 2/6

Bromsgrove. postion. & turnp. 2/6 — horses to Worcester 13/6

Worcester. postiln. & turnp. 3 — entt. 9/9 — horses to Winch. castle 16/ servts 1/6

Winchcastle. postiln & turnp. 3/6 — horses to Moreton 14/

Moreton. postiln. & turnp. 3/ — entt. 2/

Hynston [Enstone]. horses from Moreton, postiln. & turnp. 16/. horses to Woodstock 7/

Woodstock. postillion & turnp. 3/

JEFFERSON, MEMORANDUMS

Hagley.[42] Now Ld. Wescot. 1000. as. No distinction between park and garden. Both blended, but more of the character of garden. 8. or 9. labourers keep it in order. Between 2. and 300. deer in it, some few of them red deer. They breed sometimes with the fallow. This garden occupying a descending hollow between the Clent and Witchbury hills, with the spurs from those hills, there is no level in it for a spacious water. There are therefore only some small ponds. From one of these there is a fine cascade; but it can only be occasionally, by opening the sluice. This is in a small, dark, deep hollow, with recesses of stone in the banks on every side. In one of these is a Venus pudique, turned half round as if inviting you with her into the recess. There is another cascade seen from the Portico on the bridge. The castle is triangular, with a round tower at each angle, one only entire; it seems to be between 40. and 50. f. high. The ponds yield a great deal of trout. The walks are scarcely gravelled.

ADAMS, DIARY

Edgehill and Worcester were curious and interesting to us, as Scaenes where Freemen had fought for their Rights. The People in the Neighbourhood, appeared so ignorant and careless at Worcester that I was provoked and asked, "And do Englishmen so soon forget the Ground where Liberty was fought for? Tell your Neighbours and your Children that this is holy Ground, much holier than that on which your Churches stand. All England should come in Pilgrimage to this Hill, once a Year." This animated them, and they seemed much pleased with it. Perhaps their Aukwardness before might arise from their Uncertainty of our Sentiments concerning the Civil Wars.

JEFFERSON, ACCOUNT BOOK

received of mr Adams £9-9 in part towards preceding expences from our leaving London Apr. 4. which are joint.

Blenheim (D. of Marlborough's) servts 7/

Woodstock. entt. 7/ — horses to Oxford 8/ — servts. 2/

Oxford. postiln. & turnp. 2/ — doorkeepers of colleges 5/
Tatsworth [Tetsworth]. High Wycombe. Uxbridge. horse, postilns. £4-14

High Wycombe. entt. 10/10

JEFFERSON, MEMORANDUMS

Blenheim.[43] 2500. as. of which 200. is garden, 150. water, 12. kitchen garden, and the rest park. 200. people employed to keep it in order, and to make alterations and additions. About 50. of these employed in pleasure grounds. The turf is mowed once in 10. days, in summer. About 2000. fallow deer in the park, and 2. or 3000. sheep. The palace of H.2. was remaining till taken down by Sarah, widow of the 1st. D. of Marlborough. It was on a round spot levelled by art, near what is now water, and but a little above it. The island was a part of the high road leading to the palace. Rosamond's bower[44] was near where is now a little grove about 200. yards from the palace. The well is near where the bower was. The water here is very beautiful, and very grand. The cascade from the lake a fine one. Except this the garden has no great beauties. It is not laid out in fine lawns and woods, but the trees are scattered thinly over the ground, and every here and there small thickets of shrubs, in oval raised beds, cultivated, and flowers among the shrubs. The gravelled walks are broad. Art appears too much. There are but a few seats in it, and nothing of architecture more dignified. There is no one striking position in it. There has been a great addition to the length of the river since Whateley wrote.

ADAMS, DIARY

The Gentlemens Seats were the highest Entertainment, We met with. Stowe, Hagley and Blenheim, are superb. Woburn, Caversham and the Leasowes are beautifull. Wotton is both great and elegant tho neglected. Architecture, Painting, Statuary, Poetry are all employed in the Embellishment of these Residences of Greatness and Luxury. A national Debt of 274 millions sterling accumulated by Jobs, Contracts, Salaries and Pensions in the Course of a Century might easily produce all this Magnificence. The Pillars, Obelisks &c. erected in honour of Kings, Queens and Princesses, might procure the means. The Temples to Bacchus and Venus, are quite unnecessary as Mankind have

H. F. James. *View of the Leasowes and Priory*. Engraved by I. C. Stadler.
The British Museum

no need of artificial Incitements, to such Amuzements. The Temples of ancient Virtue, of the British Worthies, of Friendship, of Concord and Victory, are in a higher Taste. I mounted Ld. Cobhams Pillar 120 feet high, with pleasure, as his Lordships Name was familiar to me, from Popes Works.

Ld. Littletons Seat interested me, from a recollection of his Works, as well as the Grandeur and Beauty of the Scaenes. Popes Pavillion and Thompsons [Thomson's] Seat, made the Excursion poetical. Shenstones Leasowes is the simplest and plainest, but the most rural of all. I saw no Spot so small, that exhibited such a Variety of Beauties.

It will be long, I hope before Ridings, Parks, Pleasure Grounds, Gardens and ornamented Farms grow so much in fashion in America. But Nature has done greater Things and furnished nobler Materials there. The Oceans, Islands, Rivers, Mountains, Valleys are all laid out upon a larger Scale. — If any Man should hereafter arise, to embellish the rugged Grandeur of Pens Hill [45] he might make some thing to boast of, although there are many Situations capable of better Improvement.

April 14, 1786

JEFFERSON, ACCOUNT BOOK

gave servts at Kew 5/ — lemonade 6d. charity 6d.
pd postilion & turnpikes 16/6

JEFFERSON, MEMORANDUMS

Enfield chase. One of the 4. lodges. Garden about 60. as. originally by Ld. Chatham, now in the tenure of Dr. Beaver, who married the daughter of Mr. Sharpe. The lease lately renewed. Not in good repair. The water very fine. Would admit of great improvement by extending walks &c. to the principal water at the bottom of the lawn.

[Moor-Park] [46] Lawn about 30. as. A piece of ground up the hill of 6. as. A small lake. Clumps of Spruce firs. Surrounded by walk separately inclosed. Destroys unity. The property of Mr. Rous, who bought of Sr. Thomas Dundas. The building superb. The principal front a Corinthian portico of 4. columns. In front of the wings a colonnade, Ionic, subordinate. Back front a terras, 4. Corinthian pilasters. Pulling down wings of building. Removing deer. Wants water.

Kew. Archimedes' screw for raising water. A horizontal shaft made to turn the oblique one of the screw by a patent machinery . . .[47]

April 17, 1786

JEFFERSON, ACCOUNT BOOK

pd at Ranelagh 3/6

April 18, 1786

JEFFERSON, ACCOUNT BOOK

pd servts. at Buckingham house 24/

April 20, 1786

JEFFERSON, ACCOUNT BOOK

gave servts. at Osterly & Sion house 7/ — dinner 10/6

ADAMS, DIARY

Went with Mr. Jefferson and my Family to Osterly, to view the seat of the late Banker Child. The House is very large. It is Three houses, fronting as many Ways-between two is a double row of Six Pillars, which you rise to by

Enfield chace. one of the 4 lodges.

    garden contains ab.ᵗ 60. a.ˢ laid out originally by L.ᵈ Chatham now in the tenure of D.ʳ Beaver the man.ᵈ daur of mr Sharpe. lease lately renewed.

    not in good repair.

    the water very fine. admit of great improvement by extending walks &c to the principal water at the bottom of the lawn.

noor=park. the lawn about 30. a.ˢ

    a peice of ground up the hill on the right of 6 a.ˢ

    small lake — clumps of Spruce firs. — surround.ᵈ by walk separately inclosed. destroys Unity.

    property of mr Rous who bot of S.ʳ Tho.ˢ Dundas.

    pulling down wings of building —

    building superb — principal front ~~Ionic~~ Corinth.ⁿ portico 4. columns in front of wings a colonnade Ionic, subordinate back front, a terrass, 4. Corinth.ⁿ pilasters.

    removing deer

    wants water.

[diagram with labels: Oxford. | Buck. | Bed ford | Hertford | =inghm | Middlesex]

Page from the "Notes of a Tour of English Gardens" by Thomas Jefferson, April 14, 1786

a flight of Steps. Within is a Square, a Court, a terrace paved with large Slate. The Green House and Hot House were curious. Blowing Roses, ripe Strawberries, Cherries, Plumbs &c. in the Hot House. The Pleasure Grounds were only an undulating Gravel Walk, between two Borders of Trees and Shrubs. All the Evergreens, Trees, and Shrubbs were here. There is a Water for Fish Ponds and for Farm Uses, collected from the Springs and wet Places in the farm and neighbourhood. Fine flocks of Deer and Sheep, Wood Doves, Guinea Hens, Peacocks &c.

The Verdure is charming, the Music of the Birds pleasant. But the Ground is too level. — We could not see the Apartments in the House, because We had no Tickett. Mrs. Child is gone to New Markett it seems to the Races.

The beauty, Convenience, and Utility of these Country Seats, are not enjoyed by the owners. They are mere Ostentations of Vanity. Races, Cocking, Gambling, draw away their attention.

On our Return We called to see Sion House belonging to the Duke of Northumberland. This Farm is watered, by a rivulet drawn by an artificial Canal from the Thames. A Repetition of winding Walks, gloomy Evergreens, Sheets of Water, Clumps of Trees, Green Houses, Hot Houses &c. The Gate, which lets you into this Farm from the Brentford Road, is a beautifull Thing, and lays open to the View of the Traveller, a very beautifull green Lawn interspersed with Clumps and scattered Trees.

The Duke of Marlborough owns a House upon Sion Hill, which is only over the way.

Osterly, Sion Place and Sion Hill are all in Brentford, within Ten Miles of Hide Park Corner. We went through Hide Park and Kensington to Brentford. We passed in going and returning, by Lord Hollands House, which is a Modern Building in the gothic manner.[48]

April 26, 1786

JEFFERSON, ACCOUNT BOOK

pd seeing observatory & hospital at Greenwich 4/
Dartford. pd postillion backwards 27/6 pd do. forwards 15/ expences 1/
Rochester. pd Postillion backwds. 7/7½. do forwds. 15/7½ exp. 6d.
Sittingborne. pd Postillion backwds. 2/do. forwds 23/3
Canterbury. pd Postilln. backwds. 2/do. forwds. 22/
Dover. pd. Postillion backwds. 2/
Cash on hand £-3-sterl. and 32 Louis.

JEFFERSON, ACCOUNT BOOK

Dover. pd seeing castle 2/6

	s	d
John's account for turnpikes	8 —	10
breakfast &c	12 —	6
trifles	4 —	1
board & wages 7— 7		
	8 —12 —	5

pd him 5/ and gave him order on Colo.
Smith for £8-8

JEFFERSON, ACCOUNT BOOK

pd Payne portage of baggage £6 —	4 —	3	
custom house official	10 —	6	
entertt.	1 — 11 —	3	
	8 —	6	

gave servts 5/

France. Livres, sols. deniers.

Calais pd passage 32/8 officers of Douane 15 f 4

    pd portage 15 f 4

    gave the successor of Stern's monk at Calais 1 f 4

    pd Basein entertt. 14 f 10 servts. 3 f 6

    pd storage & repairs of carriage 27 f

    gave Petit for expences on the road 48 f

JEFFERSON, ACCOUNT BOOK

St. Omer's. gave Petit for expences on the road 120 f

Royes. gave do. for do. 120 f

JEFFERSON, ACCOUNT BOOK

gave servts. 1 f 4

Bourget. gave Petit for exp. on the road 48 f

Notes

1. Unless otherwise indicated, quotations from Adams are from *The Works of John Adams,* ed. Charles Francis Adams, 10 vols., (Boston: Little Brown & Co., 1850-1856) or from the *Diary and Autobiography of John Adams,* ed. Lyman H. Butterfield, 4 vols. (Cambridge, Mass.: Harvard University Press, 1961); and quotations from Jefferson are from *The Papers of Thomas Jefferson,* ed. Julian P. Boyd, 19 vols. (Princeton: Princeton University Press, 1950–), hereafter cited as *Papers,* or from Edward Dumbauld, *Thomas Jefferson American Tourist* (Norman, Oklahoma: University of Oklahoma Press, 1946).

2. Concerning the amendments made by Adams and Franklin, see Julian P. Boyd, *The Declaration of Independence* (Princeton: Princeton University Press, 1945), pp. 22-31. This work contains a complete account, with photographic reproductions, of the drafting of the Declaration. Roger Sherman and Robert R. Livingston were the other members of the committee, which reported to Congress on June 18, 1776. After further changes during debate, the Declaration was adopted on July 4, 1776. See also Edward Dumbauld, *The Declaration of Independence and What It Means Today* (Norman, Oklahoma: University of Oklahoma Press, 1950).

3. Quoted in John H. Hazelton, *The Declaration of Independence: Its History* (New York: Dodd, Mead & Co., 1906), pp. 162-432.

4. See Eleanor D. Berman, *Thomas Jefferson among the Arts* (New York: Philosophical Library, 1947).

5. For a recent treatment of this topic, see Helen Cripe, *Thomas Jefferson and Music* (Charlottesville: The University Press of Virginia, 1974).

6. Dumas Malone, *Jefferson the Virginian* (Boston: Little, Brown & Co., 1948), pp. 76, 164-165, 289.

7. The "Diana and Endymion, a very superior morsel of sculpture, by Michael Angelo Slodtz, done in the year 1740" praised by Jefferson, has been identified by Howard C. Rice, Jr. See François Souchal, *Les Slodtz sculpteurs et décorateurs du Roi (1685-1764)* (Paris: Editions E. de Boccard, 1967).

8. In his *Notes on the State of Virginia* Jefferson denounced the architecture of Williamsburg. On his own accomplishments as an architect, see Fiske Kimball, *Thomas Jefferson, Architect* (Boston, 1916; rpt. ed., New York: Da Capo Press, 1968).

9. On Jefferson's own practice as a gardener, see Edwin M. Betts, ed., *Thomas Jefferson's Garden Book, 1766-1824* (Philadelphia: The American Philosophical Society, 1944).

10. Adams, *Diary,* 2: 184-187.

11. *Papers,* 9: 369-375. The volume used by Jefferson as a guide book on his tour was Thomas Whately's *Observations on Modern Gardening, Illustrated by Descriptions,* 2nd ed. (London: Printed for T. Payne, 1770). Jefferson bought this book in 1785 from the estate of Samuel Henley, a professor at William and Mary. E. Millicent Sowerby, *Catalogue of the Library of Thomas Jefferson,* 4 (Washington:

The Library of Congress, 1955): 386-387. He was familiar with the book before 1771, when he recommended it to Robert Skipwith. Marie Kimball, *Jefferson: The Road to Glory* (New York: Coward-McCann, Inc., 1943), p. 161; *Papers*, 1:78. Adams noted in the margin of his copy of the 4th edition (London: Printed for T. Payne and Son, 1777) the gardens visited in company with Jefferson. Adams, *Diary*, 2:187. But he did not restrict the comments in his diary (as Jefferson did in his Memorandums) to places mentioned by Whately.

12. From 1767, the year he became a lawyer, until 1826, when he died, Jefferson conscientiously recorded his expenditures and other memoranda, in notebooks (and, for some of the earlier years, in the blank pages of almanacs); and these methodically kept volumes make it possible, as Malone said, "to follow Jefferson's movements almost, if not quite, day by day" (*Jefferson the Virginian*, p. 439). For a list showing the location of these account books, see Dumbauld, *Jefferson Tourist*, p. 242.

13. Jefferson's mention of March may have referred to his visit to Windsor Castle on March 22, 1786, before his tour with Adams.

14. On April 9, Jefferson "received of mr Adams £ 9-9 in part towards preceding expences from our leaving London Apr. 4. which are joint."

15. He seems to have been accompanied by an English servant named John. On March 28, he "pd John . . . coach & horse hire to Windsor (exclus. of 10/8 &c ante) 33/14." The entry for March 22 reads: "pd seeing castle at Windsor 5/dinner &c 11/pd for carriage & horses to & from do. &c. £ 2-13-10. in part."

The entry for March 23 states: "advanced to John 10/8—gave servt. at Stewart's 2/11," followed by payments showing that Jefferson was in London on that date ("at the Pantheon 4/16").

Marie Kimball, *Jefferson: The Scene of Europe* (New York: Coward-McCann, Inc., 1950), p. 129, says that John came with Jefferson from Paris. But Jefferson paid him off on April 27, 1786, before returning to Paris, by an "order on Colo. Smith for £ 8-8" which would be incongruous if John had been part of Jefferson's Paris household.

16. Adams, *Diary*, 2:191.

17. Account Book, entry of Apr. 16, 1786. For biographical details regarding Smith, see

Katherine Metcalf Roof, *Colonel William Smith and Lady* (Boston, Houghton Mifflin Co., 1929).

18. Adams, *Diary*, 2:186-187; Jefferson to St. John de Crèvecoeur, Jan. 15, 1787. *Papers*, 11:43-45.

19. Jefferson to Charles Thomson, Apr. 22, 1786. *Papers*, 9:400-401.

20. Adams, *Diary*, 2:187. Adams had previously visited Buckingham House in 1783 as a private citizen. At that time he was particularly impressed by the queen's German Bible, and the king's library, which contained, he thought, "every book that a king ought to have always at hand, and . . . none other." *Works*, 1:405.

21. Adams, *Diary*, 2:189-190.

22. Samuel R. Gardiner, *History of the Great Civil War*, 3 (London: Longmans, Green, and Co., 1891): 336.

23. Adams took particular pride in the success of his year-long efforts (overcoming Dutch inertia and French opposition) to obtain recognition by the Netherlands of the United States as an independent nation. He published anonymously *A Collection of State-Papers, Relative to the First Acknowledgement of the Sovereignity of the United States of America, and the Reception of Their Minister Plenipotentiary, by Their High Mightinesses the States-General of the United Netherlands* (The Hague, 1782). He had been received as minister pursuant to a resolution of April 19, 1782; and on October 8, 1782, in the "Truce Chamber" on the water side of the Binnenhof he had signed a treaty with the Netherlands on behalf of the United States. He did not wish to give any cause for offense to the Dutch by an unceremonious departure from Europe. Adams, *Diary*, 3:4, 16-17. As to his leave-taking, see *Diary*, 3:211-212, 216; and Adams, *Works*, 8:472-473, 481-483.

24. They too visited Carisbrooke Castle while awaiting the arrival of their ship. Page Smith, *John Adams* (Garden City: Doubleday & Co., Inc., 1962), 2:731-733.

25. Adams, *Works*, 1:439.

26. Adams, *Dairy*, 3:216; James Brown Cutting to Jefferson, undated, *Papers*, 8:403. For the address and response, see *Papers*, 8:402.

27. *The Adams-Jefferson Letters*, ed. Lester J. Cappon (Chapel Hill: University of North Carolina Press, 1959), 2:229.

28. For Whately's description of the grove at Esher Place, see his *Observations,* pp. 50-51.

29. Whately's account of Painshill appears in his *Observations,* pp. 184-192.

30. Whately, *Observations,* p. 192: "the greater [of five arches] is of stone, the smaller [a single arch] of wood."

31. This entry is dated June 26, 1786, and the Adamses' visit took place on June 21. Adams, *Diary,* 2:191. See text at note 16, above.

32. For Whately's comments on Woburn Farm, see *Observations,* pp. 177-182.

33.The approach to Caversham is described in Whately's *Observations,* pp. 140-144.

34. The water at Wotton is described by Whately in his *Observations,* pp. 84-88.

35. The celebrated battle of Edgehill took place near Kineton. This explains why Adams in his diary inserted the paragraph about his speech to the populace at Worcester before the one about Shakespeare, although the travelers did not reach Worcester until April 8.

36. According to Whately, *Observations,* p. 226: "Magnificence and splendor are the characteristics of Stowe; . . . the place is equally distinguished by its amenity and its grandeur." The gardens are described at pp. 213-226.

37. For Whately's description of the pyramid, see *Observations,* p. 215.

38. On the temples of Venus and Bacchus, see Whately, *Observations,* pp. 217-219. On the temples of Friendship, the Ancient Virtues, the British Worthies, and Concord and Victory (which Adams regarded as in better taste), see *Observations,* pp. 220, 224. A description of the temple of Concord and Victory at sunset "when it appears in singular beauty" is given at pp. 243-244.

39. Whately, *Observations,* p. 214, speaks of it as "a noble Corinthian arch."

40. Whately's description of the Leasowes is given in *Observations,* pp. 162-171.

41. The numbers *18* and *32* doubtless refer to the map facing page 287 at the beginning of Robert Dodsley's "A Description of the Leasowes," in *The Works, in Verse and Prose, of William Shenstone, Esq; in Two Volumes,* 2nd ed. (London: Printed for J. Dodsley in Pall-Mall, 1765), 2:287-320. Jefferson bought this book (or perhaps a first edition published in 1764) on October 10, 1765, and it may have influenced substantially his landscaping at Monticello. Marie Kimball, *Jefferson: The Road to Glory* (New York: Coward-McCann, Inc., 1943), pp. 116, 148, 160, 321. No. 28 on the map shows the location, at the end of Lover's Walk, of an ornamented urn inscribed to Maria Dolman, who was a relative of the poet and died young. The inscription ends: *"Heu quanto minus est cum reliquis versari, quam tui meminisse."* See *Works of Shenstone,* 2:307. These lines, doubtless with reference to his wife's death in 1782, were among the sentimental family relics contained in a small box which Jefferson handed to his daughter Martha two days before his death. Henry S. Randall, *The Life of Thomas Jefferson* (Philadelphia: J. B. Lippincott & Co., 1865), 3:545.

42. For Whately's account of Hagley see his *Observations,* pp. 194-206. Pope's pavilion (pp. 198, 201) and Thomson's seat (pp. 197, 201-202) made the excursion "poetical" for Adams.

43. Whately's description of Blenheim is given in his *Observations,* pp. 78-81.

44. On the site of "fair Rosamond's Bower" see Whately, *Observations,* p. 79.

45. Penn's Hill was a landmark familiar to Adams, near his home in Braintree. Page Smith, *John Adams* (Garden City: Doubleday & Co., Inc., 1962), 2:733, 735.

46. Whately, *Observations,* pp. 4-6, mentions the lawn at Moor Park.

47. This extract is followed by two diagrams with accompanying explanation of the machinery.

48. Adams, *Diary,* 3:189-190.

Jefferson:
The Making of an Architect

FREDERICK D. NICHOLS

Scale 1 square = 1'   Virginia Capitol: End elevation - Study

Thomas Jefferson. *Virginia Capitol, Richmond: front elevation.*
Massachusetts Historical Society, Boston

Foreword

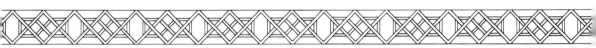

JEFFERSON'S PLACE IN THE HISTORY OF AMERICAN ARCHITECTURE AND his original accomplishments as an architect were not fully recognized until the twentieth century. The early historian of American art, William Dunlap, attributed the general plan of Monticello to Robert Mills, and even as late as 1913 Glenn Brown believed that the design of the University of Virginia was the work of Mills and William Thornton.

In 1916, Fiske Kimball set the record straight with his landmark monograph, which catalogued and published the remarkable collection of drawings by Jefferson in the Coolidge Collection at the Massachusetts Historical Society. The study did not include Jefferson's drawings for the University of Virginia and fugitive drawings and documents scattered in other American collections.

In 1961, Frederick Doveton Nichols, a former student of Kimball's and Kimball's natural successor in Jeffersonian architectural scholarship, published the definitive checklist of all surviving drawings. The ordering of this first significant group of American architectural drawings, which dated from the first plans for Monticello in 1767 to the last details of the university in the 1820s, was a major contribution to Jefferson studies as well as to American art history.

In the organization of Jefferson drawings for *The Eye of Thomas Jefferson,* Professor Nichols has been a valued colleague and friend. During a year when Jefferson's cultural role is being rediscovered and celebrated not only in the exhibition at the National Gallery but at the University of Virginia, where his rotunda has finally been restored to its original design, Professor Nichols has been a pivotal figure. His expert knowledge and enthusiasm have been important elements in both of these events. We are grateful that he was also able to turn his energy to producing this thoughtful essay as yet another contribution to the Bicentennial year, reminding us again of the genius of his neighbor on the mountain at Monticello.

WILLIAM HOWARD ADAMS

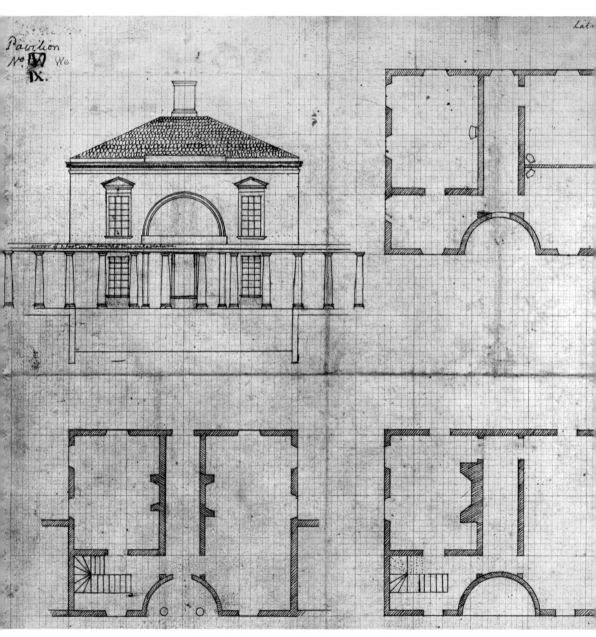

Thomas Jefferson. *Pavilion IX, University of Virginia.*
Alderman Library, University of Virginia

Jefferson: The Making of an Architect

FREDERICK D. NICHOLS

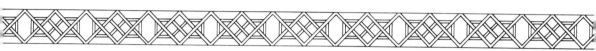

IN SPITE OF HIS GREAT ACHIEVEMENTS AS A STATESMAN AND HIS MANY other interests, Thomas Jefferson still found time to become our first great native-born architect. He was the first to make complete working drawings as well as architectural designs, and some five hundred of his architectural drawings and surveys still survive.

When Jefferson went to Europe as minister to France in 1784, he was a confirmed Palladian, as the first version of Monticello indicates. He returned, however, with his Palladian vision tempered by the influence of the Louis XVI style. Paris, with its beautiful *hôtels,* designed by the leading architects and visionary theorists of the time, had won his heart. Though scholars used to look upon the neoclassical revival in France in the late eighteenth century as a dead end, we now know that its theories were, in some cases, the basis of modern architecture. We see our own concerns reflected in the eighteenth-century interest in new towns, in workers' housing, in buildings to house large groups of people, in the emphasis on comfort, and above all in the attempts to create a new and better world.

Like many great architects, Jefferson developed late; his masterpieces— Poplar Forest, the pavilions and the rotunda at the University of Virginia — were all built after he was sixty. Poplar Forest was begun when he was sixty-three, and the university when he was seventy-four, while the rotunda was begun when Jefferson was eighty years old. Monticello was forty years in achieving its present form, and while it has enormous interest, and reflects the taste and character of its owner, as well as his growth as an architect, it lacks the unity of design found in Poplar Forest and the university.

Since there were no architecture schools in America in Jefferson's youth, he learned through building and through observation, but especially from his beloved books by English architects and Palladian theorists, most of which he had purchased before he went to Europe. Jefferson's five years in Paris came during a period of great architectural creativity there, and he had the opportunity to know some of the leading architects who were influencing all of Europe on the eve of the French Revolution.

Jefferson assembled one of the finest libraries in the country during his lifetime, and in it were most of the architectural classics. Among his books on Palladio, whom at least in his early years he considered the ultimate authority, were Leoni's translation with Inigo Jones' notes, published in London in 1742, and his earlier edition of 1715. There was a French edition, translated by Roland Fréart, Sieur de Chambray, published in Paris in 1650; and one of Jefferson's favorites, because it was portable, was another French edition published by Charles-Antoine Jombert in 1764.

Unfortunately, Jefferson does not tell us which book it was that first led him to the serious study of architecture. He does say that he purchased it from an old cabinetmaker in Williamsburg, who was fond of drink and lived by the college gate. It may well have been James Gibbs' *Rules for Drawing the Several Parts of Architecture,* London, 1732, because Jefferson used details from it in his first designs for Monticello.

Kimball states that Jefferson bought Gibbs' *Rules* in about 1769, his *Book of Architecture* about 1771 and the 1715 edition of Palladio before 1783. These were his first architectural books, but since Jefferson implies that he was still in Williamsburg when it was acquired, the *Rules* seems to have been purchased earlier than Kimball thought.

James Gibbs' influence on the architecture of colonial America was considerable due to the popularity of his two important books, *The Book of Architecture,* 1728, and *Useful and Practical Rules for Drawing the Separate Parts of Architecture,* 1732. The former was a treasury of designs for both large and small buildings and contained most of Gibbs' executed works, including such ephemera as garden casinos and gazebos. It was simple and straightforward, and displayed the influence on Gibbs' work of Palladio and of Italian mannerism.

Mount Airy in Richmond County, Virginia, completed in 1758, was adapted from a design by Gibbs, which was in turn borrowed from Palladio's Villa Saraceno at Finale. All over the colonies, too, churches were designed after the Gibbs masterpiece, St. Martin's-in-the-Fields, London. (One of the handsomest of these is St. Michael's in Charleston, South Carolina.) The mass of St. Martin's has a monumental Corinthian portico attached to the front of a pilastered building, but the cynosure is the brilliantly designed spire, which pierces the roof over the entrance. This spire was the prototype

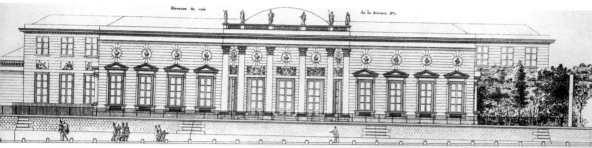

River Front of the Hôtel de Salm, Paris. Engraving by Krafft and Ransonnette

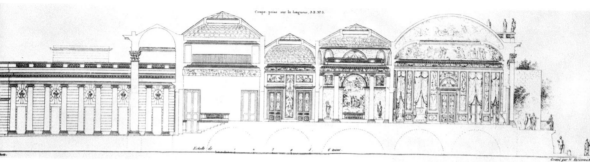

Hôtel de Salm, Paris: Section. Engraving by Krafft and Ransonnette

for that of many churches in America in the colonial period; its location was improved by placing it at the break in the mass between the portico and the nave.

Gibbs' two books had been popular for a generation before Jefferson's time, and their influence was felt to the end of the century. Besides Mount Airy and St. Michael's in Charleston, South Carolina, the entry of Samuel McIntire in the competition for the design of the capitol in Washington in 1792 was taken from Gibbs' *Book of Architecture,* plate 41, and James Hoban used plates 52 and 53 for the elevations of his plan for the president's house, which may also have been influenced by Richard Cassels' Leinster House in Dublin.

One of Jefferson's early studies for Monticello is taken directly from a plate in Gibbs which is similar to plate 41 in Palladio's second volume. It shows a portico *in antis,* a form that Jefferson was not to return to until his 1824 design for Christ Church in Charlottesville, which influenced many later churches in Virginia.

Jefferson's fondness for the octagon shape may have been inspired by Gibbs' plates 67 and 69, from which he made sketches for garden temples for the terraces at Monticello. He also considered using Chinese pavilions for the corners of the terraces, where the service wings were attached to perpendicular extensions inspired by those in Freidrich Meinert's *Schöne Land-*

baukunst. Jefferson's measured drawings in 1783 of the Hammond-Harwood house in Annapolis are a further indication of his interest in the use of semi-octagons.

After he had consulted Gibbs for the proportions of details in his first designs for Monticello, Jefferson refigured them after Palladio's proportions. This may have been the time that he purchased his first edition of Palladio. Gibbs was a Palladian only in the broadest sense, and Jefferson used his own ideas as a springboard to a more accurate, and more personal, reading of Palladio's designs.

Although Robert Morris listed himself as a surveyor, no buildings by him have been identified. However, he is remembered for his books, and through them his ideas had a considerable influence on Jefferson. The small scale of Morris' published designs appealed to Jefferson, as did the quotation from Alexander Pope on the title page of his *Essay in Defence of Ancient Architecture,* published in 1728: "Learn hence for Ancient Rules a just Esteem." Morris believed in the value of simplicity as a way of bringing architecture into contact with nature and with the ancient world. By the 1730s he was designing buildings in spheres and perfect cubes, long before the visionary architects of France became concerned with simple geometric form as an expression of ideal beauty.

Morris was a theoretician in an age when few writers were concerned with theories of architecture and concentrated, instead, on pragmatic building matters. He is the only architect of that time to have written a book, *Lectures,* in which theories only were discussed. Morris' theories and the designs with which he illustrated them were in advance of their time, and they appealed to Jefferson because of their simplicity and small scale; the grander and more elaborate English houses, which were illustrated in most of the pattern books of the eighteenth century, were far beyond the means of even the most prosperous Virginia planter.

Morris used the octagon shape even more lavishly than did Gibbs, from whose *Book of Architecture* Morris adapted several designs, particularly plate 43. Jefferson took his octagon designs for garden pavilions from both Morris and Gibbs. Plate 30 in *Select Architecture,* which Jefferson owned, shows a house with three octagonal rooms clustered about a fourth room which served as an entrance hall, a scheme not unlike the one he adopted much later for the rotunda at the University of Virginia.

While Jefferson was in Paris from 1784 to 1789, revolutionary ideas were fashionable not only in politics but in the arts, particularly among architects. When Jefferson set foot on French soil, he began a love affair with French culture that lasted the rest of his life. On September 30, 1785, he wrote about the French to his friend Charles Bellini, "Were I to proceed to tell you how much I enjoy their architecture, sculpture, painting, music, I should want words." [1] When he returned to the United States in 1789, he brought with him more than eighty cases of French furnishings. He even brought back a French chef, who stayed with him during his years in political office and who later, at Monticello, taught the cooks there some of the subtleties of French cuisine. But above all, Jefferson loved French architecture, and by the time he returned home, his library included some superb works on the subject: Philibert Delorme's *Nouvelles Inventions pour Bien Bastir,* by one of the great masters of Renaissance art, first published in Paris in 1576; Antoine Desgodets' *Edifices antiques de Rome,* 1779; and de Chambray's *Parallele de l'Architecture Antique et Moderne,* 1766. Jefferson used the Delorme volume to construct the domes at Monticello and the University of Virginia, the Desgodets for interior cornices, and the de Chambray for the orders at the University of Virginia.

Jefferson found in the polite world of the Parisians a style that agreed with his own, and in their *hôtels* and pavilions compatible ideas of design—for example in the Bagatelle, Louveciennes, and the Désert de Retz. Later, he wrote in praise of their public buildings, that he preferred for the new public buildings in Washington "the celebrated fronts of modern buildings, which have already received the approbation of all good judges. Such are the Galerie du Louvre, the Garde meubles, and the two fronts of the Hôtel de Salm." [2] The latter, especially, was to have a great influence on Jefferson's work. He carefully followed all the new developments in architecture in Paris, and he wrote to David Humphreys on August 14, 1787,

> I will observe to you that wonderful improvements are making here in various lines. In architecture the wall of circumvallation round Paris and the palaces by which we are to be let in and out are nearly compleated, 4 hospitals are to be built instead of the old hôtel-dieu, one of the old bridges has all its houses demolished and a second nearly so, a new bridge is begun at the Place Louis XV, the Palais Royal is gutted, a considerable part in the center of the garden being dug out, and a subterranean circus begun wherein will be equestrian exhibitions &c.

While he was in Europe, Jefferson took every opportunity to study the architecture of the various countries he visited. He was best acquainted, of course, with French architecture, and he preferred it above all, except for the buildings of Palladio, which he only knew through books. While making an agricultural tour through southern France and northern Italy in 1787, he briefly visited Turin, Milan and Genoa and planned to see Vicenza, the home of Palladio, on a subsequent visit, which unfortunately he never made.

Hubert Robert. *Maison Carrée and Tower at Nîmes.* Louvre

During his tour, he did visit Nîmes, and he wrote enthusiastically to Mme de Tessé,

> Here I am, Madam, gazing whole hours at the Maison Quarrée, like a lover at his mistress. The stocking weavers and silk spinners around it consider me an hypochondriac Englishman, about to write with a pistol the last chapter of his history. This is the second time I have been in love since I left Paris. The first was with a Diana at the Château de Laye Epinaye in the Beaujolais, a delicious morsel of sculpture, by Michael Angelo Slodtz. This, you will say was in rule, to fall in love with a fine woman: but, with a house! It is out of all precedent! No, madam, it is not without a precedent in my own history. While at Paris, I was violently smitten with the Hôtel de Salm, and used to go to the Tuileries almost daily to look at it. The loueuse des chaises, inattentive to my passion, never had the complaisance to place a chair there, so that, sitting on the parapet, and twisting my neck round to see the object of my admiration, I generally left with a torticollis. From Lyons to Nismes I have been nourished with the remains of Roman Grandeur.[3]

Jefferson's love of French architecture was no doubt partly inspired by his high regard for France, and while he admired the new landscape ideas of the

Claude-Nicolas Ledoux, Pavilion of Mme Guimard, Paris.
Engraving from *Maisons et Hôtels de Paris* by Krafft and Ransonnette, 1801-1802

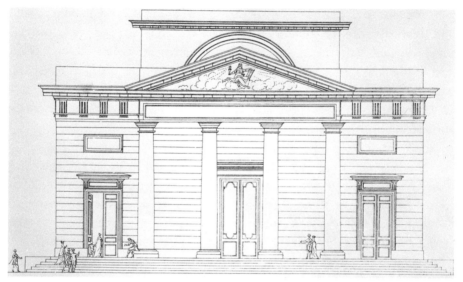

Jean-François-Thérèse Chalgrin, Saint-Philippe du Roule, Paris.
Engraving from *Maisons et Hôtels de Paris* by Krafft and Ransonnette, 1801-1802

English, he thought English architecture second-rate.[4] When he visited Germany, he was particularly impressed by buildings designed by French architects, especially the beautiful country estate of Schwetzingen, designed by Nicolas de Pigage.

Long before going to France, Jefferson had considered the design of the new capitol in Richmond. In the bill which he had presented to the House of Delegates as early as 1776, he included a revolutionary idea that provided separate buildings to house the various branches of government. In 1780, he was appointed head of a committee to erect Virginia's public buildings, and he had begun studies for a temple-form structure before he left America, as shown by the two large plans now in the possession of the Huntington Library. Europe was not to have a neoclassical temple-form public building until the building of the Madeleine, which was begun in Paris in 1807.

In his *Autobiography,* Jefferson wrote that he wished to improve the status of the arts in Virginia by

> introducing into the state an example of architecture in the classic style of antiquity, and the Maison quarrée of Nismes, an antient Roman temple, being considered as the most perfect model existing of what may be called Cubic architecture, I applied to M. Clérissault . . . to have me a model of the building made in stucco, only changing the order from the Corinthian to Ionic, on account of the difficulty of the Corinthian capitals. . . . to adapt the exterior to our use, I drew a plan for the interior, with the apartments necessary for legislative, executive, & judiciary purposes. . . . These were forwarded to the Directors in 1786. and were carried into execution.[5]

Clérisseau was a prominent antiquarian and architect, but we know that except for some changes in the doors and windows and the panels over them, the idea for the capitol was entirely Jefferson's. As Jefferson said, the model was Clérisseau's chief contribution.

At this time Jefferson was also interested in the design of a prison for solitary confinement, which was to be built in Richmond according to a most advanced design. He wrote later in his Autobiography,

> With respect to the plan of a Prison . . . I had heard of a benevolent society in England which had been indulged by the government in an experiment of the effect of labor in *solitary confinement* on some of their criminals, which experiment had succeeded beyond expectation. The same idea had been suggested in France, and an Architect of Lyons had proposed a plan of a well contrived edifice on the principle of solitary confinement. I procured a copy, and as it was too large for our purposes, I drew one on a scale less extensive. . . . It's principle . . . but not it's exact form, was adopted by Latrobe in carrying the plan into execution.[6]

This is the prison in Richmond, built in the form of a semicircle, and it exists, much altered, to this day.

It should be remembered that at the time of Louis XVI, French domestic architecture had reached its zenith. Louis XV had left the court nearly bankrupt, and so artists, architects, *ébénistes,* and sculptors who had formerly worked on buildings for the king, were available for private projects. Great palaces were out of fashion. It was chic to build small pavilions and town houses with mezzanines, where elegance, privacy, and intimacy were the rule.

It is said that an English visitor to Monticello once wrote that except for the fact that Jefferson and his daughters were speaking English, he would have thought he was in a house in France. This is not surprising, because its owner's predilection for light and air dictated his use of the octagon shape and of long French windows. As the American workmen either could not or would not build casements, Jefferson had to use the triple-hung window, which he may have invented.

Whether he was the owner of a house or not, Jefferson could never live in one for long without planning changes, and when he settled in Paris in the delightful Hôtel de Langeac at the Grille de Chaillot on the Champs Elysées, he began making sketches for improvements to both the house and the garden. Some changes proposed by Jefferson seem to have involved a rearrangement of rooms on the mezzanine level, which was in itself undoubtedly a novelty to the American, being the intermediate floor between the ground-floor reception area and the elegant first-floor apartments above.

Jefferson was familiar with the great plantation houses of Tidewater, Virginia, but in those houses the rooms were, in many cases, all-purpose — for example, a separate room for dining did not come into fashion until after the Revolutionary War. Thus, he found in the house on the Champs Elysées a luxurious privacy unknown in America. A high wall surrounded the property, assuring complete privacy. There was one main entrance and a large courtyard, with a smaller one for service, beyond which were stables, servants' quarters, and coach houses. Inside were many features which Jefferson later used in his own domestic designs. The entrance hall had an octagonal end, and a circular hall led both to the dining room and to two salons. The larger salon projected into the garden, and so the end of the room, which was oval, was light and airy with three long windows to the floor. On an upper floor was an oval vestibule opening into an oval sitting room, which projected also into the garden, so that one side was lighted with a great bay. Three bedroom suites each consisted of a sitting room, a bedroom and a dressing room. The services included two sets of servants' stairs, as well as water closets, or *lieux à l'anglaise.*

On the exterior there was a handsome modillion cornice, which, along with the bas reliefs on the main floor, added a classical touch. But even more important for their influence on Jefferson's later designs were those floor-to-ceiling windows, protected by iron or stone railings when they did not open upon a terrace. At Monticello, Jefferson built these railings of wood and added elements from Chinese trellises in Halfpenny's book. The lower height of French *hôtels* influenced Jefferson's later remodeling of Monticello, and he wrote, "All the new and good houses (in Paris) are of a single story. That is of the height of 16 or 18 f. generally, and the whole of it given to rooms of entertainment; but in parts where there are bedrooms they have two tiers of from 8 to 10 f. high each, with a small private staircase. By these means great staircases are avoided, which are expensive and occupy a space which would make a good room in every story."

Jean-François-Thérèse Chalgrin. *Elevation of the Hôtel de Langeac, Paris.*
Bibliothèque nationale

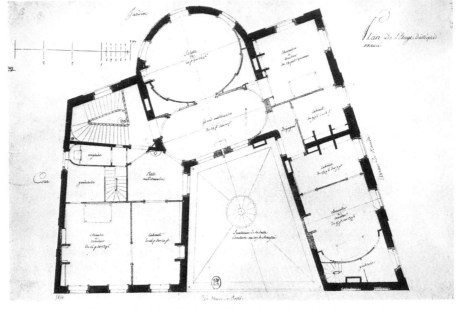

Jean-François-Thérèse Chalgrin. *Plan of the Hôtel de Langeac, Paris.*
Bibliothèque nationale

Besides the Hôtel de Langeac, other private residences in and around Paris influenced Jefferson's architectural ideas. He visited the Bagatelle in the Bois de Boulogne, which was designed by Bélanger for the comte d'Artois, who, when only seventeen, had bet his new sister-in-law, Marie-Antoinette, that he could have the house built in only sixty-four days. An army of workmen started on September 23, 1777, working around the clock, and finished the house on November 25 at a cost of three million *livres.* On the main floor there was an entrance vestibule in the center, with an oval dining room on one side and an octagonal billiard room on the other. In the rear was a circular salon with a boudoir on one side and a bathroom on the other. Upstairs on the mezzanine floor were five small bedrooms, all with alcove beds and dressing rooms, two studies, and *lieux à l'anglaise.* The long French windows of the salon opened directly on the rear terrace and garden.

The gardens at Bagatelle, which were the most famous in the new naturalistic style, were laid out between 1778 and 1780 by Bélanger and were executed by Thomas Blaikie, the Scottish gardener. There was a Swiss chalet, a philosopher's grotto in the Gothic style, a pharoah's tomb, and a paladin's tower. Many of these picturesque elements were planned, but never fully executed, for the gardens at Monticello.

Another house that Jefferson admired was the pavilion at Louveciennes, designed for Mme du Barry by Claude-Nicolas Ledoux. It was described by Pidansat de Mairobert in 1777 as

> situated on a considerable eminence, whence is enjoyed one of the most gorgeous and extensive views possible. . . . The interior consists of a hall for dining with a service room on the left, a cloak-room on the right, and a parlour with two drawing rooms on either side. There are no bedrooms. . . . The most celebrated artists have endeavoured to enrich this delightful residence with their labours. The ceiling of one of the side rooms was executed by Bisard. Its motto is *Ruris Amor.* It depicts pleasures of the country. On the other side is painted a hazy sun and four large pictures by Fragonard, which describe the amours of shepherds and seem to be an allegory of the adventures of the mistress of the house. . . . Art, however, appears to have less exerted itself here in grand masterpieces than in miniature ornaments, such as chimney-pieces, fireplaces, sconces, girandoles, chandeliers, cornices, gilding and goldsmith's works, locks, bolts, etc., every part of which is so exquisitely finished that they might all be exhibited as models of perfect workmanship. . . .

Much of the decoration was by the craftsman Gouthière.

Jefferson owned the book, *Plans des Maisons de Paris* by Krafft and Ransonette, 1801-1802?, in which the pavilion of Mme du Barry was published.

Hôtel de Brunoy, Paris. Engraving from Gallet, *Stately Mansions*

The house also had a mezzanine, from which little balconies opened on the two-story dining room. The house was arranged in a manner Jefferson sometimes used or recommended for a sloping site: while the main floor was at the entrance level, the garden side was of two stories, to take advantage of the slope of the land. But the detail that he was to remember was the semicircular portico, or exedra, in which a screen of columns was placed in front of a niche. This device he used later with great success at Pavilion IX at the University of Virginia.

Other buildings by Ledoux which Jefferson knew and commented upon were the *barrières* of Paris. These were the tollgates erected at the gates of Paris for collecting taxes from all who entered them. One was erected outside of Jefferson's window on the Champs Elysées, the Barrière du Roule. These are some of the most imaginative works of Ledoux, and the few that remain today are among the masterpieces of romantic classicism.

A study of the visionary architects of the late eighteenth century indicates how the great aesthetic ideas and the surge of imagination of the time transformed a *retardataire* antiquarian style into an advanced movement. In France, the anti-rococo sentiment began in the 1760s. The avant-garde artists were concerned with a return to the classical equilibrium of the arts which had flourished under Louis XIV. The following decade marked the height of the antiquarian impulse, and by 1784, when Jefferson arrived in Paris, French architects had gone beyond the slavish copying of antiquity to rediscover what they considered the "natural" sources of architecture and of beauty which had given rise to the designs of antiquity. At that time, Paris was the center for architectural study, and in Paris, architectural theory was dominated by Ledoux and Boullée, whose executed buildings Jefferson was certainly familiar with, and whose visionary designs he may have seen.

Boullée had designed Chaville, home of the comtesse de Tessé, which Jefferson visited and where he may even have met the architect. Boullée was the first to adopt Palladio's idea of making a house harmonize with its setting, an aim with which we may be sure Jefferson agreed. Boullée also experimented with skylights; he installed them at Chaville in 1764. Jefferson was perhaps inspired by the French architect when he installed the great skylights over his bedroom and dining room at Monticello, and added smaller ones over the two new staircases and in the attic hall.

Like Boullée, Jefferson believed in the perfectability of man through education, and both of them, along with Ledoux, believed in the importance of planning cities. Jefferson studied carefully the modification of Paris that was going on at the time. He collected over two dozen plans of leading cities, while he was in Europe, and loaned them to L'Enfant, to whom he gave advice, when the latter was planning the city of Washington.

Ledoux, Boullée and Jefferson were all excellent writers, but where the vastness of the Frenchmen's schemes made many of them impractical, Jefferson's designs were always a hard-headed combination of the pragmatic and the aesthetic. Like Palladio, Jefferson was a born builder, while Boullée produced, for the most part, beautiful, visionary drawings, which, with his teaching, provided the basis of his influence. Boullée had designed a church and at least five *hôtels* in the Louis XVI style with some innovations; his only building outside Paris, the Château de Chaville for Jefferson's friends the de Tessés, has disappeared.

Ledoux, Boullée and other romantic classicists found inspiration in the plain surfaces and simplicity of the houses of the poor. Clarity and precision dominate Boullée's style: ornament is used only in a symbolic manner. Boullée believed that the bare wall represented nobility and the sadness of death. The interests of the visionary architects had begun with the building of private houses, palaces and churches, and evolved to town planning and buildings of a grand and collective nature. In their view, the natural man, the noble savage, and individual freedom went hand-in-hand with the nobil-

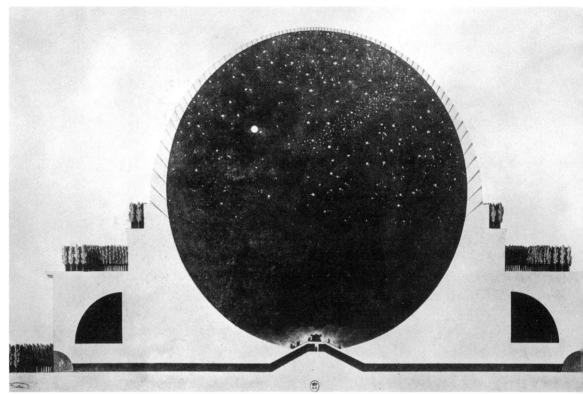

Etienne Boullée,*Cenotaph to Newton, Section, at Night.* Bibliothèque nationale

ity of Roman architecture — even though it was the buildings of imperial Rome rather than those of republican Rome which were admired and studied.

Boullée, like Jefferson, had in his library the works of Rousseau and the latest scientific treatises, which helped to form his theories of revolutionary architecture. He admired Isaac Newton extravagantly, as he admired science, so it is no wonder that his great project for a cenotaph to Newton should have been one of his most dramatic designs. He believed the only proper way to memorialize a great scientist was with a pure geometric form. The drawings of Newton's monument are impressive. The drawings show a sphere set below grade, with an altar, brightly lit. The sphere was entered by low tunnels, and the striking first impression was of a great globe, whose dome was studded with stars by night and lit in a blaze of light by day. On the exterior, the dome was set in a portion of a cylinder and surrounded by rows of trees, like the Tomb of Hadrian in Rome. The gigantic scale is as ambitious as the imagination of the architect of this design, which is dated 1784, the year Jefferson arrived in Paris.

Whether or not he knew their later, or visionary, work, Jefferson would have pleased Ledoux and Boullée with the two masterpieces of his old age, Poplar Forest and the University of Virginia. In these buildings Jefferson achieved a perfection of pure geometric form that rivaled that of Ledoux's designs at Chaux. At Poplar Forest, his retreat near Lynchburg, Jefferson designed a house based on the octagon; the outside walls, the rooms, the terraces, and even the privies took that shape — all, that is, except the dining room in the center of the house, which was pyramidal in form, square in plan, and lit by a skylight.

Various Palladian and French influences are to be found in all the houses designed by Jefferson. Except for Poplar Forest, most of his plans have T-shaped circulation with a longitudinal corridor, entered by means of a wide entrance hall. This last, with the drawing room on axis, provided the ubiquitous summer living room. But the domes he admired so much in Paris never became popular. His friends thought them an unnecessary luxury, and the one on Monticello was the only dome he ever managed to erect on a house. Most of his house plans are the eminently practical one-story Palladian type set on a high basement, which, if the site allowed, was one story in front and two stories on the garden side. Except for his alterations to town houses which he rented in Philadelphia and Paris, and his designs for the president's house, all of his house plans were for plantations. Along with his Palladian plans, he also used mezzanines, which were characteristic of Palladio and were popular in Paris.

The most obvious Palladian features of his houses were the four porticos on each side, derived from the Villa Rotonda. As his sites invariably had good views in all directions, these porches were useful as well as decorative. At Monticello he used two Doric porticos on the main axis of the house, with arcades instead of porticos at either end. Bremo is not, strictly speaking, by Jefferson, although it was built by workmen trained by him. General J. H. Cocke, who helped with the design, and was responsible for the plans for the Palmyra courthouse, put John Neilson's name in the cornerstone as architect. At any rate, without Jefferson's help (Jefferson had recommended to General Cocke that he follow Palladio's books and rules for proportions as the surest way to get a handsome house at Bremo) Bremo would not be as Jeffersonian as it is, with a T-shaped plan, which Jefferson had developed, and four porticos: a large Doric one in front, two diminutive ones on the ends, and a portico *in antis* on the river side. At Barboursville there are only two porches, but they were approached by ramps rather than the usual steps, a feature adapted from Palladio's Villa Emo at Fanzolo.

Jefferson attached great importance to the quality of domestic architecture, writing to his young friends John Rutledge, Jr., and Thomas Shippen, "As

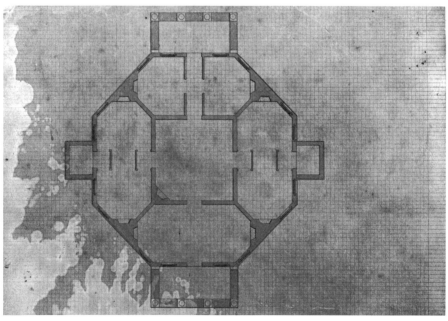

Thomas Jefferson. *Poplar Forest, garden elevation and first floor plan*.
University of Virginia, Alderman Library

we double our numbers every twenty years, we must double our houses. Besides, we build of such perishable materials, that one half of our houses must be rebuilt in every space of twenty years, so that in that time, houses are to be built for three-fourths of our inhabitants. It is, then, among the most important arts; and it is desirable to introduce taste into an art that shows so much." [7]

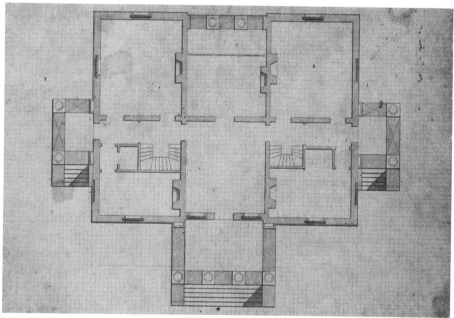

Thomas Jefferson. *Bremo, elevation and plan.* University of Virginia, Alderman Library

The design of the University of Virginia admirably reflects Jefferson's theories of architecture, as well as of education. He set it up as a free university, in which there were no required courses, no degrees, and no compulsory chapel. A student could stay for six months or six years, and when he decided that he had an education, he was free to leave. The complex was designed for two hundred students and ten faculty members, and a committee of the latter was established to administer the university. There was a pavilion for each faculty member, with his school room on the first floor along with a study-dining room; in the basement was storage space and the kitchen; on the second floor was a drawing room with two bedrooms and a dressing room. When a faculty member married and needed extra space, Jefferson specified that the extra rooms added at the rear of the house must follow the original lines. For the students, there were one hundred dormitory rooms, each for double occupancy. Six "hotels," or dining halls, were provided, and in each a different language was to be spoken at the table.

The design of the complex is similar to that of the Château de Marly, built for Louis XIV near Versailles, which Jefferson had visited. Marly had a main building for the king and twelve pavilions in two lines of six for the courtiers. In Jefferson's design, the rotunda is the focal point, with five pavilions on each side of the lawn, separated by students' rooms. Jefferson increased the apparent length of the lawn by two baroque devices: the railings above the colonnades decrease in height as they near the rotunda, and the space between each pavilion decreases as one approaches the rotunda.

The University of Virginia is the culmination, in Jefferson's old age, of a lifetime of aesthetic and intellectual concern. Not only was he the sole arbiter in building design, but he personally decided on the curriculum, chose the faculty, and coaxed a reluctant state legislature into providing funds. He wanted the students, when they returned home to the Deep South or the far West, to have known the greatest examples of the Roman orders of architecture, so that they could properly embellish the new buildings on the frontier. His designs for the pavilions are all temple forms, some of which had parapets in wood, drawn from various ancient structures. Their orders were taken from de Chambray's *Parallel of the Ancient and Modern Orders* and Leoni's edition of Palladio's *Quattro Libri.* The inscription "Latrobe" was on drawings for Pavilions VIII and IX, and it may be that the cornice and upper windows of the latter were suggested by him. Pavilion IX was taken directly from Ledoux's pavilion at Louveciennes, which Jefferson had visited. Pavilion VIII is the only one with columns *in antis,* and the general design may be the suggestion of Latrobe.

Jefferson called the rotunda the capstone of the University of Virginia. In North America, it is the supreme example of the visionary style. It is a descendant of the unrealized spherical designs of Ledoux and Boullée, particularly the latter's cenotaph to Newton. Both it and the rotunda at the University of Virginia were designed to have ceilings illuminated with stars, to extend the symbolism of the dome as the canopy of heaven. Like Boullée and Ledoux, Jefferson regarded a scientific interpretation of the antique as

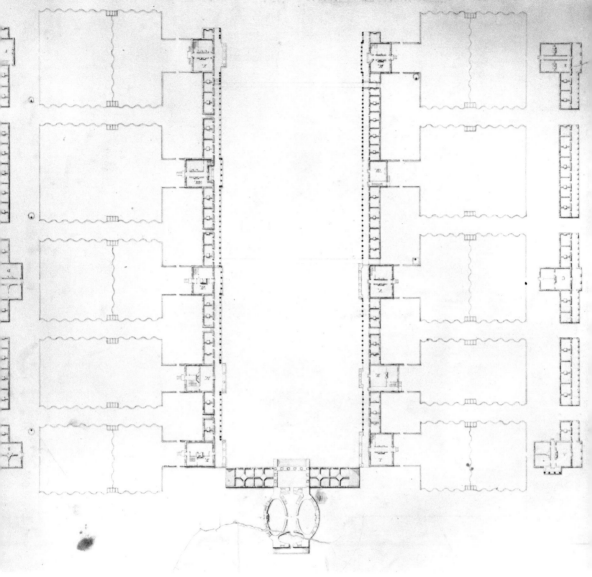

John Neilson (?). *Study for Peter Maverick's engraving published in 1822
showing first floor of the Rotunda with oval rooms and sixteen rooms in wings.*
Virginia State Library, Richmond

the only sure road to a universal architecture, and thus for the rotunda design
he adapted the Pantheon at one-half scale, reintroducing the podium on
which it rested before the foundation was obscured by the debris of millenia.
As befitting the rotunda's smaller size, Jefferson used only six columns and
eliminated the extra pediment; the building, with its native red brick and
white moldings, took on a distinctly American character.

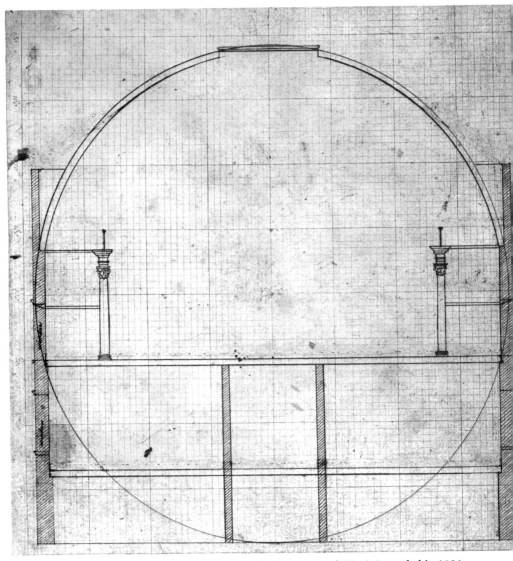

Thomas Jefferson. *Rotunda: Section of the rotunda, University of Virginia,* probably 1821.
University of Virginia, Alderman Library

On the inside, Jefferson designed the dome room, which was to be a library, at exactly the proportions of the Pantheon, but he used a continuous peristyle instead of a series of exedras. Below, he designed two floors of oval rooms, served by a dumbbell-shaped entrance hall. Similar ovals, inscribed in a cylinder, are to be found at the Désert de Retz, near Marly, which Jefferson had visited and admired in France.

The rotunda, then, represents all that was important to Jefferson; in three dimensions it is a reflection of his dearest hopes and ideals. Its light and airy

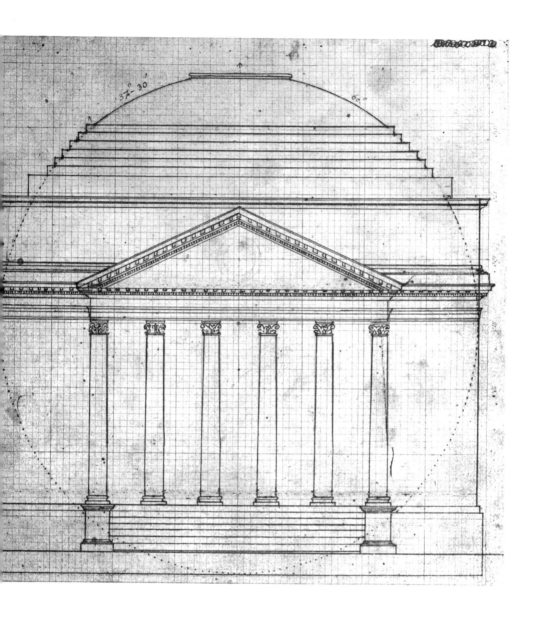

rooms, white woodwork against white plaster, are among the most beautiful spaces ever created in America. The ingenious and subtle adaptation to the sloping site, the purity of the geometric forms, and the unity of design, all combine to make this a masterpiece, an ordered and beautiful spatial experience, tied to a noble setting. As the Pantheon in Rome had been dedicated to the pagan gods, so Jefferson dedicated his rotunda to his beloved books, which, through education, guaranteed, in his view, human freedom and happiness.

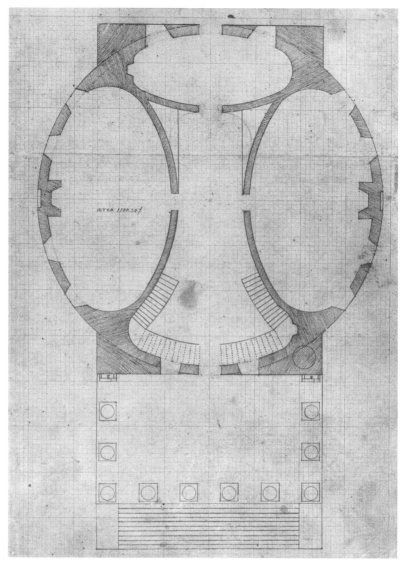

Thomas Jefferson. *Plan of the first floor of the rotunda, University of Virginia,*
probably 1821. University of Virginia, Alderman Library

Jefferson wished to be remembered for only three accomplishments, because they were the things he had done for the people. On his tombstone he
instructed that the following words be inscribed:

Author of the Declaration of American Independence,

Of the Statute of Virginia for Religious Freedom,

And Father of the University of Virginia.

But he will also be long remembered for the grandest and most beautiful
complex of buildings in North America, whose influence spread over the
land, giving our country much of the classical heritage that Jefferson so
ardently desired.

Notes

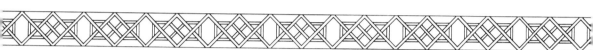

1. John P. Foley, *The Jeffersonian Cyclopedia* (New York: Russell and Russell, 1967), p. 46.

2. Bernard Mayo, ed., *Jefferson Himself* (Charlottesville: University Press of Virginia, 1942), pp. 176-177.

3. Sarah N. Randolph, *The Domestic Life of Thomas Jefferson* (Charlottesville: The Thomas Jefferson Memorial Foundation, 1947), pp. 80-81.

4. Randolph, *Domestic Life,* pp. 56-57.

5. Paul Leicester Ford, ed., *The Writings of Thomas Jefferson, 1* (New York: G. P. Putnam's Sons, 1892-99): 63-64.

6. Ford, *Writings of Jefferson,* 1:64-65.

7. Andrew A. Lipscomb and Albert E. Bergh, eds., *The Writings of Thomas Jefferson, 17* (Washington, D.C.: Thomas Jefferson Memorial Association, 1903): 292.

Thomas Jefferson and the Planning of the National Capital

PAUL F. NORTON

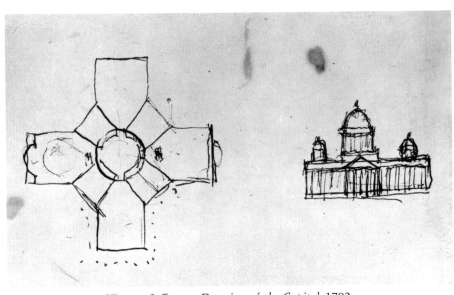

Thomas Jefferson. *Drawing of the Capitol,* 1792.
Massachusetts Historical Society, Boston

Foreword

WITH ALL OF OUR PERSPECTIVE OF HISTORY AS WELL AS OUR EXPERIENCE in organizing vast enterprises and constructing complex institutions, the wisdom and skill of the Founding Fathers as planners of visionary proportions still astonishes us. Not only were they able to hammer out a new system of government but they could and did translate those constitutions into buildings and cities from which to govern an imperfect union. As Professor Norton has pointed out, the establishment of a capital city was essential to the ultimate success of the experiment and no one saw this more clearly than Washington and Jefferson.

With all of their preoccupation with the struggle to keep the new government on its feet and moving in the face of overwhelming problems, it is remarkable how much time and informed thought they were able to give to the plans of the new federal city on the Potomac and their concern for its ultimate appearance, especially in the design and construction of the public buildings.

Washington's secretary of state, who had just returned from Paris where he had been exposed to new and advanced ideas in architectural design, was generally recognized as a man of taste with more than a passing acquaintance with architecture as a discipline and skill. He had long been a critic of the architecture of his native state, complaining bitterly in his *Notes on the State of Virginia* about the sad example set by its public buildings. If government itself failed to provide a high standard in design, the public could hardly be expected to develop critical standards for their own houses, churches and schools.

Professor Norton has focused particularly on Jefferson's role in the evolution of the plans for the capitol building and his collaboration with Benjamin

Latrobe. As the story unfolds throughout the documents and Professor Norton's narrative, it takes on the quality of an Athenian epic that, in Jefferson's words, did indeed look "beyond the range of Athenian destinies."

WILLIAM HOWARD ADAMS

Thomas Jefferson. *Study for the Capitol building, Washington.*
Massachusetts Historical Society, Boston

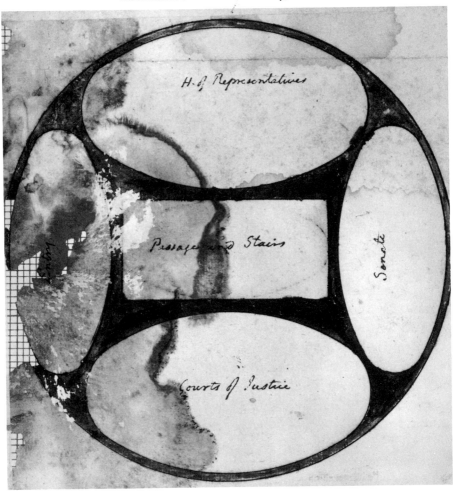

Thomas Jefferson
and the Planning of the National Capital

PAUL F. NORTON

TO PLAN A NEW CITY ON THE POTOMAC AND ERECT ITS PUBLIC BUILD-
ings was a task of such immense proportions that only men of wisdom, tact
and vision could have organized the complicated venture. Although George
Washington and Thomas Jefferson, the primary planners, were already fully
occupied with the business of government, they nevertheless were able to
give much time to the details of planning. As they well knew, without a
capital city there would be no federal union of states.

Washington and Jefferson had the most important roles in planning the
new federal city. Washington's early training as a surveyor coupled with his
knowledge of land use as a Virginia farmer complemented Jefferson's experience in unraveling legal problems and his unrivaled architectural vision.
Jefferson exerted especial influence on the design of public buildings during
his two presidential terms (1801-1809), when building construction in
Washington burgeoned. The result of the initial intense activity of these
leaders, which was not always seen by their contemporaries, was of course
the eventual growth of Washington as it is today.

As early as November 1779, Benjamin Rush, the Philadelphia physician,
noted that "some of the members [of the Continental Congress] talk of
purchasing a few square miles of territory near Princetown and erecting
public offices and buildings of all kinds for their accommodation upon it." [1]
But it was nearly two years after the Revolutionary War before any serious
plan was suggested for housing Congress.

In June 1783, the session of Congress meeting at Philadelphia was
threatened by the approach of mutinous unpaid troops from Lancaster.
Forced to adjourn and reunite at Princeton some days later, members of
Congress earnestly debated the question of a safe and permanent location for

191

the government. A vote on the question was not taken until October 6, after Congress had moved to Annapolis. It showed that New Jersey and Maryland were equally favored.[2] After many futile attempts to agree on a location, a motion calculated to satisfy everyone was put forward to erect two sets of buildings, one on the banks of the Delaware, the other on the Potomac! [3]

Considerable doubt arose among legislators as to the wisdom of erecting two sets of federal buildings, so Congress postponed action until it met in Trenton in the fall of 1784. Of the several resolutions proposed, all were abandoned. Two more years passed before Congress renewed its efforts to establish a federal city; [4] yet the final decision was left for the Congress which assembled in New York on March 4, 1789, under the rules of the newly written Constitution. After much debate, this Congress prepared a bill selecting Germantown, Pennsylvania, as the site and providing 100,000 dollars for buildings. The bill was accepted by the House but was postponed by the Senate until the next session. In the meantime the City Council of New York remodeled its city hall, which had been used by the British as a prison, and renamed it Federal Hall in the hope of persuading Congress to remain permanently in New York.

The New York City Council's choice of the Frenchman Pierre-Charles L'Enfant, an engineer during the Revolutionary War, to improve and redecorate Federal Hall was significant in several ways.[5] L'Enfant's splendid work on that project recommended him as a logical choice for architect and planner of the future federal city. Eager to secure a position, L'Enfant wrote to President Washington offering his services and emphasizing his superior engineering ability.[6] This offer was made ten months before the president signed the Residence Act which established a permanent seat of government on the Potomac and a temporary residence for Congress at Philadelphia until 1800.[7]

In October 1790, President Washington made a preliminary investigation of land near Georgetown along the Potomac. Then in November Jefferson, always thinking several steps in advance, made notes relating to the Residence Act that are interesting because they show how closely he stayed in touch with architectural affairs. He suggested that "the Commissioners should have some taste in architecture, because they may have to decide between different plans." And more specifically he added, "The Commissioners will no doubt submit different ones formed by themselves, or obtained from ingenious architects." Among further random thoughts, Jefferson made the first reference to obtaining plans by competition. "Should it be thought proper," he said, "to excite emulation by a premium for the best, the expence is authorized, as an incident to that of the Buildings." [8]

Commissioners were appointed by the president in January 1791, with duties centered at first on land survey and apportionment and on the selection of designers and builders for the public buildings. Washington joined them in March for further investigation. On March 9, L'Enfant arrived at Georgetown with a letter of instruction from Jefferson. "You are desired to proceed to Georgetown," said Jefferson, "where you will find Mr. Ellicott employed in making a survey and map of the Federal territory. The special object of asking your aid is to have a drawing of the particular grounds most likely to be approved for the site of the Federal town and buildings." [9] Quite clearly Jefferson was becoming directly involved with the formation of the city as a whole, but in particular with the public buildings; and it is the latter that held the greatest interest for him as steps were taken to procure adequate designs. Ellicott and L'Enfant were hindered by the weather in their attempts to prepare plans for the president, however. "I am only at present to regret," said L'Enfant, "that an heavy rain and thick mist which has been incessant ever since my arrival here, does put an insuperable obstacle to my wish of proceeding immediately to the survey. . . . As far as I was able to judge through a thick fog, I passed on many spots which appeared to me really beautiful and which seem to dispute with each other who commands the most extensive prospect on the water." [10] When Washington arrived at the end of March, he rode over the dismal terrain and made agreements with local landowners for the purchase of property.

After proceeding to Mount Vernon, Washington wrote to L'Enfant describing further duties and enclosing two sketches (one by Jefferson) as aids to planning the city. Jefferson's sketch, as Washington pointed out, was "drawn under different circumstances," that is, when it appeared to Jefferson that there was little likelihood of landowners in the easterly area (Carrollsburg) coming to a satisfactory agreement of sale. He therefore confined his planning to a stretch of the Potomac and the northern bank of Tiber Creek. Almost the same relationship existed in L'Enfant's final plan; that is, the capitol to the east is united by public ways to the president's house to the west.

Early in April 1791, L'Enfant reported to Jefferson on his progress and inquired about the number and type of public buildings desired. It is interesting to discover that L'Enfant brought with him no maps of European cities, and he soon found himself hopelessly lost without reference data. "I would be very much obliged to you, in the mean time," he begged of Jefferson, "if you could procure for me whatever map may fall within your reach — of any of the differents grand city now Existing such as — for example — as london — madry — paris — Amsterdam — naples — venice — genoa

— florence. . . ." [11] Jefferson obliged by sending in the return mail the plans of twelve cities gathered during his own European travels.

In the same letter to L'Enfant Jefferson made a strong statement about the public buildings, which were ever his greatest interest. "Whenever it is proposed to prepare plans for the Capitol," he said, "I should prefer the adoption of some one of the models of antiquity which have had the approbation of thousands of years; and for the President's house I should prefer the celebrated fronts of modern buildings which have already received the approbation of all good judges. Such are the Galerie du Louvre, the Garde meubles; and two fronts of the Hôtel de Salm." That Jefferson should suggest to a Frenchman that he make designs for the president's house like those of his native city was more than a proposal which would flatter the architect; it came from Jefferson's personal experience in the city which he believed was the cultural center of Europe. And the Hôtel de Salm eventually influenced the design of the president's house, although L'Enfant was not the architect. As for the capitol, Jefferson did not succeed in having an ancient building imitated, as will be demonstrated.

From Jefferson's plans, Ellicott's survey, and his own ramblings over the unprepossessing terrain, L'Enfant gradually traced the outline of a city and filled in the complicated set of roadways in the form of a grid overlaid with diagonal avenues leading from important bridges and highways to the principal points such as the sites of the capitol building and the president's house. At the end of June it was presented to the president, accompanied by a long explanatory report. Among the remarks on the capitol those mentioning the qualities of the most acceptable location are worth quoting. "After much menutial search for an elligible situation, promoted I may say from a fear of being prejudiced in favour of a first opinion I could discover no one so advantageously to greet the congressional building as this on the west of Jenkins heights which stands as a pedestal waiting for a monument, and I am confident, were all the wood cleared from the ground no situation could stand in competition with this. some might require less labour to be rendered agreeable but after all assistance of arts none ever would be made so grand and all other would appear but of secondary nature," [12] wrote L'Enfant. Jenkins Heights, with its long view westward across the flat land of the Potomac Valley, was the site accepted by Washington and it is where the capitol stands today.

Amusing, though not as incredible at that time as it sounds to us now, was L'Enfant's fantastic concept of "leting the tiber return in its proper channel by a fall which issuing from under the base of the Congress building may there form a cascade of forty feet heigh or more than one hundred waide which would produce the most happy effect in rolling down to fill up the canall and discharge itself in the Potowack...." Ledoux and other French romantics had had similar ideas, but the more practical Americans rejected this kind of display.

About the middle of August, L'Enfant's plan of streets and avenues was essentially complete; and it has survived to the present day, though buildings along its routes have been replaced many times, with only a few of the original ones remaining. Once he had the plan under control, L'Enfant began to give his attention to designs for the public buildings, and he wrote to Secretary of State Jefferson asking him for drawings of the Richmond state capitol for architectural guidance.[13] L'Enfant knew of course that this building had been modeled after the Maison Carrée at Nîmes, a building admired by Jefferson as one of the most perfect of ancient monuments. The story of Jefferson's designs for the state capitol, produced with the help of the French architect Clérisseau, need not be told here, but it is important as a demonstration of the taste which Jefferson cultivated in France under the dual influences of neoclassicism and romanticism. Jefferson's design was the first in America to fully develop the exterior appearance of an ancient temple in the design of modern building. The success of the Richmond capitol encouraged him to promote the designing of another.

During the summer and into the fall of 1791 the president and Jefferson pressed the commissioners of the Federal City to finish the surveying, to make a feasible plan for selling lots, and to make contracts for materials for construction of the public buildings. However, several circumstances arose that put great difficulties in their way. L'Enfant's plan was supposed to be engraved in the number of ten thousand copies at Philadelphia so that buyers could see the positions of lots in Washington, but unaccountably the engraving was not done in time, nor would L'Enfant produce a plan during the sale in October. George Washington's comments on this fiasco, always directly to the point, were that L'Enfant's "pertinacity would, I am persuaded, be the same in all cases and to all men. He conceives, or would have others believe, that the sale was promoted by withholding the general map, and thereby the means of comparison; but I have caused it to be signified to him that I am of a different opinion." [14] Following upon this was the case of the house of Daniel Carroll of Duddington. Washington had persuaded Carroll, the largest property owner in the district, to cooperate with the government by selling much of his land for the new city. In November Carroll was having a new brick house built for himself when with little warning L'Enfant had the house destroyed because it protruded into the land selected for New Jersey Avenue. Because of his outspoken opposition to the ideas of both

Washington and the commissioners, it was only a matter of few months before L'Enfant was dismissed.

The commissioners had thought in October that L'Enfant would soon produce plans for the capitol and president's house. They wrote to Washington, stating, "We have requested him [L'Enfant] to prepare a draft of the public buildings for our inspection, and he has promised to enter on it as soon as he finds himself disengaged. He can have recourse to books in Philadelphia and can not have it here." [15] In December, diggers were ordered to prepare ground for foundations on "Federal Square" for the capitol. Clay was dug for both the capitol and the president's "Palace" as L'Enfant preferred to call it. But no one ever caught a glimpse of the actual plans for either building. Washington was under the impression that L'Enfant had made some drawings, as he wrote to Jefferson saying, "The Plans of the buildings ought to come forward immediately for consideration. I think Mr. Walker said yesterday he [L'Enfant] had been showing the different views of them to Mr. Trumbul." [16] A week later, at the end of February, L'Enfant was dismissed and Jefferson commented that "Majr. Lenfant had no plans prepared for the Capitol or government house. he said, he had them in his head." [17] In sending his deep regrets to L'Enfant at the loss of the architect's services, Washington said that he had counted upon L'Enfant's genius to produce designs of high merit in lieu of "advertising a premium to the person who should present the best." [18] However, it was Jefferson, not Washington, who first suggested procuring designs by means of a competition.

Jefferson had noticed how well established the custom in Europe was of holding competition, whereas in America only one competition had been held, that for the Library Company of Philadelphia in 1789, won by Dr. William Thornton — a versatile gentleman soon to become prominent in Washington. Although Jefferson's notes for the Residence Act in November 1790 and for the commissioners' meeting of September 8 alluded to the possibility of holding a competition, the idea was not announced until the beginning of March 1792. In September Jefferson had made "a sketch or specimen of advertisement" for possible release to the newspapers. It was sent at some point to the commissioners in Washington, returned by them to the president, who altered some parts and returned it to the commissioners on March 6 accompanied by a letter from Jefferson exhorting them to make all effort to hasten the completion of various public works. Jefferson also included a similar notice of competition for the president's house.

Washington, in the Territory of Columbia

A Premium

Of a LOT in this City, to be designated by impartial judges, and FIVE HUNDRED DOLLARS; or a MEDAL of that value, at the option of the party; will be given by the Commissioners of the Federal Buildings, to the person who, before the fifteenth day of July, 1792, shall produce to them the most approved PLAN, if adopted by them, for a CAPITOL, to be erected in this City; and TWO HUNDRED AND FIFTY DOLLARS, or a MEDAL, for the Plan deemed next in merit to the one they shall adopt. The building to be of brick, and to contain the following compartments, to wit:

A Conference Room ⎱ sufficient to accommo-

A Room for the Representatives ⎰ date 300 persons each.

A Lobby or Antichamber to the latter

A Senate Room of 1200 square feet area

An Antichamber or Lobby to the last

These rooms to be of full elevation.

12 Rooms of 600 square feet area each, for Committee Rooms and Clerks' Offices, to be of half the elevation of the former.

Drawings will be expected of the ground plats, elevations of each front, and sections through the building of such directions as may be necessary to explain the internal structure; and an estimate of the cubic feet of the brickwork composing the whole mass of the walls.

The Commissioners.[19]

March 14, 1792.

A Premium

of 500 dollars, or a Medal of that value, at the option of the party, will be given by the Commissioners of the federal buildings to the person who before the _____ day of _____ next shall produce to them the most approved plan for a President's house to be erected in the city of Washington & territory of Columbia. The site of the building, if the artist will attend to it, will of course influence the aspect & outline of his plan, & its destination of the building will point out to the artist him the number, size & distribution of the apartments. it will be a recommendation of any plan that if the central part of it may be detached & erected for the present, with the appearance of a complete whole, and the other parts added be capable of admitting the additional parts in future if they shall be wanting.[20]

Once the competition was announced nothing more could be accomplished with the building operations until the middle of July when the designs were to be submitted. By July 15, 1792, the appointed day, the commissioners had received ten designs for the capitol building.[21] For two days Washington, Jefferson and the commissioners considered the plans and found merit in several, though none were judged entirely satisfactory. They favored the design by Stephen Hallet without approving of certain aspects of it.[22]

The superior designs of James Hoban for the president's "Palace" were quickly approved. L'Enfant had already set out stakes for his version of the president's house.[23] He had envisioned a much larger building as appropriate to the stature of the nation's leader. Hoban's smaller design, unexpectedly good, was declared superior to the domed villa, submitted anonymously, by Jefferson himself. Jefferson's motive seems to have been less to win a contest than to supply a reasonable design in case all others were inadequate. His was a simplified Palladian design with a superimposed dome not unlike the wooden one over the Halle aux Bleds, or Grain Market, in Paris before it burned and was revaulted with a metal dome. It was not this building that Jefferson had earlier suggested as a model for L'Enfant; instead he had asked the architect to consider the Louvre, the Gardes Meubles, and the Hôtel de Salm. It is clear that Hoban became aware of Jefferson's preferences, as his designs bear strong resemblances to the Hôtel de Salm.

Encouraged by the judges, Stephen Hallet and another top competitor, Judge George Turner, came to Washington to consult on modifications to their plans for the capitol that might ensure acceptance. But the commissioners reported late in August, "None appeared so compleate in the whole as to fix a decided Opinion which did not appear to be essential at this time, to the Progress of the Execution, therefore . . . the final Decission is put off." Their inability to reach a quicker decision was owing to a desire for quality in design and fairness to the contestants. "Tho limitted in the means," they said, "we are determined to embrace a Plan which may from its extent, its Design, and Taste do credit to the Age. . . ."[24] Gradually Hallet's plans won the preference of the commissioners, though they were unwilling to accept them as presented by the architect. Hallet felt so close to winning the coveted prize that in a frenzy of work he produced a whole series of new drawings, each calculated to include all the latest suggestions made by the commissioners. Still the commissioners told Jefferson in mid-October that

> the plan which he has exhibited, and which was drawn by our directions, after his fancy piece, does not meet altogether with our approbation, Nor does it appear to be agreeable to his own taste and judgement — We had given him a sketch of the internal arrangements which we thought would be most happy — It appears not to have been possible to accomodate

the exterior of the fancy piece, to those arrangements — We have therefore desired him to make any departure from it he may approve of in his future Plan; Consulting the President, and yourself on the subject — We have not a doubt of his possessing the highest merits in his line; as every thing he has exhibited, tho' not approved of, has still evinced more taste, and practical skill, than has appeared in any of the numerous ones with which we have been favoured.[25]

The inconclusive results of the capitol competition must have become known to all, so it is perhaps not surprising that another set of designs, by Dr. William Thornton of Philadelphia fame, should have been received by the commissioners. Although very late with respect to the rules of the competition, the new designs were apparently not too late to be considered. It seems that no promise was ever made to build the winning design, and therefore the commissioners maintained the right to select any plan they chose. When Dr. Thornton submitted his design, it was received without prejudice by the secretary of state to hold for the president's inspection.[26]

William Thornton, unlike Hallet, was not a professional architect. He was born in the West Indies in 1759, studied medicine at the University of Edinburgh (receiving his M.D. in 1784), and in 1787 came to New York. He shortly moved to Philadelphia, married, and by October 1790 had returned to his estates in Tortola, W.I. It was only in November of 1792 that he came again to Philadelphia, heard of the competition for the capitol, and began to make a design from books, using his own natural sense of good taste.

Thornton's architectural models were chosen so well that his design immediately caught the eye of the president. Jefferson enthusiastically reported to the commissioners Washington's feelings and those of others in Philadelphia who had viewed the plans. "Doctor Thornton's plan of a capitol has been produced," he said, "and has so captivated the eyes and judgment of all as to leave no doubt you will prefer it when it shall be exhibited to you; as no doubt exists here of its preference over all which have been produced, and among its admirers no one is more decided than him whose decision is most important. It is simple, noble, beautiful, excellently distributed, and moderate in size." [27] After receiving this communication from Jefferson the commissioners had little to do but accept the design when they saw it in early March, brought by the architect himself who wished to explain details of the plans directly to the commissioners. Thornton brought also a letter of introduction from President Washington conveying sentiments similar to those already expressed by Jefferson — "Grandure, Simplicity and Convenience." [28] With less certainty and some special reservations the commissioners were pressed to a quick decision and by the middle of March had told

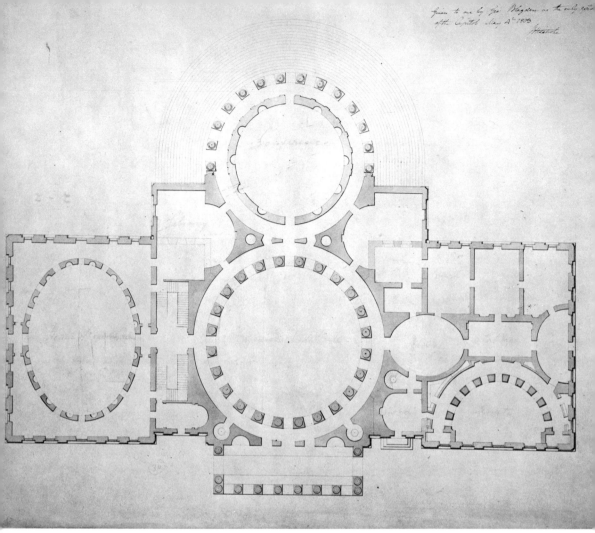

Hallet, who expected his design to win the prize, the final result. Admittedly the contest was not carried out strictly according to the advertisement of it and was thus open to criticism which could be answered only by an appeal to the public good. "Neither the Doctor or yourself can demand the Prize under the Strict Terms of our Advertisement," said the commissioners, "but the Public has been benefited by the Emulation Excited and the End having been answered we shall give the reward of 500 Dollars and a Lot to Dr. Thornton — You certainly rank next and because your Application has been exited by particular request, we have resolved to place you on the same footing as near as may be, that is to allow a Compensation for everything to this Time 100£ being the value of a Lot and 500 Dollars." [29] The official letter announcing to Thornton his winning of first prize did not go to the doctor until the president had given his final approval of the plans in early April.[30]

Realizing that the time left for completing the capitol for Congress was fast disappearing and that the whole federal enterprise of settling in Washington might collapse if the capitol were not ready in time, the commissioners pressed Thornton to disclose his scheme immediately so that they might "mark out the ground and make preparations and even begin to lay the Foundation this fall." [31] Some time during the next two months Hallet and others saw the plans of Thornton and criticized them as impracticable. This is not surprising since Thornton was only an amateur. In fact it soon appeared that Thornton had little conception of how to construct a large building. His was the contribution of beauty and monumentality, the qualities for which his design was accepted by Washington and the commissioners, who themselves had little knowledge of the technical aspects of construction.

As Thornton was quite evidently unable to supervise or even make working drawings for construction, the commissioners, who had been bowled over by the quick decision of Jefferson and Washington to accept the design, were now helplessly holding plans for a building which could not be built. In their predicament they ill-advisedly turned to Hallet as obviously competent to draw buildable plans. They even felt some measure of obligation to him because they had led him to make designs following their suggestions as though he would ultimately be the architect. Their report at this moment to Washington reflected their unsettled minds. "We had desired Mr. Hallet," they said, "to study Doct. Thornton's plan of a Capitol, we thought it prudent that the whole together and every part seperately should be in the mind of some person who was to see to the execution, perhaps it may be Hallet — perhaps not, he has simplified and abridged the plan, we have had not great time to consider it . . . we wish for your Instructions." [32]

Washington's reaction to the commissioners' letter was to put everything into the hands of Jefferson, with a few strong remarks on the case.

> It is unlucky, he said, that this investigation of Doctor Thornton's plan, and estimate of the cost had not preceeded the adoption of it: but knowing the impatience of the Carrollsburg interest and the anxiety of the Public to see both buildings progressing; and supposing the plan to be correct, it was adjudged best to avoid delay. It is better, however, to correct an error, though late, than to proceed in a ruinous measure, in the adoption of which I do not hesitate to confess I was governed by the beauty of the exterior and the distribution of the appartments, declaring then, as I do now, that I had no knowledge in the rules or principles of Architecture, and was equally unable to count the cost. But, if there be such material defects as are represented, and such immense time and cost to complete the buildings, it would be folly in the extreme to proceed on the Plan which has been adopted. [33]

Jefferson hastily called a meeting in Philadelphia hoping to settle what had by now become an acrimonious dispute. Hallet and James Hoban came from Washington to join Thornton and Carstairs, a builder whom Thornton had chosen as an adviser, for the discussions with Jefferson. The meeting was well reported by Jefferson in his usual concise manner. The strongest objections to Thornton's design were the following:

> 1st The intercolonnation of the western and central peristyles are too wide for the support of their architraves of stone: so are those of the doors, in the Wings.—2nd the Collonnade passing through the middle of the conference room has an ill effect to the eye and will obstruct the view of the members: and if taken away the ceiling is too wide to support itself — 3d The floor of the Central peristyle is too wide to support itself — 4. The stairways on each side of the conference room want head room — 5. The windows are in some important instances masked by the Galleries — 6. many parts of the building want light and air in a degree, which renders them unfit for their purposes.[34]

Such formidable difficulties could hardly be overlooked, particularly since those present, including the builder brought by Thornton, all disapproved of one or another aspect of the design. Hallet, knowing beforehand of the objections to Thornton's design, brought with him a revised one which Jefferson referred to as "Dr. Thornton's plan, rendered into practicable form."

In his role as final judge, Washington was obliged to separate the proposed changes which were based on personal ambition and professional jealousy from those designed to correct real flaws, for by now Hallet was evidently trying to revise Thornton's plans to become his own, slipping in this and that new idea ostensibly to satisfy the objections raised by one or another person. Jefferson and Washington were well aware of this but believed that by giving judicious and explicit instructions and having the commissioners oversee the operations, that Hallet's talents could be applied without destroying the project as conceived by Thornton. "The plan produced by Mr. Hallet," wrote Washington, "altho' preserving the original ideas of Doct Thornton, . . . was pronounced by the Gentlemen on the part of Doct Thornton, as the one which they, as practical Architects, would chuse to execute — Besides which you will see that, in the opinion of the Gentlemen, the plan executed according to Mr. Hallet's ideas would not cost more than one half of what it would if executed according to Doct Thornton's." As to professional ambition Washington added, "It has been intimated that the reason of his [Hallet's] proposing the recess instead of a portico, is to make it in one essential feature different from Doct. Thornton's plan."[35] James

Hoban, who was already superintending construction of the president's house, was instructed to lay the foundations for the north and south wings of the capitol, leaving the plan of the central portion for future discussion. On the first of August the commissioners could report back to Washington that "a considerable force is imployed in digging at the Capitol and the Hands will begin to lay the foundation of it as soon as they quit the President's House." [36]

On September 18, 1793, a gala parade with bands and costumed members of several Masonic lodges celebrated the placing of a cornerstone for the capitol. It bore a silver plaque engraved as follows:

> This southeast corner-stone of the Capitol of the United States of America, in the City of Washington, was laid on the eighteenth day of September, 1793, in the thirteenth year of American Independence, in the first year of the second term of the presidency of George Washington, whose virtues in the civil administration of his country have been as conspicuous and beneficial as his military valor and prudence have been useful in establishing her liberties, and in the year of Masonry, 5793, by the President of the United States, in concert with the Grand Lodge of Maryland, several lodges under its jurisdiction, and Lodge No. 22, from Alexandria, Va., Thomas Johnson, David Steuart and Daniel Carroll, Commissioners; Joseph Clark, R. W. Grand Master, *pro tem.;* Joseph Hoban and Stephen Hallate, architects; Collin Williamson, master mason. [37]

Clearly these sentiments were not composed by either Washington or Jefferson both of whom would have vigorously objected to the names of Hoban and Hallet as "architects."

At the end of 1793 Thomas Jefferson left Washington's cabinet for retirement at Monticello; his influence on the construction of both the capitol and president's house thus ceased for a time. However, it is well to bear in mind what happened during the intervening years. Hoban was retained by the commissioners as superintendent of the capitol and the president's house, while Hallet became assistant superintendent for architectural matters. [38] Still smarting from his rejection as architect of the capitol, Hallet refused in the spring of 1794 to provide further detailed plans, which by then were essential to continue construction. The commissioners discovered that Hallet had not only overreached his authority by giving directions to the workmen but also intended to introduce new changes to the plans. "In general nothing has gone from us," the commissioners told Hallet, "by which we believe you could infer that you had the chief direction of executing the work of the Capitol or that you or anybody else were to introduce into that building any departure from Doct Thornton's Plan without the President's or Commissioner's approbation." [39] Two days later Hallet was dismissed.

William Thornton had meanwhile taken up residence in Georgetown, close to the Federal City, and in the summer of 1794 he replaced one of the commissioners, placing himself in a position where he could wield authority over the city and in particular keep an eye on the capitol building as it gradually grew on Jenkins Hill.

Without a supervising architect the work at the capitol lagged until John Trumbull, painter and secretary to the American minister to England, heard of Hallet's dismissal and recommended the young George Hadfield, winner of a gold medal in architecture at the Royal Academy where he had been one of Trumbull's classmates. Reluctant at first to appoint still another architect, the commissioners soon said: "We are convinced of the necessity of constant attention to adjust the various members of the work to preserve an elegant correspondence — A Superintendent of great ability, whose time will be wholly engaged is therefore requisite." [40] Hadfield arrived to take up his duties on October 15, 1795, receiving the appointment of superintendent of the capitol. As though it were endemic to the position, the thought of revising the plans soon occurred to Hadfield. When these changes were mentioned to Washington, he replied that "I should have no objection, . . . as the present plan is nobody's, but a compound of everybody's, to the proposed change," [41] but the commissioners, with Thornton in the midst, thought otherwise and refused any alterations. [42]

Steady but slow progress was maintained on construction at the capitol for the next three years under Hadfield's direction. The very real danger existed that if the public buildings were not ready for Congress and the president, then Congress might be persuaded to settle elsewhere. "It may be relied on," warned Washington, "that it is the progress of that building [the Capitol], that is to inspire, or depress public confidence . . . it is essential on the score of policy, & for the gratification of the public wishes, that this work should be vigorously prosecuted in the manner I have suggested. — And I require it accordingly." [43]

Although Jefferson returned to public life in March 1797 as vice president under Adams, he had little contact with architecture in Washington except to witness its progress as he journeyed from Philadelphia to Monticello. A disagreement between Hadfield and the commissioners over plans for executive buildings and perhaps some other contributing circumstances led to the architect's dismissal in May 1798, and James Hoban again assumed superintendence of the capitol. In spite of the innumerable problems arising constantly over labor, materials and plans, the north wing of the capitol and a portion of the president's house were ready for occupation in November 1800, when the government was established in Washington. On this occasion

President John Adams in his annual address to Congress, which was gathered in the capitol, said with confidence, "I congratulate the people of the United States on the assembling of Congress at the permanent seat of their Government; and I congratulate you, gentlemen, on the prospect of a residence not to be changed. Although there is cause to apprehend that accommodations are not now so complete as might be wished, yet there is great reason to believe that this inconvenience will cease with the present session." [44]

The election of Thomas Jefferson as third president and his subsequent appointment of Benjamin Henry Latrobe as surveyor of public buildings opened a period of great architectural importance for the new nation. It is hard for us to imagine today how uninviting the city was for members of Congress and the hundreds of others associated with the central government. Many must have felt as did John Davis, the London traveler, who arrived in time to hear Jefferson give his inaugural address on the fourth of March 1801. "When I heard the speech of Mr. Jefferson," the president's admirer remarked, "there was nothing more to detain me among the scattered buildings of the desert." [45] Jefferson soon brought considerable pressure to bear on Congress to appropriate funds for continuing construction, but spending money was not popular, nor was the city of Washington. Even as late as 1803 legislators were making resolutions to remove the seat of government to another place.

In the fall of 1801 it was expected that there would be an increase in the membership of the House of Representatives, and as a result new space would be needed for them. Hoban made three plans that would allow the House to use the south wing of the capitol expanded for this need, though in an unfinished state. Thornton's original plan for the representatives had an oval room inscribed within a rectangle, matching the exterior design of the north wing. Of Hoban's three plans Jefferson preferred the one suggesting that the walls of the oval room be built one story high, while leaving the exterior walls at the foundation level. It was the cheapest scheme and the one least likely to interfere with construction whenever that began again. [46] The oval hall of brick was completed with a temporary roof in time for the representatives' next meeting.

As Congress became active in Washington it wished to have made control over the affairs of the city and, after receiving a series of reports from them, decided to abolish the positions of the commissioners on June 1, 1802, in favor of a single superintendent. The position was promptly filled by Jefferson's appointee, Thomas Munroe, the former clerk of the commissioners. [47] This appointment had no immediate architectural consequences. "The state of the public buildings . . .," declared Munroe in December 1802, "is the same as at the last session of Congress, or not materially changed." [48]

While the commissioners were being replaced by a superintendent, Jefferson was searching for an architect with the training and experience requisite to complete the neglected capitol. In Boston there was Charles Bulfinch, and there were men available in the class of carpenter-builders, but none except Benjamin Henry Latrobe were professionally trained architects. Latrobe had designed and supervised the construction of the Richmond penitentiary in 1797, basing his plan on studies made by Jefferson a decade earlier.[49] Latrobe had spent three years in the office of the well-known London architect Samuel Pepys Cockerell and another three years attempting to establish his own business. Unsuccessful in the latter and depressed over family circumstances, Latrobe sailed for America and arrived here in March 1796, looking for a new life in the land where his mother was born. That Latrobe should have been selected rather than some more practical man of experience is, I believe, owing to the importance Jefferson always gave to education and quality in the arts. Latrobe's education, he soon discovered, was as good as or better than his own; and there was little doubt about his artistic ability. Yet Jefferson did not appoint Latrobe as architect for the capitol immediately. Instead he invited him to prepare estimates for docks, locks and an arsenal, as though to test his talents. Latrobe accepted the assignment and made a beautiful set of drawings carefully thought out and accompanied by estimates that he submitted to Jefferson before the end of 1802.[50] In any case, Jefferson could not make an official appointment until Congress had appropriated funds for construction of public buildings.

Perhaps the most cogent reason for Congress to agree on an appropriations bill early in 1803 was the personal discomfort of the members in the unfinished capitol. After much debate, the important "Act concerning the city of Washington" was passed by both houses on March 3, 1803,[51] appropriating fifty thousand dollars to be used, under the direction of the president, for making necessary repairs and alterations to the capitol and other public buildings. The act had the effect of giving confidence to dwellers, builders, and land speculators who were uncertain as to the future of the government in Washington. The citizens were acutely aware of the tentative nature of the new city as the speculator Thomas Law was quick to notice: "Last year Congress, by voting a sum of money for the capitol and by resolving not to alter the plan of the city, banished forever all doubts, and in consequence more houses have been built since that decisive crisis than in any preceding year." [52]

Immediately after the passage of this act Jefferson wrote to Latrobe asking him to become the surveyor of public buildings, an office not mentioned in

Benjamin Henry Latrobe. *Drawing of the Capitol,* presented to Jefferson.
Library of Congress

the act, though tacitly understood as necessary to carry it out. Jefferson told him it was important to appear in Washington immediately so that contracts could be let for materials and financial arrangements could be made.[53] The president was confident that Latrobe would accept, even though the salary offered was small and the job was a dubious honor, to judge from the experiences of former capitol architects. Latrobe did accept, and his first task was to prepare a lengthy report to the president on the state of the capitol, not hesitating to mention faults in construction. It concluded with a list of desirable alterations.[54]

Since Latrobe's report is the basis for practically all his later successes and difficulties, it is well to review it in some detail. The first section of the report was devoted to a description of the blunders Latrobe maintained he had found in Thornton's plans and to an enumeration of mistakes in construction. He attacked the disparity between the exterior appearance and the interior functions. For example, in Thornton's design the façade consisted of a ground-level story of heavily drafted stonework, above which stood a magnificent portico establishing the level of the principal (second) floor. The monumental staircases at both the east and west sides ascended to the portico level where large doorways led to an interior vestibule. But corridors from the vestibule led only to offices and galleries of the legislative rooms. To reach the main legislative floor it was necessary to descend a flight of steps equal to that already ascended on the exterior. In the Hall of Representatives Latrobe noted a very high colonnade, which, when superimposed on a low arcade, exhibited "a poverty of design." The illogical arrangement of floor levels was later explained to Latrobe by Dr. Thornton himself. He said that in the original plan the legislative halls were on the principal floor, but that owing to a circumstance he had lowered the halls by one story. At the same time he claimed to have made the columns of the exterior portico shorter and smaller in diameter so that no change would be necessary in the total height of the building, and yet the basement story would be sufficiently increased in height to allow ample vertical space inside the halls.

The "circumstance" referred to by Thornton seems to have been the change in plan accepted by Jefferson in 1801 for accommodating the representatives in the south wing by lowering the level of their Hall one flight. If this was meant as a final solution (which I doubt) then Jefferson must have been more than a little surprised to read Latrobe's strong criticism of Thornton's alterations that the president himself had approved. Latrobe said that he "fully communicated and explained" his ideas to Thornton, but evidently he made a tactless approach for which Thornton never forgave him.

On the one hand, the Senate chamber in the north wing was fragile, Latrobe said, and showed bad workmanship. On the other hand, he thought the central grand vestibule equal in magnificence to any building in Europe. He had few objections to the Hall of Conference, where the two legislative bodies could meet concurrently, because it was properly located at the level of the porticos. He called it a "beautiful part of the plan," and only objected that the space beneath was not usable.

The south wing, where only foundations and the temporary Hall of Representatives had been constructed, became the butt of Latrobe's most vigorous criticism, particularly since the north wing, already built, could not be materially changed. Under the heading of "Use and Convenience," Latrobe found too little space for offices and committee rooms. The lobby was objectionable as it would surround the legislative hall and prevent a good view of the House floor by the representatives and House officers. Furthermore, the legislators would have to pass through this public lobby, inconveniently mingling with the public, in order to reach their private rooms.

Under objections "as they respect safe practicability" Latrobe stressed the unsafe relationship of the two tall masonry walls (the exterior and the interior elliptical hall), which had no connecting links and therefore no mutual buttressing. Furthermore, Thornton's plan called for a domed roof,

90x120 feet, supported by thin masonry walls at a height of about sixty feet from the ground. These walls, opened by Latrobe for inspection, had been built by erecting two thin casings and filling the space between with loose stones. The architect asserted that no wall like this could possibly bear the weight of a domical vault nor even remain in vertical alignment very long. "I want the courage," he said, "necessary to embolden me to attempt it."

Concerning architectural taste Latrobe betrayed his predilection for the Greek and Roman styles tempered by more recent Italian and English design. He opposed the rococo of the eighteenth century, saw beauty and utility only in the work of the ancients, and believed that his immediate predecessors had often mishandled architectural forms. In place of the ellipse and other forms which he considered unattractive, the architect pointed out that recently (in Europe) "both architects and scene painters have substituted in their room parallelograms bounded by semicircles" as closer to the elegance and purity of antiquity.

Latrobe accepted his position under no misapprehensions about the troubles which might arise over designing and building the capitol. The careers of Hallet and Hadfield, he pointed out, were already ruined, as he believed, through no fault of their own. "The utmost praise I can ever deserve in this work," he said to Jefferson, "will be that of *la difficulté vaincue.*" [55] In spite of his long list of criticisms of the capitol and its plans, Jefferson recognized Latrobe's great talents, accepted the report, and advised him to get the building operations for the year under way without delay.

Inhibited by the condition set by the president, that no changes would be allowed in Thornton's plans unless he agreed to them, Latrobe could not quickly make the alterations he had proposed. However, he began his campaign of change at the risk of an argument with Jefferson by preparing a new plan for the south wing with a semicircular hall, like "that of the ancient theater." In arguing his case for a Roman theater form, Latrobe told Jefferson that the best shape for acoustics, vision, and oratory had always been a semicircular room, not an ellipse. His plan showed a hall for 360 members, each seat facing the speaker's chair which was at the center of the south side. In the two southern corners he inserted circular stairs, ten feet in diameter, providing access to the public galleries. The area known as the recess (between the Hall of Representatives and the grand vestibule) was in Thornton's plan not adequately lighted. By adding an open court and making a smaller grand staircase with skylights this problem was solved. [56]

Jefferson fully expected Latrobe to move to Washington after his appointment. But Latrobe's salary was small and his family increasing. He arranged instead to make frequent short trips to Washington while maintaining an architectural practice in Philadelphia. From Jefferson's point of view this was a great disadvantage, because the job obviously could not be as well directed from one hundred miles away. To cover the immediate problems of construction in Washington, Latrobe appointed John Lenthall as clerk-of-the-works. Lenthall, a skilled carpenter, managed very well and must be given great credit for organizing the construction work so successfully. Latrobe, of course, saw nothing uncommon in not being on the construction site every minute. The London architects, whose methods he well understood, also employed clerks-of-the-works and only visited the site at convenient intervals. The architect's major effort was spent on perfecting the plans and working drawings and keeping the accounts with suppliers and workers. The restless president was not satisfied and spent many anxious hours examining plans and inspecting the actual work in progress. His motives were always for the public good, which he thought would be best served by expediting the construction of the capitol. Thus when he interfered with Latrobe's schedule in late April 1803, Jefferson caused much embarrassment all around by telling Lenthall that the old unsound walls were not being taken down fast enough. Then with characteristic precision and thoroughness the president wrote to Latrobe asking for a stone-cutting schedule for the next twenty-three weeks and a progress report from Lenthall each week.[57] Since Lenthall complied with this request, we now have an almost day by day record of work accomplished until the middle of the summer.[58] At this point Lenthall, overworked in the hot, humid summer, with little extra time or energy, neglected to send any more reports. Jefferson had left the city for Monticello. Lenthall probably thought (very mistakenly) that the president would no longer want reports. In August Jefferson wrote anxiously to the superintendent asking that the usual report be sent.[59] When building superintendent Thomas Munroe questioned Lenthall on his failure to send the report, Lenthall replied that he had not received essential information from Latrobe. This excuse Munroe related to Jefferson: "He [Lenthall] is surprised and embarrassed in consequence of not having seen or heard from Mr. Latrobe since he was here early in July, and is at a stand for want of instructions in some cases he tells me, and particularly with regard to repairs & alterations at the President's house and north wing of the Capitol and for want of some materials which Mr. Latrobe was to procure and send forward."[60]

The responsibility for building the capitol, so well bestowed upon the versatile president, now became for him an all-important project. He insisted that the capitol be given preference over every other public work, including the president's own house.[61] The caustic, popular poet, Thomas Moore, saw

210

the neglect of the latter in another light. "The President's house, a very noble structure," Moore said, "is by no means suited to the philosophical humility of its present possessor, who inhabits but a corner of the mansion himself, and abandons the rest to a state of uncleanly desolation, which those who are not philosophers cannot look at without regret." [62]

The whereabouts of Latrobe during the critical summer of 1804 is explained by his correspondence in the fall. Supposing that his plans and instructions to Lenthall were sufficient for the buildings in Washington, he was very eager to work on a project that he hoped might become more lucrative and had begun exploring the area between the Chesapeake and Delaware Bays for the Chesapeake and Delaware Canal Company in order to locate an economical canal route. While surveying, he found it impossible to write to Lenthall owing to difficulties of communication.[63] This ill-advised canal venture lost for Latrobe much of the confidence Jefferson had placed in him, upset Lenthall's tight schedule of work, and brought public condemnation upon him for inattention to duties. These criticisms were partially, though not wholly, misplaced.

To prevent leakage during the winter sheet-iron roofing for both the president's house and the north wing of the capitol had been ordered in May from Samuel Mifflin of Philadelphia.[64] Yet in September the prospect of getting the metal in time was indeed bleak, for during the summer an unusual drought had compelled most of the Pennsylvania furnaces to shut down. Still more serious, owing to its effect on manpower in Philadelphia, was an epidemic of yellow fever, which had raged during the summer with devastating effects.[65] Though aware of these difficulties Jefferson was no less keen to have the public buildings watertight for the session of Congress convening in October. He wrote to Latrobe exhorting him to throw his fullest energies into procuring the missing materials.[66] Latrobe obediently made inquiries at Mifflin's iron mill, and good news was forthcoming, for he could tell the president early in October, with evident relief, that roofing iron would be ready for his homes in Charlottesville and at Washington.[67] Even the new iron roofing ordered for the Senate, using a "zig-zag" design suggested by the president, was rolled and ready for shipment by the end of November.[68] After the near disaster of the fall, Latrobe declared to Lenthall, "As to what people say, I don't care a straw, provided I have nothing to say against myself." [69]

Latrobe was in Washington from December 1803 to March 1804 to make contracts for stone and other materials for the next working season. During that time, an argument arose between him and Jefferson over the manner of covering the Hall of Representatives. Thornton's original plans

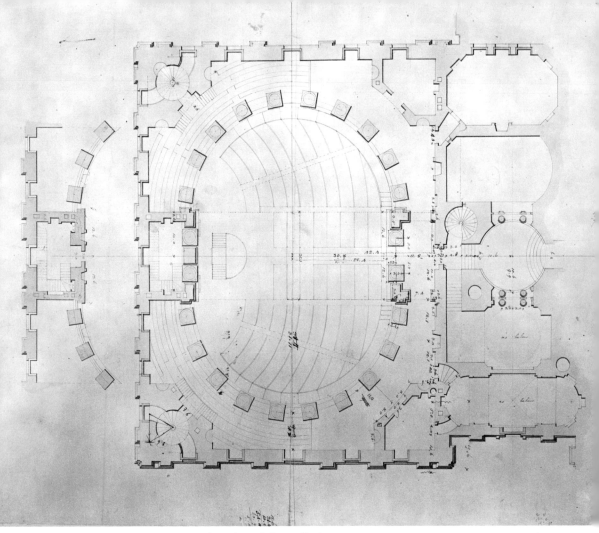

Benjamin Henry Latrobe. *Plan of the Hall of Representatives,* U.S. Capitol, March 1804.
Library of Congress

had called for a semicircular dome, but made no mention of central lighting. Latrobe made a series of sketches showing the effect of four different schemes, none of which he said appealed to him personally, as he wanted a room of an entirely different shape.[70] These sketches showed a ceiling like that over the Halle aux Bleds in Paris,[71] which was greatly admired by Jefferson while he was in France. It was circular in form and had an open market court in the center, surrounded by a vaulted aisle used as a granary. Later the open court was covered by using the vaulting system devised by the Renaissance architect Philibert Delorme, a system which consisted of small curved beams fastened by wooden pegs that converged at the center of the dome like the ribs of a Gothic vault.[72] The interstices were glazed, furnishing ample light for the interior and giving the magnificent effect of a radiating sunburst. According to Jefferson, "It was the most superb thing on earth!"[73]

The moment had now arrived when Latrobe believed he must make a strong plea for change in the designs of the capitol, or give in entirely. He first met with the president and then with his arch rival, Dr. Thornton, believing that he could point out the inherent mistakes in the doctor's plans without offense and thereby gain his approval. Instead his attempt ended in a violent outburst of tempers. Thornton would agree to nothing Latrobe proposed; in fact, he refused to discuss the plans. The futility of this conversation was summed up by Latrobe afterward: "I judged very ill in going to Dr. Thornton." He told Jefferson, "In a few peremptory words he in fact told me that no difficulties existed in his plan but such as were made by those who were too ignorant to remove them." [74] Jefferson's reply was that "in order to get along with any public undertaking it is necessary that some stability of plan be observed — nothing impedes progress so much as perpetual changes of design." [75] Of course, Jefferson actually preferred Thornton's design of an elliptical Hall of Representatives and therefore opposed any changes on aesthetic grounds, saying that the design would "be more handsome and commodious than anything which can now be proposed on the same area." Jefferson was willing to admit that erecting a dome over an ellipse was not an easy task, but he believed that Latrobe, a man of genius, should be able to do it.

As a measure of economy Jefferson in 1803 had suggested substituting wooden for stone columns in the plans for the Hall of Representatives; now he wanted to use bricks molded to fit the curve of a column and covered with plaster in imitation of antique stone columns. He knew from his copy of Palladio's architectural writings that the idea was sanctioned by this master of the Renaissance and therefore could be proposed to a professional. Latrobe rejected Jefferson's proposal in favor of building with solid stone, based on his continuous preference for the manner of the Greeks.

Latrobe never lost an opportunity to point out to Jefferson the faults in Thornton's plans, as though repetition would eventually undermine the president's convictions. Latrobe attacked from every angle. "If I felt the slightest respect for the talents of the original designer *as an architect*," he quipped, "I should be fearless as to myself, but placed as I am on the very spot from which Hallet & Hadfield fell, attacked by the same weapons, & with the same activity, nothing but a very resolute defense can save me." [76]

Unsuccessful at persuading Jefferson to allow him to replace Thornton's plans, the architect reluctantly worked with the old scheme. "I am laboring at the plan, retaining the elliptical colonnade," Latrobe told Lenthall.

My conscience urges me exceedingly to throw the trumpery, along with my appointment into the fire. When once erected, the absurdity can never be recalled & a public explanation can only amount to this that one presi-

213

dent was blockhead enough to adopt a plan, which another was fool enough to retain, when he might have altered it. The only discovery which I have made, in elaborating the thing, . . . is, that the Doctor was born under a musical planet, for all his rooms fall naturally into the shape of fiddles, tamborines, & mandolines, one or two into that of a harp.[77]

The elliptical form bothered Latrobe incessantly, until at last he decided to give it up and replace it with two semicircles abutting a parallelogram.[78] Jefferson naturally protested the new scheme but consented to speak with Thornton about it. Much to his surprise Thornton fully agreed to the idea. The roll of new designs sent to Jefferson at the end of March contained five large drawings — each described in the accompanying letter. Of these, two are lost, the third is a plan of the Hall of Representatives, the fourth an elevation of the hall displaying the Corinthian order using the order of the Tower of the Winds in Athens as a model, and the fifth an elevation of the hall with the Doric order as found in Vignola's book of architecture and taken by him from the Theater of Marcellus in Rome.[79] Jefferson promptly replied, seeming to accept the designs and agreeing with Latrobe that the elevation with the Corinthian would best satisfy the situation; his criticisms, in fact, were very minor.[80] At last Latrobe believed he had won a victory, but he was not altogether reassured, for no absolute word was given as to either removing the freestanding temporary hall, now called the "Oven," or fully accepting the new designs. In fact misunderstandings now occurred so frequently that only a meeting of all parties could have settled the issues. Such a meeting was never to take place.

By the middle of the summer Jefferson had given up his defense of Thornton's plans and gave orders for the removal of the "Oven," it having been pointed out to him that to build the outer walls without bonding them to an inner wall would cause a very unsafe condition. But owing to a mis-understanding the outer wall was, in fact, carried up without bonding, much to the mortification of Jefferson who had urged the legislators to move from their hall so that the construction could be done properly.[81]

Another act, including an appropriation for the south wing, was passed hastily by Congress on January 25, 1805, two months earlier than the previous year, approving the sum of $130,000.[82] Jefferson wrote to Latrobe the following day urging him to come speedily to Washington, adding, "The appropriation has been made in confidence that we will finish the south wing this year, leaving the north one for the next year." [83] Now that the exterior walls were reaching the cornice level, where there was 147 feet of external ornamental entablature and twenty-four Corinthian capitals to cut for the interior of the Hall of Representatives, it became necessary to find skilled stonecarvers. Almost no one was available in the country for this purpose, and to meet the emergency Latrobe and Jefferson decided to import artists from Italy. They asked Philip Mazzei, the Italian physician, merchant, and horticulturist, who was now returning to his native land, to act as intermediary. Mazzei agreed, but it was a long time before anything was heard from him. In September Mazzei could finally write saying that he had located two sculptors, Giuseppi Franzoni and Giovanni Andrei, whom he considered "superior to the work they are required for, and remarkable for good morals and excellent temper." [84] They each had young Italian wives and children, all of whom would make the journey as soon as they could arrange passage. The sculptors arrived early the following year.

Jefferson doubtless was frequently annoyed by Latrobe's continuous activity elsewhere than in Washington. The architect, on his part, found the president's stubbornness frustrating, yet he always held Jefferson in the highest esteem, as the following episode illustrates. Lenthall had received a very frank letter from Latrobe. In his reply he cautioned Latrobe that mail sent via the president might well be seen by the latter. In fact, Latrobe's most recent letter had been opened as is attested to by Jefferson's note attached to it. "Th. Jefferson presents his compliments to Mr. Lenthall and sends him a letter this moment received inclosed from Mr. Latrobe. Being handed him among his own he broke it open without looking at the superscription; but seeing Mr. Lenthall's name at the head of it, he closed it instantly and assures him on his honor he did not read one other word of it." [85] Unfortunately the last paragraph of Latrobe's letter was less than complimentary to the president. "I am sorry," he wrote, "that I am cramped in this design by his [Jefferson's] prejudices in favor of the architecture of the old french books, out of which he fishes everything, but it is a small sacrifice to my personal attachment to him to humor him, and the less so, because the style of the colonnade he proposes is exactly consistent with Hoban's pile, a litter of pigs worthy of the great sow it surrounds, & of the Irish boar, the father of her." [86] He went on to write one of the finest sketches of Jefferson ever composed.

He is one of the best hearted men that ever came out of the hand of Nature and has one of the best heads also. But he thinks, writes, and acts differently from others; and who ever does that must submit to abuse, let the new road he travels be ever so much shorter, cleaner, and pleasanter. As a man, I never knew his superior in candor, kindness, and universal information; — as a political character he has not his equal anywhere in patriotism, right intentions, and uniform perserverance in the system he has conceived to be the most beneficial for his country. — Nothing in fact exists, in his whole character, on which to fasten ridicule and censure but his manner, and a few oddities of appearance and of conduct which are perfectly innocent and probably very right.[87]

As the time approached to cover the south wing with a roof, Latrobe became less and less convinced that a design imitating the Halle aux Bleds in Paris (like the design he had grudgingly made for Jefferson early in 1804) would satisfy the conditions for a legislative hall. While a leaking roof or imperfect lighting might not disturb the use of a granary or exchange hall, Latrobe said with fine understatement that "a single leaky joint, dropping upon the head or desk of a member will disturb the whole house." [88] After mentioning all possible reasons for replacing this with another scheme he sent two notes to Jefferson, who characteristically and quite sharply replied,

> I cannot express to you the regret I feel on the subject of renouncing the Halle au bles lights of the Capitol dome. That single circumstance was to constitute the distinguishing merit of the room, & would solely have made it the handsomest room in the world, without a single exception. . . . The only objection having any weight with me is the danger of leaking, & I had hoped that art had resources for that where the expense would not have been an obstacle. . . . I cannot take on myself to say that leakage can be prevented in opposition to the opinion of practical men. I leave therefore the decision on the abandonment of the idea entirely to yourself, & will acquiesce in that.[89]

This reply left only one course open for Latrobe; since his professional ability had been challenged, he was obliged to use some form of skylight. Within a week Latrobe had contrived a new way of lighting the Hall of Representatives and admitted to Jefferson that he had "an embryo idea." Soon he made drawings to illustrate it. The major drawing, dated November 28 (1805), shows that he intended to substitute five roughly rectangular panel lights for each long ribbed skylight. This method reduced the number of joints and each pane of glass could be framed in wood on three sides, with the fourth left free for drainage. Jefferson was entirely satisfied, in fact elated, over the new proposal. "It would be beautiful [as the Halle aux Bleds] & more mild mode of lighting, because it would be an original & unique, & I knew that all experience had proved that a skylight of a single pane, bedded in wood, was easily secured from leaking." [90] Although problems never ceased to arise, the others that arose in 1805 were not as serious as the skylights.

The slow progress made on the capitol during the preceding three years

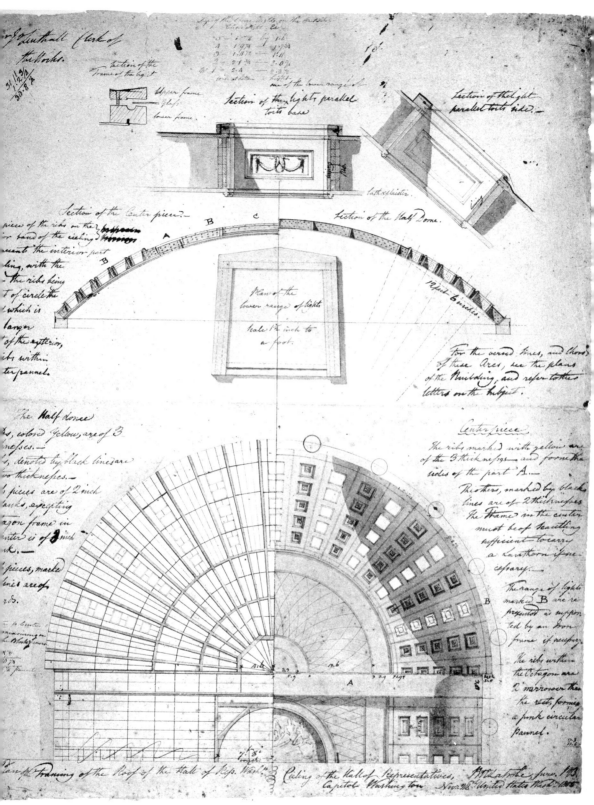

Benjamin Henry Latrobe. *Ceiling, Hall of Representatives*, U.S. Capitol, 1805.
Library of Congress

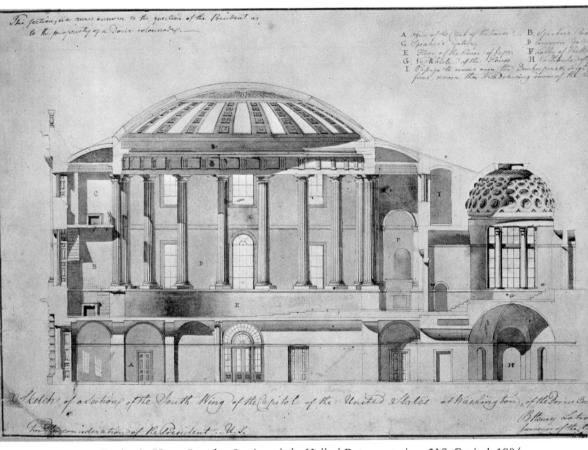

Benjamin Henry Latrobe. *Section of the Hall of Representatives,* U.S. Capitol, 1804.
Library of Congress

induced the representatives to urge Jefferson to employ more stringent measures toward ensuring the readiness of their hall for the session convening in
the autumn of 1806.[91] In his usual methodical way Jefferson sent an inquiry
to Latrobe asking when the internal order of columns would be completed,
when the entablature would be able to carry the roof, when the roof would
be ready for the sash lights, and how many men would be needed for each
job. He demanded frequent progress reports from Lenthall, even though he
himself might be absent from Washington when they came due. Latrobe's
prepared statement of expected progress on the building optimistically answered these requests.[92] The persistent legislators who frequently complained
that their quarters were not complete were the same who invariably made
late appropriations. The difficulties produced by their procrastination cannot
be overemphasized, particularly in a city of fragile existence, where doubt
continued about its validity as a seat of government. It was not until the

end of April in 1806 that funds became available for the new year so that men could be hired and materials bought. Considering that masons and carpenters were scarce and that many building materials could not be supplied locally, it would have been logical to make appropriations a year in advance; but this never occurred.

The reports submitted bimonthly by Lenthall at first showed steady progress on the part of the capitol referred to as the recess, that is, the section between the south wing and the central area reserved for a domed room. Against the best principles of building construction, each part of the capitol was erected separately, like modular additions of today but without the materials and techniques that would make it feasible. For example, the recess would have its foundations, arched vaults and vertical walls all built at a later stage than the wing, and the north wall had to be carried up its entire height without a solid masonry connection on either side. To the north side was the area reserved for the central building which had not even been designed. "It was without exception," said Latrobe, "the most desperate attempt at Walling I ever saw." [93] The recess was to serve as a ground floor entrance with the second floor having a vestibule as an ornamental public entrance to the Hall of Representatives. The vestibule gave Latrobe ample opportunity to display his decorative skill. His beautiful rendering of its dome with octagonal coffers and crowning oculus was much admired by all who passed through the vestibule to the monumental hall beyond. The masonry dome was designed with a chain of iron imbedded at its base for added strength, a precaution Michelangelo took for the great dome of St. Peter's.[94]

As the season wore on, Lenthall's progress reports showed that work was lagging. Jefferson learned from George Blagden, the master mason, that the lack of stonecutters held back the work. Jefferson tried to hire more men only to find that none were available. He sent an urgent request to Latrobe in Philadelphia,[95] but Latrobe could do no better even after threatening the master cutters there by telling them he would pay higher wages in Washington.[96] Advertisements in the papers of New York, Baltimore, and Albany brought forth no one. As a last resort Latrobe sent Robert Mills, his assistant, to Albany, where cutters were at work on additions to the state capitol.[97] By one means or another, twenty-four men were found by the middle of August in the northern cities, but only eight ever arrived in Washington, and two of these disappeared after receiving their expenses to the city.[98] Washington was regarded not only as providing little security in jobs, but also as having an unhealthy climate, and it was difficult to lure men to work there.

The more the work lagged the greater was Jefferson's concern. He told Latrobe that "price must not be regarded" in hiring laborers.[99] But stone did not arrive from the quarries, so that instead of hiring more men Lenthall reported, "They go away murmuring," and "will not be easily collected again when wanted." [100]

In October 1806 Lenthall was still struggling to cover the Hall of Representatives for the winter. He reported to Jefferson that Latrobe had directed him to place framing in the roof for some of the planned panel lights but to cover them for the present with roof sheathing and to insert at the center of the ceiling a lantern, or cupola, that would satisfactorily illuminate the interior.[101] If thought advisable at a later time, the cupola could be removed and the panel lights uncovered. Latrobe had suggested a cupola in August because he feared that the glass for the lights, which had been ordered from Germany in 1805, would not arrive in time. He arranged, therefore, to have Lenthall prepare a cupola as an emergency measure.[102] Jefferson apparently took little notice of this proposal of Latrobe's, since it was presumably temporary. This maneuver, under the guise of expedience, was actually an attempt by Latrobe to circumvent the president's insistence on a ceiling like that of the Halle aux Bleds. "The skylights in the dome of the Representatives chamber," Jefferson curtly replied to Lenthall, "were a part of the plan as settled and communicated to Mr. Latrobe. That the preparation for them has not been made, & the building now to be stopped for them, has been wrong." [103] The president's criticism brought forth a long explanation from Latrobe in which he introduced several ingenious reasons for preferring a cupola. He said that the frames for the panel lights were not prepared because the glass had not yet arrived. He remarked too that panel lights produced leakage, condensation, high cost, etc., and that, "so spangled a ceiling, giving an air of the highest gaiety, will I think destroy the solemnity that is appropriate to the object of the edifice." Turning his argument another way he said, "As all the Architecture is solid & projected, its whole effect will be lost by the destruction of *determinate shadows,* on which it depends," and he implied this would not be the case with cupola lighting. He ended his lengthy letter with a final slur on the original design by saying that the cupola will "exceedingly relieve the insipidity arising from the Squareness of these Masses." [104]

The natural consequence of his letter was to prolong the dispute. When Jefferson returned to Washington from Monticello in October, he observed that the cupola had been built, to which he had no objection, but the roof had not been framed for the panel lights. Furthermore, since Congress could not now expect to use the room during the ensuing session, there was no point in erecting the cupola. To smooth troubled waters Jefferson patiently and kindly said to Latrobe, "Be assured that in the whole of this business I have permitted no sentiment to arise unfriendly to you. I saw a departure from the plan & it was my duty to bring it back to its course. I ascribed it more to your absence than any thing else." [105]

With Latrobe back in Washington late in the year, construction proceeded steadily; Latrobe could report in November that half the roof had received its panel light frames, which had been hastily manufactured.[106] He presented a drawing of the capitol to the president, based upon a scaled plan made by his apprentice Robert Mills, perhaps as a gift of reconciliation. It represented the completed building with a central rotunda and a splendid eastern portico.[107]

In the year 1807 Congress made its annual appropriation early, and work began toward the end of March.[108] All went well until one Sunday morning in the middle of April a heavy rain began pelting the capitol unceasingly and continued until Monday afternoon. During this time much damage was done. Although the openings left for the glass panel lights had been covered with boards and the rest of the roof with sheet iron, the rain still blew fiercely into the cracks and gradually seeped through to the newly plastered ceiling. The plaster, not yet set, disintegrated, falling off in soft chunks from the soaked planks. The damage caused Latrobe to complain once again of the folly of using skylights. In discouraging tones he wrote to Jefferson, "The practical mischief which we have experienced in trusting to any thing but a solid continuous roof, in which leakage is impossible, and the dread of a repetition in the new wing of the scenes which the leakage of the old one has occasioned, together with all the considerations formerly laid before you, depresses my courage, & deprives me entirely of spirit in proceeding with the work." And he added, "Can[not] beauty still be sacrificed to the *certainty* of practical security?" [109]

To Latrobe's renewed appeal for a cupola Jefferson remained adamant, observing that "it is with real pain I oppose myself to your passion for the lanthern [cupola], and that in a matter of taste, I differ from a professor in his own art." To place a cupola over a dome was to Jefferson, the lover of classical architecture, an anachronism. "I have supposed the Cupola an Italian invention," he said, "produced by the introduction of bells in the churches, and one of the degeneracies of modern architecture." [110] Latrobe lost no time in answering. He admitted that his own "principles of good taste are rigid in Grecian architecture, . . . but the forms and the distribution of the Roman and Greek buildings which remain are in general inapplicable to the objects and uses of our public buildings." Yet the classical tradition had to be converted into functional modern architecture. "The question would be as to its [a cupola's] real or apparent utility in the place in which it appeared," he continued, "for nothing in the field of good taste, which ought never to be at warfare, with good sense, can be beautiful which appears useless or unmeaning." [111] His plaintive words went unheeded.

Once more, in August, a thirty-six-hour storm soaked the roof of the south wing causing many leaks and staining the ceiling, entablature, and colonnade. The trouble was in the joints between the sheets of iron roofing. The putty had cracked from frost and allowed the water to enter. Then the water flowed downward until it met an obstruction that raised the level of the water until it surged over the joints and poured into the room below. Angry over this latest catastrophe, Latrobe sat down and once more wrote an appeal to the president. "Of the total destruction of my individual reputation," he wrote,

> of the personal disgrace, I should incure after the censure implied by my reports, of my predecessors, I say nothing. . . But this one public consideration which seems to involve higher interests. Your administration, Sir, in respect to public works, has hitherto claims of gratitude & respect from the public, & from posterity. It is not flattery to say that you have planted the arts in your country. . . . I am not ashamed to say, that my pride is not a little flattered & my professional ambition roused, when I think that my grandchildren may at some future day read that after the turbulence of revolution & of faction which characterized the two first presidencies, — their ancestor was the instrument in *your* hands to decorate the tranquillity, the prosperity, & the happiness of your Government. Under this stimulus, I have acted; and I hope, . . . obtained an influence over the feelings & opinions of congress which without some fatal disaster or miscarriage would ensure the progress & completion of all your objects of which you can make me the instrument. I am now in despair. [112]

The architect offered two remedies: first, to erect the cupola and shingle the roof continuously; and second, to shingle only between the panel lights, leaving a furrow at each side of the glass framework to discharge the rain water. Naturally the president chose the latter as it was closer to the original design. And not surprisingly Latrobe replied that "I should have been the happiest man in the United States had you adopted my first instead of my second proposition. But you have not, & I must now pluck up the courage of a Man who marches to meet certain death at the breach, — and do my duty without inquiring the result of what it enjoins." [113]

In September 1807 Latrobe sent the president a design he had long been preparing that demonstrated his ideas on renovating the roof of the north

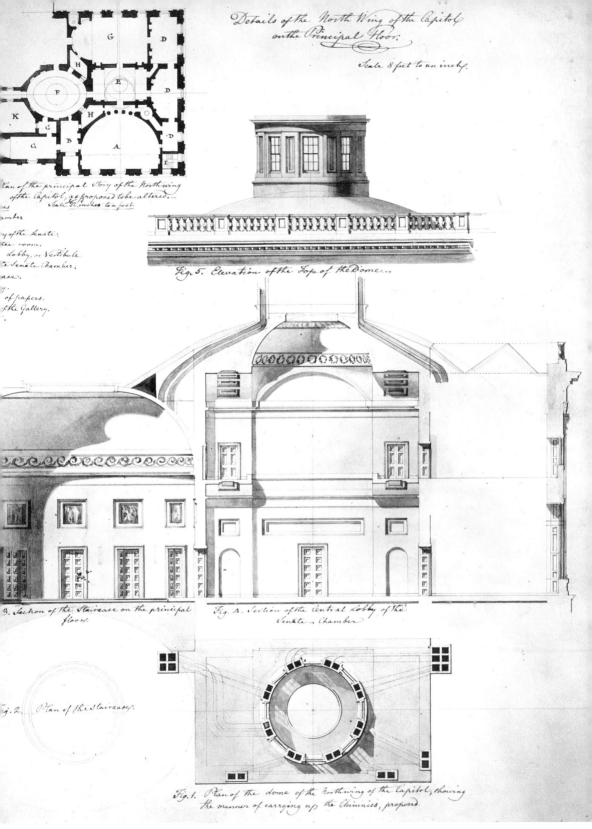

Details of the North Wing of the Capitol on the Principal Floor.

Scale 8 feet to an inch.

Plan of the principal Story of the North wing of the Capitol, as proposed to be altered.
Scale 32 inches to a foot.

Fig. 5. Elevation of the Top of the Dome.

3. Section of the Staircase on the principal floor.

Fig. 4. Section of the Central Lobby of the Senate Chamber.

Fig. 2. Plan of the Staircase.

Fig. 1. Plan of the dome of the north wing of the Capitol; shewing the manner of carrying up the Chimnies, proposed.

Benjamin Henry Latrobe. *Roof of the North Wing*, U.S. Capitol, September 1807.
Library of Congress

wing.[114] It was drawn with masterly technique and neatly tinted with water-colors to give it depth and beauty. Six figures showed the intricacies of the roof construction. By this visual means Latrobe hoped to persuade the president of the advantages in collecting all sixteen chimney flues over the Senate lobby ceiling and raising the stacks to protrude through the roof high enough to prevent "overblowing." The chimneys, gathered in a circle, were drawn in the shape of a cupola that Latrobe was quick to point out was "chosen a termination for the North [roof], which is consonant to my ideas for the South roof, from predilection rather than necessity." [115] Latrobe argued for a cupola, he said, because the previous irregular positions of the chimneys had caused many of the roof leaks complained of by the legislators. He noted also that the chimneys would enhance the building's appearance if they were gathered in this manner, instead of rising from the roof like separate stumps in a burned forest. Jefferson's succinct answer to these pleas again defeated Latrobe's plans. "I like well all your ideas," wrote the wily president, "except that of introducing a Cupola to cover the chimnies. The eye is so habituated to the sight of chimnies & connects with them the idea of utility so intimate-ly, that their natural ugliness loses much of it's impression. come out of the roof in whatever way they may, I do not think they will present such a difformity as a Cupola, so much increased by there being none on the other wing. indeed it is evident that a cupola on the one wing necessarily calls for a corresponding one on the other. I need not here repeat the objections to that." [116] Not waiting this time for a reply, Latrobe proceeded to carry out his chimney scheme, telling himself that if Jefferson would not agree to a cupola he could always cap the chimney area with a skylight.[117]

The Hall of Representatives, now open for the first time, gave much satisfaction to its users except in one unfortunate way — the acoustics. The irregular surfaces in the room echoed unceasingly, inhibiting debate, making confusion in place of clarity. An investigating committee was appointed headed by the Honorable W. W. Bibb,[118] and the opposition newspapers in the large cities broke out with exaggerated abuse of the new room, with which many of the legislators obviously agreed. Latrobe slyly noted that, although the room was acoustically poor, "yet they report the debates as regularly and minutely as if they caught every word." [119]

At least one part of the south wing was given very high praise: the coffered ceiling of the circular vestibule to the Hall of Representatives.

The acoustical committee, referred to above, decided to ask Latrobe for advice. He suggested hanging fringed, baize curtains between the columns in the hall to absorb part of the sound.[120] One of the architect's drawings (dated February 1808) shows two columns cut at their midsections with a curtain between hanging nearly to the socle upon which all the columns were raised. This plan was carried out and proved partially successful.[121]

In his March 1808 report to the president,[122] Latrobe gave the cost of each wing of the capitol revealing some surprising results. The cost of the north wing, which had been built under the direction of the commissioners, exceeded by fifty thousand dollars Latrobe's south wing that was constructed much more durably and with better materials. Where the north wing had wooden joists, beams and roofers, Latrobe used masonry vaults, and where the north wing had inferior sculptural work, Latrobe had employed skilled sculptors from Italy, and so on. Although this economy in construction should have sounded very pleasant to the legislative ear, it was overshadowed by the impropriety of having exceeded the appropriations by a substantial amount in 1807. The delicacy of this matter was never appreciated by Latrobe, who seemed to believe that common sense should dictate to Congress the need for completing the capitol and that it should praise his unstinting efforts in this direction. But Jefferson knew otherwise. "When I was obliged to state it [the deficit] to Congress," Jefferson remonstrated, "I was never more embarrassed than to select expressions, which, while they should not charge it on myself, should commit you as little as possible. as short as that message was, it was the subject of repeated consultations with the heads of departments separately, to help me to find expressions which should neither hurt your feelings or do you any injury." [123]

The final version of the appropriations bill, passed April 25, 1808,[124] included money for the deficit on the south wing, for masonry work on the interior of the north wing, and for finishing the interior of the south wing. Although passage of the bill showed that the congressmen were confident of the architect's abilities and good intentions, a note of discontent still lingered. Lest Latrobe should be rash in his victory over the payment of the south wing deficiency, the president immediately settled upon a plan for the very careful dispersal of funds for the ensuing year — a pay-as-you-go plan. This he communicated to Latrobe, with a warning: "You see, my Dear Sir, that the object of this cautious proceding is to prevent the possibility of a deficit of a single Dollar this year. The lesson of the last year has been a serious one, it has done you great injury, & has been much felt by myself — it was so contrary to the principles of our Government, which make the representatives of the people the sole arbitors of the public expense, and do not permit any work to be forced on them on a larger scale than their judgment deems adopted to the circumstances of the nation." [125]

Latrobe blamed the deficiency, in part, on an unsatisfactory method of keeping accounts. He was allowed no access to the account books and therefore did not know each year how much of the appropriation had been spent. Furthermore, Latrobe reminded Jefferson that during the entire previous year (1807) the president had urged him to complete the south wing at all costs. "I was expressly ordered to hire more workmen," Latrobe wrote, "& not on any account whatever to neglect to get the house ready by the Session." [126] In his reply Jefferson excused himself for not knowing the state of the appropriations when he requested more workmen for the capitol and quietly told Latrobe that opinions drawn from certain congressmen were not necessarily agreed to by him. At the end Jefferson added a generous word characteristic of his magnanimity: "I thank you for the opportunity given of making this explanation. If all, to whom falsehoods are carried for purposes of embroiling, had been equally just, I should have saved to them as well as myself the uneasinesses of a silent separation for causes never made known." [127]

As Jefferson's second presidential term ended, so did his influence on politics and the arts in America. In relation to the city of Washington and the construction of the capitol and the president's house, he became only an interested bystander. He continued to receive for many years at Monticello friendly, informative letters from Latrobe, but their combined efforts and frequent disagreements were of the past. "After laboring for 6 years here for the public," Latrobe wrote, "I find myself an object of suspicion & hatred, & persecuted by the most unmanly abuse in the public papers. To have injured my private fortune, and wasted the best years of my life in successful labors for the public avails me nothing. . . I should not complain, but for the last 10 years of my life I have never been mentioned in the papers but to be slandered, nor has one solitary paragraph ever hinted that I might possibly possess honesty, taste, or skill." [128] Jefferson's cheering reply was: "I think that the work [the capitol] when finished will be a durable and honorable monument of our infant republic, and will bear favorable comparison with the remains of the same kind of the ancient republics of Greece & Rome." [129]

With the change in presidency there also came a change in the relationship between the new president and the surveyor of public buildings. James Madison, though a friend of Latrobe, saw the latter's position as of less consequence, since he regarded buildings literally as piles of stone and mortar, and found them far less inspirational than did Jefferson. When the War of 1812 brought public building operations in Washington to a standstill, construction was replaced with destruction. The British burned several government buildings in 1814; the greatest damage was to the capitol, whose interior was entirely gutted. The stone walls remained standing and were reused in the new plans which Latrobe drew for the rejuvenated building. He now had the opportunity to make designs to his own taste for the interiors of both wings and the central building and had the last word, in opposition to the architectural principles of Jefferson. However, the former president, who saw the public will more clearly, was not surprised when he heard the news of Latrobe's resignation in 1817, brought about mainly by the constant controversy which had placed him at odds with many persons in Washington.

Yet in words which must have pleased Latrobe, since they came directly from the man who represented the best in American culture of his time and who had been so very instrumental in planning the city of Washington, Jefferson wrote of the capitol from his seclusion at Monticello saying that it was "the first temple dedicated to the sovereignty of the people, embellishing with Athenian taste the course of a nation looking far beyond the range of Athenian destinies." [130]

Notes

1. Lyman K. Butterfield, ed., *The Letters of Benjamin Rush*, 1 (Princeton: Princeton University Press, 1951): 245. Rush to George Morgan, Nov. 8, 1779.

2. William Tindall, *Origin and Government of the District of Columbia* (Washington: U.S. Government Printing Office, 1908), Appendix I.

3. Tindall, *Origin*, p. 41.

4. The delay may have been because preparations were still being made for the Constitutional Convention, at which decisions would be made having a strong bearing on this problem. Tindall, *Origin*, p. 51.

5. H. Paul Caemmerer, *The Life of Pierre Charles L'Enfant* (Washington: National Republic Pub. Co., 1950).

6. Caemmerer, *L'Enfant*, pp. 127-130.

7. Julian P. Boyd, ed., *The Papers of Thomas Jefferson*, 12 (Princeton: University Press, 1965): 163-208. Hereinafter cited as *Papers*.

8. Saul K. Padover, ed., *Thomas Jefferson and the National Capital* (Washington: U.S. Government Printing Office, 1946), pp. 30-36. Notes written Nov. 29, 1790.

9. Caemmerer, *L'Enfant*, p. 135.

10. Caemmerer, *L'Enfant*, p. 136.

11. Caemmerer, *L'Enfant*, p. 146.

12. Caemmerer, *L'Enfant*, p. 152.

13. Governor B. Randolph to D. Stuart, July 25, 1791. The plans were sent with this letter. National Archives, Record Group 42, Letters of the Commissioners.

14. Caemmerer, *L'Enfant*, pp. 175-176.

15. National Archives, Record Group 42, Letters of the Commissioners. Commissioners to Washington, Oct. 21, 1791.

16. John C. Fitzpatrick, ed., *Writings of Washington*, 31 (Washington: U.S. Government Printing Office, 1931-1944): 482-483. Washington to Jefferson, Feb. 22, 1792.

17. Padover, *Jefferson*, pp. 109-112. Jefferson to Thomas Johnson, Mar. 8, 1792.

18. Caemmerer, *L'Enfant*, pp. 214-215. Washington to L'Enfant, Feb. 28, 1792.

19. *Documentary History of the Construction and Development of the United States Capitol Building and Grounds* (Washington: U.S. Government Printing Office, 1904), p. 15.

20. Padover, *Jefferson*, p. 106. The premium notice was enclosed in a letter of Jefferson to commissioners, Mar. 6, 1792.

21. The entries received were as follows: Stephen Hallet, Jacob Small, James Diamond, Samuel Dobie, Samuel McIntire, Robert G. Lanphier, Charles Wintersmith, Andrew Mayfield Carshore, Philip Hart, and Abram Faw. See S. F. Kimball and Wells Bennett, "The Competition for the Federal Buildings, 1792-1793," *Journal*, of the American Institute of Architects, 7 (1919): 8-12, 98-102, 202-210, 355-361, 521-528; and 8 (1920): 117-124.

22. Little is known of Hallet's accomplishments before he came to America in about 1787. However, he was sufficiently well trained as an architect to be admitted to the class of *Architectes experts* in 1785. Architects of this

class were regarded as professionally just below the Academicians. National Archives, Record Group 42, Letters of the Commissioners. Commissioners to Hallet, July 17, 1792.

23. National Archives, Record Group 42, Letters of the Commissioners. Commissioners to Washington, July 19, 1792.

24. National Archives, Record Group 42, Letters of the Commissioners. Commissioners to Blodgett, Aug. 29, 1792.

25. Letters of the Commissioners. Commissioners to Jefferson, Oct. 14, 1792.

26. Letters of the Commissioners. Commissioners to Jefferson, Dec. 5, 1792; and commissioners to Thornton, Dec. 14, 1792.

27. Padover, *Jefferson,* p. 171. Jefferson to Daniel Carroll, Feb. 1, 1793.

28. Letters of the Commissioners. Washington to commissioners. Mar. 3, 1793.

29. Letters of the Commissioners. Commissioners to Hallet, Mar. 13, 1793.

30. Letters of the Commissioners. Commissioners to Thornton, Apr. 5, 1793.

31. Letters of the Commissioners. Commissioners to Thornton, Apr. 5, 1793.

32. Letters of the Commissioners. Commissioners to Washington, June 23, 1793.

33. Padover, *Jefferson,* pp. 181-183. Washington to Jefferson, June 30, 1793.

34. Letters of the Commissioners. Jefferson to Washington, July 17, 1793, enclosed in a letter of Washington to commissioners, July 25, 1793. The plans commented upon here apparently no longer exist.

35. Letters of the Commissioners. Washington to commissioners, July 25, 1793.

36. Letters of the Commissioners. Commissioners to Washington, Aug. 1, 1793.

37. Glenn Brown, *History of the United States Capitol,* 1 (Washington: U.S. Government Printing Office, 1900): 16.

38. National Archives, Record Group 42, Proceedings of the Commissioners, Sept. 23, 1793. Published in *Documentary History,* p. 29.

39. *Documentary History,* p. 31. Commissioners to Hallet, June 26, 1795.

40. Letters of the Commissioners. Commissioners to Washington, Jan. 2, 1795.

41. *Documentary History,* pp. 36-37. Washington to commissioners, Nov. 9, 1795.

42. *Documentary History,* pp. 37-38. Commissioners to Washington, Nov. 18, 1795.

43. *Documentary History,* pp. 77-78. Washington to commissioners, Feb. 15, 1797.

44. *Documentary History,* pp. 91-92. Fourth annual address of President John Adams, Nov. 22, 1800.

45. John Davis, *Travels of Four Years and a Half in the United States of America during 1798, 1799, 1800, 1801, and 1802,* ed. A. J. Morrison (New York: H. Holt and Co., 1909), p. 203.

46. Padover, *Jefferson,* pp. 210-211. Jefferson to commissioners, June 2, 1801.

47. *United States Statutes at Large,* 2 (Boston: Little, Brown & Co., c. 1855): 175.

48. *American State Papers, Class 10, Miscellaneous,* 1 (Washington: Gales and Seaton, 1834): 337-338. Munroe to Jefferson, Dec. 20, 1802.

49. Latrobe Papers, Maryland Historical Society, Baltimore. Letter of Latrobe to Jefferson, Mar. 28, 1798. For Latrobe see: Talbot Hamlin, *Benjamin Henry Latrobe* (New York: Oxford, 1955), and Paul F. Norton, bibliography of Latrobe in The American Association of Architectural Bibliographers, *Papers,* 9 (Charlottesville: The University Press of Virginia, 1972): 51-84.

50. Paul F. Norton, "Jefferson's Plans for Mothballing the Frigates," Proceedings of the United States Naval Institute, *82* (July 1956), 736-741.

51. *Annals of Congress* 7-2 (Washington: Gales and Seaton, 1851), p. 1601. Act of Mar. 3, 1803.

52. Thomas Law, *Observations on the intended canal in Washington city* (Washington: published anonymously, 1804).

53. Padover, *Jefferson,* pp. 296-297, two letters of Jefferson to Latrobe, Mar. 6, 1803.

54. Jefferson Papers, Library of Congress. Latrobe to Jefferson, Apr. 4, 1803.

55. Padover, *Jefferson,* pp. 340-341. Latrobe to Jefferson, Feb. 27, 1804.

56. Latrobe Papers, Library of Congress. Latrobe to Lenthall, May 6, 1803. A sketch in this letter shows a circular staircase and an open court to the west.

57. Jefferson Papers, Library of Congress. Jefferson to Latrobe, Apr. 23, 1803.

58. Jefferson Papers, Library of Congress. Reports from Lenthall, for Latrobe, to Jefferson beginning with the date of May 7, 1803, and continuing through the summer.

59. This letter is not known to exist. It is mentioned in a letter of Munroe to Jefferson, Aug. 31, 1803. Jefferson Papers, Library of Congress.

60. Jefferson Papers, Library of Congress. Munroe to Jefferson, Aug. 31, 1803.

61. Jefferson Papers, Library of Congress. Jefferson to Munroe, Sept. 12, 1806.

62. Thomas Moore, *The Poetical Works of Thomas Moore*, 2 (London, 1840): 297. Moore had resigned from a minor government service position in Bermuda and was meandering through the United States on his way to Canada and home to England. His stay in Washington lasted a little less than a week. Moore was critical of the Democratic (Jeffersonian) party, in all probability because of the imagined lack of ceremony observed by the president towards Moore's English friends, Mr. and Mrs. Anthony Merry, who were residing in Washington. Moore says that when Merry, the British minister to the United States, waited upon the president in full dress ready to deliver his credentials, Jefferson was very informally wearing slippers and Connemara stockings, which greatly upset Merry. The situation was soon reversed when Mrs. Merry began to wear gaudy costumes shockingly displaying more than the usual amount of flesh. She raised the eyebrows of diplomats on both sides of the Atlantic by insisting on her right to enter the dining room on the president's arm. See the letter from Moore to his mother, June 13, 1804, in Lord John Russell, ed., *Memoirs, Journal, and Correspondence of Thomas Moore*, 1 (London, 1853): 161; and the letter of Mrs. Smith to Mrs. Kirkpatrick, Jan. 23, 1804, in Gaillard Hunt, ed., *The First Forty Years of Washington Society* (New York, 1906), p. 45.

63. Jefferson Papers, Library of Congress. Latrobe to Jefferson, Nov. 30, 1803.

64. Latrobe Papers, Library of Congress. Latrobe to Lenthall, May 18, 1803. Latrobe was a partner in the iron business, and Mifflin the manager of the iron mill. The mill was run by surplus power from the city waterworks (designed by Latrobe).

65. Thomas Paine wrote an essay on yellow fever in 1806, but, although his perceptions were shrewd and close to the fact, he completely overlooked the deadly mosquito. John Melish in relating a conversation with Jefferson said, "The president observed, that it [Paine's essay] was one of the most sensible performances on that disease, that had come under his observation." John Melish, *Travels through the United States of America in the Years 1806, & 1807, and 1809, 1810, & 1811* (Belfast: J. Smyth, 1818), p. 150. Paine's essay was published in the appendix.

66. Jefferson's letter has not been preserved. It was enclosed with a letter to Munroe and is mentioned in Munroe's letter to Jefferson, Sept. 16, 1803. Jefferson Papers, Library of Congress.

67. Jefferson Papers, Library of Congress. Latrobe to Jefferson, Oct. 2, 1803.

68. Latrobe Papers, Library of Congress. Latrobe to Lenthall, Nov. 27, 1803.

69. Latrobe Papers, Library of Congress. Latrobe to Lenthall, Nov. 11, 1803.

70. Jefferson Papers, Library of Congress. Latrobe to Jefferson, Feb. 18, 1804.

71. Gabriel Vauthier, "La Halle au blé," *Bulletin of the Société de l'histoire de Paris et de l'Ile-de-France*, 53 (1926), 62ff; Dora Wiebenson, "The Two Domes of the Halle au Blé in Paris," *The Art Bulletin*, 55 (June 1973), 262-279.

72. Philibert de l'Orme, *Architecture de Philibert de l'Orme* (Rouen, 1648), bk. 10, pp. 279ff. Jefferson owned a copy of an earlier edition (Paris, 1576) that he acquired while in Paris. It was sold to Congress in 1815 for its new library.

73. *Papers*, 10: 443-454. Jefferson to Maria Cosway, Oct. 12, 1786.

74. Padover, *Jefferson*, pp. 340-341. Latrobe to Jefferson, Feb. 27, 1804.

75. Padover, *Jefferson*, pp. 342-343. Jefferson to Latrobe, Feb. 28, 1804.

76. Jefferson Papers, Library of Congress. Latrobe to Jefferson, Feb. 28, 1804.

77. Latrobe Papers, Library of Congress. Latrobe to Lenthall, Mar. 8, 1804.

78. Latrobe Papers, Library of Congress. Latrobe to Lenthall, Mar. 10, 1804.

79. Jefferson Papers, Library of Congress. Latrobe to Jefferson, Mar. 29, 1804. Latrobe owned a copy of James Stuart and Nicholas Revett, *The Antiquities of Athens*, 1 (London: 1762), in which the Tower of the Winds is described and illustrated. He probably owned

a copy of Giacomo Vignola, *Li cinque ordini di architettura et aguita de lopere* (Venezia, c. 1750), in which the Doric order of the Theater of Marcellus is illustrated.

80. Padover, *Jefferson,* pp. 344-345. Jefferson to Latrobe, Apr. 9, 1804.

81. Jefferson Papers, Library of Congress. Jefferson to Munroe, Aug. 4, 1804; and Jefferson to Latrobe, Oct. 5, 1804.

82. *Statutes,* 2:311.

83. Jefferson Papers, Library of Congress. Jefferson to Latrobe, Jan. 26, 1805.

84. R. C. Garlick, *Philip Mazzei, Friend of Jefferson* (Baltimore: Johns Hopkins Press, 1933), pp. 150-153. Mazzei to Latrobe, Sept. 12, 1805.

85. Jefferson Papers, Library of Congress. Jefferson to Lenthall, May 5, 1805.

86. Latrobe Papers, Library of Congress. Latrobe to Lenthall, May 3, 1805.

87. Latrobe Papers, Library of Congress. Latrobe to Lenthall, May 11, 1805.

88. Jefferson Papers, Library of Congress. Latrobe to Jefferson, Aug. 31, 1805.

89. Jefferson Papers, Library of Congress. Jefferson to Latrobe, Sept. 8, 1805.

90. Jefferson Papers, Library of Congress. Jefferson to Latrobe, Oct. 31, 1806.

91. Jefferson Papers, Library of Congress. Jefferson to Latrobe and Lenthall, Apr. 20, 1806.

92. Jefferson Papers, Library of Congress. Statement of the probable progress of work on the south wing of the capitol during the season of 1806, Mar. 12, 1806.

93. Jefferson Papers, Library of Congress. Latrobe to Jefferson, Aug. 15, 1806.

94. Latrobe Papers, Library of Congress. Latrobe to Lenthall, June 25, 1806.

95. Jefferson Papers, Library of Congress. Jefferson to Latrobe, July 1, 1806.

96. Latrobe Papers, Library of Congress. Latrobe to Lenthall, July 3, 1806. Also Jefferson Papers, Library of Congress. Latrobe to Jefferson, July 5, 1806.

97. Latrobe Papers, Library of Congress. Latrobe to Lenthall, July 19, 1806.

98. Jefferson Papers, Library of Congress. Latrobe to Jefferson, Aug. 15, 1806.

99. Jefferson Papers, Library of Congress. Jefferson to Latrobe, July 18, 1806.

100. Jefferson Papers, Library of Congress. Lenthall to Jefferson, Aug. 1, 1806.

101. Jefferson Papers, Library of Congress. Lenthall to Jefferson, Oct. 20, 1806.

102. Jefferson Papers, Library of Congress. Latrobe to Jefferson, Aug. 27, 1806.

103. Padover, *Jefferson,* pp. 371-372. Jefferson to Lenthall, Oct. 21, 1806.

104. Latrobe Papers, Library of Congress. Latrobe to Jefferson, Oct. 29, 1806.

105. Jefferson Papers, Library of Congress. Jefferson to Latrobe, Oct. 31, 1806.

106. Jefferson Papers, Library of Congress. Latrobe to Jefferson, Nov. 11, 1806.

107. Latrobe Papers, Library of Congress. Latrobe to Lenthall, Sept. 1, 1806. Also Jefferson Papers, Library of Congress. Latrobe to Jefferson, Nov. 17, 1806.

108. *Documentary History,* pp. 128-131. An act making appropriations for the south wing, etc., approved Mar. 3, 1807. Jefferson Papers, Library of Congress. Latrobe to Jefferson, Mar. 23, 1807.

109. Jefferson Papers, Library of Congress. Latrobe to Jefferson, Apr. 14, 1807.

110. Padover, *Jefferson,* pp. 386-387. Jefferson to Latrobe, Apr. 22, 1807.

111. Padover, *Jefferson,* pp. 389-392. Latrobe to Jefferson, May 21, 1807.

112. Padover, *Jefferson,* pp. 394-396. Latrobe to Jefferson, Aug. 13, 1807.

113. Jefferson Papers, Library of Congress. Latrobe to Jefferson, Aug. 21, 1807.

114. Jefferson Papers, Library of Congress. Latrobe to Jefferson, Sept. 14, 1807.

115. Jefferson Papers, Library of Congress. Latrobe to Jefferson, Sept. 14, 1807.

116. Jefferson Papers, Library of Congress. Jefferson to Latrobe, Sept. 20, 1807.

117. Jefferson Papers, Library of Congress. Latrobe to Jefferson, Sept. 24, 1807.

118. Latrobe Papers, Maryland Historical Society. Latrobe to Hon. W. W. Bibb, Dec. 14, 1807.

119. Latrobe Papers, Library of Congress. Latrobe to Lenthall, Nov. 21, 1807.

120. Latrobe Papers, Maryland Historical Society. Latrobe to Hon. William Stedman, Jan. 5, 1808. In his report to Jefferson, Mar. 23, 1808, in *Annals of Congress* 10-1 (Washing-

ton: Gales and Seaton, 1851), pp. 2750-2759, Latrobe analyzed the acoustical difficulties.

121. Latrobe Papers, Maryland Historical Society. Latrobe to John Kae, Jan. 22, 1808. The curtains had not yet arrived, so Latrobe wrote to the supplier to rush the order. The advantages of the curtains are discussed in a letter of Latrobe to Colonel William Duane, Feb. 29, 1808, in the Latrobe Papers, Maryland Historical Society.

122. *Annals* 10-1, pp. 2750-2759.

123. Jefferson Papers, Library of Congress. Jefferson to Latrobe, Mar. 15, 1808.

124. *Statutes,* 2: 499. "An act to make good a deficit in the appropriation of eighteen hundred and seven, for completing the public buildings, and for other purposes." Approved Apr. 25, 1808.

125. Padover, *Jefferson,* pp. 414-416. Jefferson to Latrobe, Apr. 26, 1808.

126. Padover, *Jefferson,* pp. 420-427. Latrobe to Jefferson, May 23, 1808.

127. Padover, *Jefferson,* pp. 429-432. Jefferson to Latrobe, June 2, 1808.

128. Latrobe Papers, Library of Congress. Latrobe to Jefferson, Aug. 28, 1809.

129. Padover, *Jefferson,* pp. 462-463. Jefferson to Latrobe, Oct. 10, 1809.

130. Padover, *Jefferson,* pp. 470-471. Jefferson to Latrobe, July 12, 1812.

"A Peep into Elysium"

GEORGE GREEN SHACKELFORD

Foreword

JEFFERSON'S LIFE IS THREADED WITH THE STRANDS OF ITALIAN CULTURE. His earliest education in the classics was undoubtedly the foundation and the stimulus of this interest, but it manifests itself in his study of the language; his friendship with Philip Mazzei, the Tuscan intellectual who became his neighbor; his taste in music — Pergolesi, Boccherini, Vivaldi and Clementi are indexed in his library — and above all in the architecture of Andrea Palladio.

Before the Revolution, Mazzei became a part of Jefferson's circle of friends in Virginia and so charmed his host during a visit to Monticello that Jefferson gave him a tract of two thousand acres bordering his own estate. In Mazzei, Jefferson found a most congenial neighbor and friend, who shared his taste in art, music, literature and the cultivation of the grape. In coming to America, Mazzei had brought with him a number of Tuscan laborers, and the two gentlemen farmers pursued their interest in viticulture together. The Virginian's hope of producing an acceptable Italian wine in his native Albemarle County dramatizes Jefferson's strong interest in Mediterranean culture and in Italy particularly, and is the background to Professor Shackelford's account of the American minister's brief visit to Italy in 1787. That visit, a "peep into Elysium," has always frustrated Jeffersonian scholars because its brevity did not allow Jefferson to adequately see and record his responses to the architecture, ancient culture and art which so fascinated him.

In 1785, Jefferson had written to John Banister, Jr., advising him to pursue his studies in Rome. "The advantages of Rome are the acquiring a local knowledge of a spot so classical and so celebrated; the acquiring the true pronunciation of the latin language; the acquiring a just taste in the fine arts, more particularly those of painting, sculpture, architecture, and music." In other words, the resources of Rome could provide the essentials of a European education superior to any other place. Eventually, however, Rome would not be a part of Jefferson's own travels in pursuit of education.

Professor Shackelford has carefully sifted the letters, account books and traveler's guides to reconstruct the two weeks of the Italian trip. Disconcerting gaps in the record have been filled by carefully pinpointing the location of art collections, architecture and ruins along Jefferson's itinerary, and Professor Shackelford provides possibilities, where Jefferson's notes are vague or non-existent, for the Virginian's excursions into the Italian culture.

When he returned to Paris, Jefferson wrote his friend Maria Cosway, who had been born in Florence, to explain that time and distance had curtailed his travels in 'Elysium.' "Was not this provoking?" he complained, and students ever since have agreed, but now with some mitigation as a result of Professor Shackelford's researches presented here.

WILLIAM HOWARD ADAMS

"A Peep into Elysium"

GEORGE GREEN SHACKELFORD

THOMAS JEFFERSON'S APPRECIATION OF THE FINE ARTS DEPENDED ON associations with other persons, on books and on personal observation. As a young man at Williamsburg in the 1760s he was fortunate in the companionship of the cultivated royal governor of Virginia, Francis Fauquier, at whose table he enjoyed "rational and philosophical conversation," and with whom he would afterward join in impromptu musical performances.[1] In the 1770s, he became a firm friend of Charles Bellini, who taught Italian at the College of William and Mary, the enthusiastic Florentine addressing the future author of the Declaration of Independence as "My dearest Thomas."[2] Both men did much to mold Jefferson's taste. Although Jefferson, the provincial, could not then embark on a grand tour, he had recourse to books in which he studied the monuments of Roman civilization that led cultivated Europeans to Italy.

In 1787, during his term as minister to France, Jefferson did travel briefly in Italy. He then satisfied his most immediate goal of learning about rice cultivation and milling in the plain of the Po. But he was also able to savor, if hastily, some of the cultural glories of northern Italy — and to further his knowledge of those subjects in which, as he wrote to Bellini, Europeans excelled: "architecture, sculpture, painting [and] music."[3] But even as an untraveled provincial, Jefferson already had declared a cultural allegiance to Italy. As the marquis de Chastellux observed in 1782, Jefferson called his home "Monticello, . . . a name which bespeaks its owner's attachment to the language of Italy and above all the Fine Arts, of which Italy was the cradle and is still the resort."[4] Even though he had learned some Italian with Bellini's help, Jefferson relied mostly on English books for his knowledge of the ancient world and of those parts of its heritage which constituted the basis for the eighteenth century's conception of what was chaste and correct.

We do not know the name of the first architectural book Jefferson bought when he was a student of the College of William and Mary,[5] but one book which he almost certainly possessed as well as read between 1770 and 1781 was probably the source of most of what he ever knew about the art of the ancients. This was Joseph Spence's *Polymetis: or An Enquiry Concerning the Agreement Between the Works of the Roman Poets and the Remains of the Ancient Artists.* As a young man in his thirties, Jefferson must have studied carefully its forty-one folio-size illustrations by L. B. Boitard.[6] Beyond doubt, he relied on these illustrations and on Bellini's advice when he compiled the list[7] of statuary and paintings of which he desired copies for Monticello. The list was mostly complete by 1781, though he later added a few items, and from it one may fairly conclude that he desired to place in his house for decorative and didactic purposes a dozen or so English engravings and about ten six-by-twelve-foot canvases copied from masterpieces, all but one of which were Italian. He also wished to place there about a dozen statues, ranging from larger than life-size pieces to two-foot statuettes by sculptors of the Greek or Roman world or of the Italian Renaissance. He carefully noted his friend Bellini's advice that "historical paintings on canvass" of that size cost £15 sterling if copied by a "good hand." Jefferson specified terra cotta as the medium for some of the statues, and one can only speculate whether he desired plaster or marble copies of the others. From their coincident dimensions, it appears that he intended to pair many of the statues, giving an Italian arrangement to his Italian-named house.

Though the pictures Jefferson specified did not include any landscapes, his notation of Bellini's advice on the cost of "fresco painting of landscapes or architecture" makes it clear that he toyed with the idea of decorating Monticello with wall paintings. Because he specified the inclusion of engravings by Francis Hayman, as well as those by William Hogarth, we are tempted to surmise that he appreciated Hayman's capabilities as a landscapist as well as a depictor of characters like Falstaff and an illustrator of works by Milton, Don Quixote and Shakespeare.[8] At least two oil paintings cannot be identified today: a "Sacrifice of Iphigenia" and a "History of Seleucus giving his beloved wife Stratonice to his only son Seleucus who languished for her."[9]

One work, entitled "Curtius leaping into the gulph" or chasm, is, in the original, a Roman sculpture in high relief in the Borghese Gallery at Rome. Jefferson desired a copy of Pier Francesco Mola's rendering of this scene in oils, but no such work is cited in studies of that artist.[10] The others, however, were well-known masterpieces then to be found in London, Florence or

Rome. "St. Paul preaching at Athens" refers to one of the ten Flemish tapestries designed by Raphael for occasional use in the Sistine Chapel but now in the Pinacoteca Vaticana, Rome. Raphael's cartoon for this had been bought in 1623 by Charles, Prince of Wales, and is now exhibited in the Victoria and Albert Museum, London.[11] Probably Jefferson was acquainted with it from English engravings after the cartoon. By "St. Ignatius at prayer," Jefferson probably meant to refer to the seventeenth-century work by Rubens which is usually called *The Miracle of St. Ignatius* and which is in the church of St. Ambrosio at Genoa.[12] "Jeptha meeting his daughter" is an eighteenth-century painting by Sebastiano Ricci which is now in the Kress Collection at the University of Pennsylvania.[13] "Diana Venatrix," a painting by Domenichino, has been since 1620 one of the most important pieces in the Borghese Gallery at Rome.[14] "Belissarius by Salvator Rosa" was probably at Rome in Jefferson's day.[15] The same artist may have painted other versions of "the Prodigal Son," but one was sold at Paris in 1776. Jefferson may have been confused as to which artist painted this popular subject.[16] Of the six versions of "Susanna and the two Elders," which is one of the greatest works of Rubens, there is one of these seventeenth-century masterpieces in the Borghese Gallery, Rome.[17]

Three statues were to be copied in "terra cotta." "Hercules and Antaeus," more commonly called *Hercules Strangling Antaeus,* is in the original a 17¾-inch-high bronze by the fifteenth-century sculptor Antonio Pollaiuolo, which is now in the Bargello National Museum, Florence.[18] "The two wrestlers" is a Greek masterpiece of the fourth-century, now in the Uffizi Gallery, Florence.[19] "The Rape of the Sabines (3 figures)" refers to the 1583 work in marble by Giambologna which is in the Loggia de' Lanzi, Florence.[20] The "Messenger pulling out a thorn," better known as the *Spinario,* is in the original a bronze of little less than three feet in height, which is now in the Palazzo dei Conservatori, Rome.[21] The "Roman slave whetting his knife" is a celebrated statue known as the *Knife Grinder.* This third-century B.C. marble copy of a work from Pergamon was found at Rome in the fifteenth century and is now in the Uffizi Gallery, Florence.[22]

The eight remaining statues on Jefferson's list were approximately life-size. The "Venus of [the] Medicis" is the marble from Hadrian's villa at Tivoli which was brought to Florence in 1680 and is now in the Uffizi Gallery.[23] The "Hercules Farnese" was in Rome in Jefferson's day, but it is now in the National Museum at Naples.[24] The famous "Apollo Belvedere" is a fourth-century Roman marble copy from a lost Greek original. Pope Julius II acquired the copy at the beginning of the sixteenth century, and it is now in the Museo Pio Clementino of the Vatican.[25] "Antinous" was located by Jefferson at Florence. He probably meant to refer to the statue then being renamed *Meleager,* which was then at Rome and which is now in the Capitoline Museum; [26] but one cannot be sure. "The Dancing Faunus" is also called the *Dancing Satyr.* It is a marble copied from a lost bronze and is in the Villa Borghese, Rome.[27] "The Gladiator at Montalto" almost certainly refers to that commonly known as the *Borghese Warrior* or *Fighting Gladiator* which was copied from a lost original in the Imperial Villa at Anzio and signed by Agasias. Prince Camillo Borghese sold the copy to Napoleon in 1806, and it is now in the Louvre Museum, Paris.[28] The "Myrmillo expiring" is better known as the *Dying Gaul* or the *Dying Gladiator.* A Myrmillo was a special kind of gladiator, armed with a sword, shield and helmet bearing a fish *(mormylos)* design. It is now in the Capitoline Museum, Rome.[29] "The Gladiator reposing himself after the engagement (companion of the former)" is more commonly called *The Boxer.* It was signed by Appolonius, son of Nestor, and is now in the Museo delle Terme at Rome.[30]

Certainly Jefferson was inspired by some of the greatest works of painting and sculpture that have survived from antiquity and the Renaissance. Fiske Kimball in *Thomas Jefferson, Architect* [31] was the first to devote much attention to Jefferson's profound interest in all the fine arts. And though many writers have hailed Jefferson as the American Palladio, responsible for introducing his countrymen to the principles of architectural neoclassicism, it was not until the 1940s that it was discovered what Italian buildings he had in fact seen.[32] Nor did historians often note which persons had helped form Jefferson's taste, though these included his architectural colleague, Charles-Louis Clérisseau; the artists, John Trumbull and Maria Cosway; Louis XVI's *directeur des bâtiments,* comte d'Angiviller; Baron Friedrich Melchior Grimm, the art and music critic; and talented connoisseurs like Fauquier in Williamsburg and Mme de Tott in Paris.[33] These people and others prepared Jefferson for what he was to see and to think of the fine arts in Italy. Yet, Jefferson "despised the artificial canons of criticism," saying that "when I have read a work in prose or poetry, or seen a painting, a statue, etc., I have only asked myself whether it gives me pleasure, whether it is animating, interesting, attaching? If it is, it is good for these reasons." [34]

One of those who most shaped his artistic taste was Mrs. Maria Cosway, an Anglo-Italian beauty of London and Paris society in the 1780s. One can only speculate on the nature of their friendship, but there is no doubt that they shared interests in architecture, education, music, nature, and especially painting. He practiced his Italian on her, and he sometimes was able to persuade her to leave her often frenetic social life and leisurely examine the paintings located in the royal palaces in and about Paris. Doubtless she spoke to him on such occasions about the paintings in Florence, where she had grown up and to whose academy she had been elected as a youthful painter, or about those in Turin, where she had spent a year before coming to London in the early 1770s.[35]

There was some talk of creating a public art gallery in Paris in Jefferson's day, although entrée to the royal collections was easy for gentlemen to obtain. He must have found the biennial exhibitions of paintings at the Salons [36] an inadequate substitute for those pictures in Italy which he had marked for special attention while in America, but he relished the opportunity to see original works of art. In his *Notes on the State of Virginia*, Jefferson had written that part of the commonwealth's plan for general education was to establish "a public library and gallery, by laying out a certain sum annually in books, paintings and statues." [37] In fact, however, only Jefferson seems seriously to have contemplated an art gallery for Virginia, and the legislative bill for a research library and gallery died a-borning.[38] Later, he was more successful in his patronage of the federal capital and in 1815 he sold his library to the fledgling Library of Congress. Benjamin Latrobe wrote to Jefferson in 1807, "It is not flattery to say that you have planted the arts in your country. The works already in this city are monuments to your judgement and of your zeal and taste. The first sculpture that adorned an American public building perpetuates your love and protection of the arts." [39]

Within the concept that the fine arts possess an essential unity, Jefferson's interest in sculpture and painting is as important as his more familiar concern with architecture. There has been general approbation of his interest in and influence on the latter, and no one seems to have condemned Jefferson either for having bastardized neoclassicism or for having imprisoned Americans in architectural patterns two millenia out-of-date and a hemisphere removed from their place of origin. Neoclassicism was the mode of all the fine arts in Jefferson's day, and he preferred it almost to the exclusion of its medieval, baroque, and Georgian predecessors. Like his contemporaries, he believed that his age was harmoniously attuned both to the Renaissance and to the classical era. Remarkably, many of those who accept Jefferson's taste in architecture condemn his taste in painting and sculpture, although according to the standards of his time the three arts were inseparable. They castigate him for his occasional excessive praise for neoclassical paintings that were the rage everywhere in the Western world and for his alleged reference to "the old red faded things of Rubens." [40]

At least once, Jefferson backed down when an artistic friend, Mme de Tott, showed him the error of his extravagant praise.[41] Jefferson's taste, however,

241

was more catholic than is generally recognized: he thought enough of Rubens to display at Monticello a copy of his *Diogenes and His Lantern,* and he also possessed three copies of works by Raphael. Of Jefferson's paintings, four of the forty-six portraits, four of the twenty-seven biblical scenes and one of the fifteen mythological scenes have been recovered and hung in the parlor of Monticello, where once there were forty-eight paintings. Within the standards of his day, in the young United States of America, Jefferson was a considerable art collector, even though, except for portraits, few of his paintings were originals. Then, as now, the greatest works of the old masters were in museums or royal collections; only copies were available to the general public. When he could obtain an original by a good contemporary, such as Duplessis, the Peales, Houdon, Benjamin West, or Trumbull, he did so. Fiske Kimball, the former director of the Philadelphia Museum of Art, declared that Jefferson was "the first American connoisseur and patron of the arts." [42]

Jefferson himself observed that his appreciation of the fine arts was acquired more through books than by firsthand observation.[43] His biographers have often noted his indebtedness to architectural and gardening books, but none have alluded to the guidebooks that he used in European cities, not merely to get about from one place to another but as sources of information about noted buildings and art collections. The Virginia bibliophile kept these guidebooks in his library and later lent them to L'Enfant for his plans of the city of Washington.[44] By referring to these and to contemporary and near-contemporary travelers' accounts, we can describe many of the monuments and paintings that Jefferson saw in northern Italy and hazard some speculation upon their influence on his mature taste in the fine arts. Because he relied so heavily on his three principal Italian guidebooks, *Guide pour le voyage d'Italie en poste,*[45] *Nouva guida di Milano,*[46] and *Beautés de Génes,*[47] he did not himself make notes on much more than agricultural, financial, and utilitarian matters during his hurried Italian tour. At its conclusion, he had so strained his constitution that he suffered a spell of sickness which, after his official correspondence was done, long left him unable to write detailed letters to his familiars about what he had seen during what he told Maria Cosway had been only "a Peep . . . into Elysium."[48]

Alas! Jefferson never went to Rome [49] to improve his concept of what was chaste and correct; nor did he go to Venice or Vicenza to see a building designed by Palladio. Thomas Jefferson gained his only first-hand knowledge of Italy in the spring of 1787 when he traveled through the Piedmontese provinces of the king of Sardinia, the Austrian duchy of Milan, and the Republic of Genoa. As minister resident at Paris and former treaty commissioner, he had unsuccessfully asked for authority from Congress to go there officially to survey opportunities for American commerce. Although Secretary for Foreign Affairs John Jay could grant him leave only to travel for his health, the minister comported himself as though his status as a commercial agent had been approved.[50] He imposed upon himself a strict timetable and limited itinerary from which he did not depart in order to gratify his architectural and artistic interests.[51]

In planning his journey from Nice to Turin to Milan to Genoa and back to Nice, Jefferson was prepared for the discomfort, noise, dirt, and disorder along the way. He employed a valet named Petitjean for the whole trip, and he hired additional local valets and messenger boys to show him the lay of the land in strange cities.[52] Jefferson, ever a humane man, steeled himself in advance against being "persecuted" by the sound of the "cruel whip of the postillion." [53] There were, however, compensations for such disagreeable sensations, even though he customarily made light of his sightseeing visits to palaces, art galleries, and museums. In a splendid letter to Lafayette, he welcomed the chance to "see what I have never seen before and shall never see again. In the great cities, I go to see what travelers think alone worthy of being seen; but I make a job of it, and generally gulp it all down in a day." [54]

When Jefferson later suggested a seven-month continental itinerary for Thomas Mann Randolph, Jr., he recommended spending most of the time in and about the great cities: after prolonged study in the vicinity of Paris, a month each at Rome and Naples; two weeks at Florence; a week each at Geneva, Genoa, Milan, and Turin; four days each at Bordeaux and Marseilles; three days each at Leghorn and Dijon; two days each at Lyons, Nantes, and Nîmes; and one day each at Nice and Pisa.[55] He himself was never to go east of Milan or south of Genoa; at both he spent less time than he wished.

When Jefferson crossed the Var River from France into the kingdom of Sardinia on April 10, 1787, he had been absent from Paris for six weeks.[56] It is likely that he did not secure his visas until he determined at Marseilles that he would go to Italy. In preparation for this eventuality, however, he had arranged with the Parisian banker Ferdinand Grand for a letter of credit and a list of bankers on whom he might draw along his way.[57] He had not sought letters of introduction from the Sardinian ambassador to the court of Versailles, the conte di Scarnafis, an unrelenting advocate of absolutism who had been haughty in transmitting his government's refusal to enter into a commercial treaty.[58] However, Jefferson had secured a few letters of scholarly introduction from the philosophical abbés Arnoux and Chalut,[59] from his one-time Albemarle neighbor Filippo Mazzei, who was then at Paris seeing through the press his *Recherches sur les Etats-Unis*,[60] and from a Milanese gentleman named Gaudenzio Clerici, whom Jefferson may have met in America and who claimed friendship with David Ramsay, the South Carolina botanist and historian. More dilettante than *philosophe,* Clerici was a cousin of a prominent noble family of Milan. In vain, he urged the American minister leisurely to enjoy "the serenity and mildness of the Italian climate [which made that country] the Garden of Europe." Jefferson may have not been aware of the younger man's interesting and important associations, since he did not attempt to see Clerici when passing through the latter's countryside along the Ticino between Novara and Milan. In later years, however, he guided to Clerici's door a number of young Americans on their grand tour.[61]

When Jefferson discovered that he could not learn about Italian rice at Marseilles,[62] he determined to travel in Italy for the briefest period necessary to accomplish that purpose. Ever a discriminating bibliophile, Jefferson was to buy maps and guidebooks of Turin, Milan, and Genoa, both for immediate use and for subsequent rumination.[63] The American diplomat proceeded to the Piedmontese port of Nice, whence he arranged to cross the Maritime Alps through the Tende Pass and then to descend the plain of the Po as far as the rice fields situated in the great triangle between Vercelli, Milan, and Pavia.[64]

While refreshing himself at Nice, Jefferson visited the royal botanical garden and called upon some of the persons to whom he carried letters of introduction.[65] The American diplomat declared that Nice was handsome, possessed good accommodations, and enjoyed a "superb" climate. The rather straitlaced Virginian lamented that its society was "gay and dissipated," but he may have told himself that such was the natural consequence of absolutism in the kingdom of Sardinia.

Learning that the snows were "not yet enough melted to allow carriages to pass," Jefferson engaged at Nice mules and muleteers to convey him, his valet, and his portmanteau through the Tende Pass. The road through the pass was then considered an engineering marvel, by whose sixty-nine *lacets,* or hairpin curves, one ascended to the 4,230-foot-high Col de Braus.[66] In good weather, Jefferson assured Maria Cosway, "You may go in your chariot in full trot from Nice to Turin, as if there were no mountain,"[67] using the system of engaging successive teams of horses to draw one's chaise from one way station, or post, to the next about ten miles distant. He noted, and perhaps ate as a local delicacy, the speckled trout of the River Roya in its stretches just below the great Gorge of Saorgo. "Further on," Jefferson wrote, "we come to the Château of Saorgo, where a scene is presented, the most singular and picturesque I ever saw. The castle and village seem hanging to a cloud in front. On the right is a mountain cloven through to let pass a gurgling stream; on the left a river over which is thrown a magnificent bridge. The whole form a bason, the sides of which are shagged with rocks, olive trees, vines, herds, etc." [68] He went so far as to declare to Mrs. Cosway, "I insist on your painting it." [69] The château was a fortresslike castle "in the Oriental style"; in 1792, the French destroyed it and its adjacent fortified barracks. In its wild, romantic setting the château must have resembled a Shangri-la, set on an irregular triangular platform whose three nearly equal sides were about seventy yards in length. [70] It is tempting to give to Maria Cosway's painting of a frowning structure situated on roseate cliffs above a rocky mountain torrent the title *The Château of Saorgo*. [71]

Once he reached the plain of the Po, the flat countryside permitted Jefferson to travel swiftly in a two-horse carriage with a postillion and an extra horse. During the four changes of post horses between Cuneo and Turin, he jotted down impressions of the rich agricultural lands through which he passed. [72] He lunched at Racconigi, the site of the palazzo of the Carignano branch of the house of Savoy, whose park and gardens have been attributed to Louis XIV's landscape architect, André Le Nôtre. The façade of the edifice is about a hundred yards from the village and separated from the latter only by a *grille,* but Jefferson did not record entering either the grounds or the palazzo, famous for its great soaring rococo hall. Not far from Racconigi he crossed the Po where it was about fifty yards wide on a wooden roadway built on "swinging batteaux" that were moored to the river bank by cables supported at their midsection by canoes. Another American traveler remarked that the canoes used on the Po near Turin were dugouts, just like the canoes of the North American Indians; it is curious that Jefferson, a collector of Indian artifacts and recorder of their languages and customs, did not make a similar observation. [73]

Jefferson arrived at Turin in the late afternoon of April 16 and took lodgings at the Hôtel d'Angleterre for what proved to be a four-night stay. He must have followed local custom by joining at common table about a dozen persons for a *table d'hôte* dinner. Unfortunately, the American epicure commented only on the wines of the region, a "red wine of Nebiule," similar to the present-day Fraisi, which he found so "pleasing" that he noted, "It is about as sweet as the silky Madiera, as astringent on the palate as Bordeaux, and as brisk as Champagne." He also noted favorably the "thick and strong" red wine of Monferrato, similar to today's Dolcetti. [74]

Once Jefferson determined that he could not obtain at Turin the desired information about rice, he felt free to devote several days to cultivating his appreciation of the history and fine arts of Piedmont, of which Maria Cosway surely had told him. On the first and second nights of his visit, he attended

Bernardo Bellotto. *Vedute dell'antico ponte sul Po a Torino*. Galleria Sabauda, Turin

comedies at what may have been the semiprivate theater of the duca di Carignano. He devoted the daylight hours of April 17 and 18 so completely to sightseeing that he left little time for business.[75] Former Treaty Commissioner Jefferson was painfully aware that the king of Sardinia had rebuffed America's invitation to negotiate a treaty of amity and commerce, saying that he would not consider such a move until U.S.-Sardianian trade through Nice had expanded enough to make it mutually advantageous.[76] At Turin, Jefferson bought £13.10 worth of "maps," which certainly included the guidebook *Italie en poste* and perhaps Carlo Bianci's *Nuova guida di Milano,* too.[77]

In seeing the sights of Turin, it was conventional to devote a morning to the Palazzo Reale, the Duomo, the adjacent royal chapel of the Santissima Sindone, and the church of San Lorenzo.[78] Characteristically, Jefferson did not record his sensations upon viewing these. One could reluctantly conclude that he might have agreed with his fellow classicist, the Irish Jesuit priest John Chetwode Eustace, that Guarino Guarini and Filippo Juvara, the

246

principal architects of Turin's palazzi and churches, were too baroque in preferring

> the twisted, tortured curves and angles of Borromini, to the unbroken lines and simple forms of antiquity. Novelty, not purity, and *prettyness* instead of majesty, seem to have been their sole object. Hence, this city does not . . . present one chaste model, one single grand specimen in the ancient style, to challenge the admiration of travelers. Every edifice . . . , whether church or theatre, hospital or palace, is encumbered with whimsical ornaments, is all glare and glitter, gaiety and confusion. In vain does the eye seek for repose, the mind long for simplicity. Gilding and flourishing blaze on all sides, and we turn away from the gaudy show, dazzled and disgusted.[79]

It would have been remarkable if Jefferson had expressed approbation of Guarini's churches of Santissima Sindone and San Lorenzo. A man of his own times, he doubtless agreed with his bitter critic and fellow American, Theodore Dwight, that these early eighteenth-century churches "had nothing remarkable, except the non-descript barbarisms of their cupolas."[80]

Because Jefferson had a letter of introduction to the abbé Deleuze, a professor of the academy, he surely visited the University of Turin and the academy and archives.[81] Before the 1790s, the university occupied a position more similar to universities of the Renaissance and to the one that Jefferson was to found in Virginia than to its contemporary institutions. Students were "considered as part of the court, and admitted to all its balls and amusements." According to Eustace, the university was housed in a "most extensive building" of two stories built about an arcaded court; it boasted a library of "more than fifty thousand volumes," a museum noted for its "numerous collection of statues, vases, and other antiquities; . . . a hall of anatomy, admirably furnished, and an observatory." Furthermore, the university was "endowed for twenty-four professors, all of whom gave daily lectures." Associated with, but not a part of, the university was the academy, which enjoyed "a considerable degree of reputation,"[82] and which Jefferson must enviously have contemplated, and felt the irony that the despot-ridden Piedmont should possess a gallery and research library, while the virtuous Commonwealth of Virginia refused to support one.

Apparently the news that an American savant was in the city spread enough to make Jefferson an object of momentary curiosity. Gaudenzio Clerici later wrote him that "the . . . Marquis de Cacciapiatti and his Brother the Chevalier told me . . . of either having seen or having heard the Monsr. de Jefferson was, at the time of their coming thro' Turin, quietly philosofizing in the Capital."[83]

Guarino Guarini. *SS. Sindone*. From Guarini, *Architettura Civile,* 1737

Jefferson engaged a carriage to visit the basilica church of Superga and the royal palazzi of Moncalieri and of Stupinigi. The sight of the mountain of Superga from the banks of the Po is far more compelling than that of Monticello from the Rivanna, but the view from both of those eminences reveals rolling plains to the east and high mountains to the north and west. Since it was, after all, Jefferson who popularized the name Piedmont as an American geographic term, he may have exclaimed over the similarities of terrain, but he made no note of it. The basilica, built both to commemorate Piedmontese success in breaking the French seige of 1706 and to serve as a royal mausoleum, was a monument to be looked at: the scale of its classical portico, curved interior, forest of pillars, and carved reredoses is very grand. After this excursion, Jefferson recorded only his irritation over a custom of local coachmen. Although it took an hour for their six-horse carriages to ascend the mountain, on the descent they raced "to prove the brilliance of themselves and of their steeds."

It was not the season for the court to be in residence at Moncalieri when Jefferson visited its Palazzo Reale located on the southern slope of the mountain of Superga. The reddish, rectangular complex with its round corner towers had been rebuilt often, but one could still discern that it once had been a fortress. From observing there lessers members of the house of Savoy and retired courtiers, the sturdy American republican may have thought that the palazzo gave tangible illustration of the diminishing relevance of monarchical institutions.[84]

At Stupinigi the Palazzina di Caccia or hunting lodge had been begun in 1729. Its first and greatest architect was Fillippo Juvara, of whose work little was left after thirty years of additions and rebuilding. His initial concept was that only the king, a few courtiers, and several servants would sleep in the lodge; all others would come from Turin, five or six miles to the north-east, only when invited. The edifice was to be one room thick, giving maximum visual effect for the least expense. Its great room, the *salone centrale,* was a stage for sumptuous entertainment located at the junction of four wings, two of which were devoted to royal apartments and two to banqueting halls. When Jefferson visited Stupinigi, the palazzina had become a palazzo, swollen to accommodate the prolific royal family and their entourage. The *salone centrale* had been raised from its original two stories to three, and it presented on its ceiling a fresco of Diana departing at dawn for the chase and on its roof a huge statue of a stag. Sacheverell Sitwell has endorsed the statement that this room is "one of the most successful of baroque interiors," but Richard Pommer in his authoritative work on Piedmontese architecture makes it clear that, however fine Stupinigi had been to begin with, this room and the building of which it is a part had become quite a different place by the time Jefferson saw it.[85]

Before leaving Turin, Jefferson must have seen and may have inspected some of the nine "hospitals" of the city, which under the auspices of church and state provided many social services in addition to medical and nursing care — "provisions and employment to the poor, education to the orphans, a dowry to unmarried girls, and an asylum to the sick and decayed."[86] One would like to think that one so keenly desirous as Jefferson of support for such services in Virginia visited these hospitals, but his ecclesiastical suspicions may have prevailed. There was no uncertainty, however, of his interest in Turin's straight streets and broad avenues inherited from Roman days, but he did not say that they reminded him of Philadelphia, as did Timothy Dwight. His protégé William Short later declared that Turin was "the handsomest city . . . in Europe on account of regularity" both of streets and of buildings, even though the surface of the latter appeared more "unfinished" than that of English and American urban dwellings.[87]

Jefferson's postchaise brought him to the Albergo dei Tre Re in Vercelli, the rice-market town, on April 19. There he made a clandestine arrangement to see how rough rice was husked and to smuggle some seed rice out of the country on his own person, a daring exploit, since Sardinian law prescribed death as the penalty for exporting seed rice. Ultimately, Jefferson and others determined that the Italian milling process did not differ substantially from that employed in South Carolina, but they decided that the rice grains of the two places were different. Right or wrong, his South Carolina friends to whom he sent seed rice preferred their own variety. After clearing customs and crossing the River Agogna the next day, Jefferson hastened through Novara to Milan, where he lodged at the Albergo Reale.[88]

In Milan, the conte Francisco dal Verme[89] befriended Jefferson and directed him "to those objects which precisely merited most attention" in the Lombard capital during his visit of three nights and two days. An acquaintance of Benjamin Franklin and John Adams and a man who had visited the United States in 1783-1784, dal Verme was good company as well as good cicerone, and Jefferson subsequently sent him from Paris a gift of books which included his own *Notes on the State of Virginia*. Jefferson also directed to dal Verme his protégé, William Short, and several young Americans on their grand tour. It is likely that Jefferson and his new-found Milanese friends, enlightened aristocrats, discussed the controversial reforms decreed by the Hapsburg Emperor Joseph II in the duchy of Milan. The conte dal Verme was a man to Jefferson's liking. Not only did the nobleman tell him about a pendulum odometer suitable for carriages, but he displayed an interest in the scientific and pseudoscientific interests of the age. Making a gracious reference to the marquis de Chastellux's account of his visit to Jefferson at Monticello, dal Verme exclaimed that he would like to "be transported in a Baloon" to America.[90]

Besides dal Verme, Jefferson met also at Milan the conte Luigi di Castiglioni. Unfortunately, the American's visit was so brief that he could not have accepted, as did William Short about eighteen months later, Castiglioni's invitation to inspect his own and his relatives' villas about a dozen miles from the city on the way to the Italian lakes. From Short's account, his patron would have enjoyed such an excursion not only for the beauties of the landscape but also because Castiglioni and his in-laws proved to be "zealous botanist[s] . . ., as much attached to American plants & trees as . . . to Americans, themselves."[91]

In Milan, Jefferson singled out three houses as especially noteworthy: the Casa Candiani, the Casa Roma, and the Casa Belgioioso. The first two of these palazzi he identified as recent works by the architect Appiani, and he stated his preference for the Casa Candiani. However, it was the Palazzo Belgioioso that he described. The architect Martin had built this edifice in the mid-eighteenth century on the Via Moroni, a block north of the Piazza della Scala. Its small cabinet especially pleased Jefferson, because its ceiling was composed of small hexagons, in the center of each of which were painted alternating cameo medallions and classic busts. The salon was worthy of special remark, also, because its walls and floor were sheathed in scagliola work, or marble dust of various colors so reconstituted as to be "scarcely distinguishable from the finest marbles."[92]

It is remarkable that Jefferson did not mention the splendid Palazzo Clerici nearby, built in the first half of the eighteenth century. Among its furnishings, other than fine tapestries, is a large fresco by Giovanni Battista Tiepolo depicting how the chariot of the sun, driven by Mercury, illumines the world.[93] Stendhal observed that the Milanesi believed that the "true patent of nobility" was to build a fine palazzo. Jefferson might have concurred with Stendhal's admiration of the rather academic style of Guiseppe Piermarini's 1778 rebuilding of the La Scala Theater, and even with his acidulous observation that new "social requirements" outmoded interior arrangements appropriate to palazzi built in the sixteenth century by Palladio and his school, and that "the main features of the Italian residence which seems . . . worth preserving are the bedrooms, which are lofty [and] salubrious."[94]

Almost surely Jefferson visited what is now the Brera Gallery, then known as the Palazzo di Scienze, Lettere, e Arti, which housed a college recently secularized and expanded by Emperor Joseph II. A decade before, while a Jesuit institution of "great extent and magnificence," it had a student body of twelve hundred. Built by Francesco Maria Richini in the sixteenth century, it was a typical north Italian collegiate complex located in the central city around a courtyard and enclosed by two stories of arcaded loggias. The great picture gallery for which the Brera has been famous since 1809 was not, of course, there for Jefferson to see, but there were smaller and less notable collections of paintings and sculpture in its halls to give him "much amusement." [95]

The Biblioteca Ambrosiana was in 1787 much the same as it is today. Since Jefferson owned a good copy of Leonardo da Vinci's painting of *St. John* [96] and was fascinated by mechanical contrivances, he may have gone to the Biblioteca to view its celebrated collection of Leonardo's manuscripts and drawings. By the same reasoning, Jefferson may have gone to the refectory of the former Dominican convent attached to the suburban church of Santa Maria delle Grazie to see Leonardo's *Last Supper,* even though that fresco was flaking and fading. Despite Jefferson's anticlerical predelictions, he could not ignore the Duomo of Milan. Without knowing whether he examined its interior with care, we may assume that he climbed to its roof, just as he advised younger Americans to climb to the top of church steeples in order to perceive the scope of cities. The author of the Virginia Statute for Religious Freedom left no doubt, however, of his opinion of the Duomo in particular and of Italian churches in general: "The Cathedral of Milan [is] a worthy object of philosophical contemplation, to be placed among the rarest instances of the misuse of money. On viewing the churches of Italy it is evident without calculation that the same expense would have sufficed to throw the Appenines into the Adriatic and thereby render it terra firma from Leghorn to Constantinople." Jefferson, to be sure, was far from complaining, as did Father Eustace fifteen years later, that the enlightened despot Joseph II had curtailed construction of the Duomo. [97]

When the Ospedale Maggiore of Milan loomed up before him, Jefferson presumably relied upon his guidebook, for he recorded no data even though its secular nature should have guaranteed that he would give free rein to his longstanding interest in prisons and hospitals. Since the fifteenth century, the Ospedale's series of rectangular courts had housed the medical, nursing, and other social services of the duchy. Its buildings were of a transitional style combining Gothic and Renaissance architectural features. Sometimes referred to as Milan's Ca' Grande, there were three hundred rooms in the lazaretto or wards, and another portion of the immense edifice housed twelve hundred working convalescents. Although its rooms were airy and clean, the huge structure was surrounded by a stream whose convenience for sewage purposes must have induced fevers that periodically reduced the number of inmates.

Jefferson, the classicist, probably visited the Basilica di San Lorenzo Maggiore, where the city's major Roman remains were located — sixteen marble Corinthian columns that in the third century A. D. had led to the baths of Roman Mediolanum.[98]

Jefferson resisted the temptation to travel more widely in Italy before returning to France via Genoa. As he wrote to Maria Cosway, "I took a peep only into Elysium. I entered it at one door, and came out at another . . . I calculated the hours it would have taken to carry me on to Rome. But they were exactly so many more than I could spare. Was not this provoking? In thirty hours from Milan I could have been at [Venice]." [99]

Nor did Jefferson go to Vicenza to observe at first hand buildings whose plans Palladio had published and which the Virginian had studied. Instead, he turned south when he left Milan after breakfast on April 23. On his way he resumed his agricultural notes. He broke his journey to visit the former Carthusian monastery, the Certosa di Pavia, about five miles north of Pavia, but he remarked neither on its superb Lombard Romanesque architecture nor on its disestablishment several years earlier by Joseph II. The property of the former abbey had produced an income £1,200 a year, which the emperor diverted to support an expansion of the hospitals and educational institutions of Milan and Pavia.

At Pavia, the traveler lodged at the Albergo Croce Bianco, famous as a hostelry for more than a century. He visited the botanical gardens, but if he went elsewhere in the university of which they are a part, he did not say so. Because of his interest in educational institutions, he may quickly have taken a turn about its "noble library, grand halls for lectures, anatomical galleries, . . . and several well-endowed colleges." Since the fourteenth century, this university had produced great men, such as the scientist Volta and Pietro di Pavia,[100] the early master of the University of Paris.

From Pavia, Jefferson traveled south without significant delay to the Republic of Genoa. Discharging his old equipage and employing a new one, the weary traveler drove into Genoa, which was said to have been sited by Janus so as to face toward both Italy and France. Dissatisfied with his initial lodgings, he moved to the French-style Hôtel du Cerf, where he engaged a room overlooking the Mediterranean. During three days in Genoa he spent almost £80 in sightseeing and transportation.

Thomas Jefferson left a record of having visited only one of the city's famous palazzi and two others in its suburbs. The first of these "lofty palaces"

Torricelli (?). *Citta di Genova,* 1780. Engraved by Giovanni Lorenzo Guidotti

was the Palazzo Marcello Durazzo, then owned by the marchese Jean Luc Durazzo, to whom he brought a letter of introduction from the marchese Jean Baptiste di Spinola, a kinsman of the minister of the Republic of Genoa resident at the court of Versailles, Christoforo Vicenzo di Spinola.[101] Located on the up-hill side of the Via Balbi, this palazzo was thought to have been built in the late sixteenth century by the architect Galeazzo Alessi, reputedly a student of Michelangelo and a contemporary of Palladio; but it was more the work of Bartolomeo Bianci. It had been much improved by the later addition of an eighteenth-century façade, vestibule, and double stairway that was the work of Andrea Taglifici. Although Jefferson urged all Americans who came to Italy to go thither, he noted only a bench with straight legs and a caned seat which particularly pleased him. There was good reason for his taciturnity: his guidebook, Brusco's *Beautés de Génes,* devoted five pages to the palazzo's paintings and contained a fine illustration of the street façade.[102] According to Brusco, the frescos of the Palazzo Marcello Durazzo were executed in the Bolognese style of Jacques Bena, Simone da Pesaro, and Domenico Piola. Of about eight paintings, listed by artists and title, more than one-half were by such famous men as Caravaggio, Agostino and Annibale Carracci, Guido Reni, Rubens, Titian, van Dyke, and Veronese. Remarkably for that day, Brusco's guidebook differentiated between originals and those which were copies or "of the school of" a famous artist. Among the family portraits were several by Hyacinthe Rigaud, who had painted Louis XIV and the young Louis XV.[103]

Inasmuch as Jefferson was acquainted with marchese di Spinola, he may have visited his palazzo and possibly others of the latter's family, which had provided the patrons for Peter Paul Rubens.[104] Spinola once had made courteous inquiries about a possible treaty of amity and commerce between the two republics, and such acts were cherished by the treaty commissioners. The Genoese diplomat's palace near the Palazzo Garibaldi of that day was called the Palazzo *alla catena*. By no means so splendid as the Palazzo Marcello Durazzo, it nonetheless boasted three Guido Renis and a Correggio among about a dozen important paintings.

As a man who not only provided his own house with many windows but amplified them by skylights, Jefferson may have nodded agreement when he read in his guidebook and at the same time observed for himself that the cathedral church of San Lorenzo was "of the rather heavy gothic variety" with "badly lighted aisles." [105] As a resolute anticlerical, he was indifferent to whether the churches of Genoa were, in the words of the Irish Jesuit Father Eustace, guilty of too much "ornament and glare," but he probably agreed they possessed too little of "the first of architectural graces, simplicity." [106] Or, as Fiske Kimball put it, the "free and florid art" of Milan and Genoa awoke in Jefferson no "spiritual affinity." [107]

The Palazzo Doria Pamphili still glistens whitely on the western verge of Genoa. In Jefferson's day it was called the Palazzo Doria Principe. Whether or not Jefferson met in Paris Monsignor Guiseppi Doria Pamphili who had served as Papal Nuncio at Versailles in the early 1760s,[108] his failure to mention this "earliest" and "most familiar" of the "great" palazzi of the city fits into his usual pattern. This celebrated structure had been begun early in the sixteenth century for Admiral Andrea Doria, and it had been embellished with statuary and gardens designed by Fra Montorsoli that reached from the mountains to the shore. Jefferson, with his preference for romantic English-style gardens, presumably found its Renaissance gardens of parterres and geometric forms too old-fashioned. Brusco's *Beautés de Génes* gave this palazzo and its pleasure grounds not only a lengthy description but a full-

Giacomo Brusco. *Palazzo Durazzo, Genoa.*
From Brusco, *Descriptions des beautés de Génes et de ses environs,* 1788

page illustration which emphasized its old-fashioned forecourt and cren-
ellated, bastionlike walls along the sea.[109]

The American minister took pleasure in consulting with the marble-cutters
of Genoa about mantlepieces for future delivery to Virginia. From the crafts-
men he selected Antonio Capellano, whose establishment was situated on
the waterfront near the Ponte della Legne. When William Short passed
through Genoa two years later, Jefferson asked him to obtain prices for
carving several different "chimney pieces" for which he supplied sketches for
the architraves, freizes, and cornices. "You can tell Capellano," said Jefferson,
"that you make the enquiry for the person to whom he furnished notes of
the price of marble in April 1787, and from the circumstance I shall give
him a preference to other workmen, at an equal price."[110] Almost twenty
years later, President Jefferson employed the agency of his Florentine friend
Filippo Mazzei to recruit for work on the United States' capitol two "sculptor[s] of architectural decorations." The senior of these was Guiseppi Fran-
zoni, son of the president of the Academy of Fine Arts at Carrara, and the
other was Giovanni Andrei. The possibility that Antonio Canova might
undertake a commission for a marble or plaster statue of Liberty was soon
discarded.[111]

In visiting the suburbs of Genoa, the Virginia horticulturist was happy to view the extent and excellence of the conte Durazzo's gardens at Nervi to the east and of the principe Lomellino at Sestri to the west. He advised American travelers in later years to visit the former because it possessed a vegetable garden surpassed only by "Woburn farm in England." The flower gardens of the principe Lomellino, he exclaimed, were the "finest I ever saw out of England." [112]

Since there was no continuous road from Genoa to Nice, Jefferson embarked in a felucca on April 28, 1787, even though he was never a good sailor under the best of circumstances. Hardly out of the harbor, the little ship was beset by a fierce southwesterly wind which is called locally the *libeccio,* of which he should have had ample warning from reading Brusco's guidebook. The Gulf of Genoa was put into so nasty a chop that not only did he become "mortally sick," but the captain thought that conditions were severe enough to put into the little fishing port of Noli, about forty miles west of Genoa. Ironically, there was a good road from Genoa as far as Noli.

Abandoning his hopes of continuing a comfortable voyage on a placid sea, Jefferson decided to go on by land, "clambering [up] the cliffs of the Appenine[s], sometimes on foot, sometimes on a mule according as the path was more or less difficult." Two days of alternating between the rich, narrow pockets of coastal plain and the desolate mountains behind them would have been enough to prevent a less determined traveler from reaching Nice on May 1, 1787, and crossing the Var River into France the next day.[113] There were no roads there because Genoa believed she enjoyed military security by not building roads for her western neighbors to use as invasion routes. But Jefferson the physiocrat railed against having to traverse these *corniches,* or mountain pathways usually bearing only pedestrian traffic. Instead of these, he observed, there should be a fine road "along the margin of the sea," which would create "one continuous village" and on which "travelers would enter Italy without crossing the Alps." [114]

It is a paradox that Jefferson, the lover of art and architecture, wrote so little about the fine arts that he enjoyed while in northern Italy. Consultation of his guidebooks and pocket account book, more than of his correspondence or notes about his tour, have made possible this reconstruction of a list of the "worthy" great buildings and collections of paintings that, as he wrote Lafayette, he was in the habit of visiting.[115] Hazardous as is such a speculative synthesis, it is even more hazardous to attempt to attribute to these sights any specific influence on Jefferson. In reality, much of what he saw there was little different from what he already had seen and discussed with his intimates at Paris, or even from what he had learned from books and conversations with Bellini and others at Williamsburg. Except for the marble mantlepieces that he wanted to order for Monticello, the influence of what he saw in northern Italy was subliminal.

Even less direct was the influence of central Italy. Jefferson's interest in the monuments and collections of Rome and Florence has already been noted, but one must also take into account the advice he gave to young Americans to travel there, where he was not able to go. A good case may be made for saying that Jefferson intended to make such a trip himself in the 1790s.[116] At any rate, he made suggestions for travel that have become famous to three young men whom he called his "triumvirate": John Rutledge, Jr., of South Carolina, Thomas Lee Shippen of Pennsylvania, and his own kinsman and diplomatic protégé, William Short.[117] Shippen was called home to America while in northern Italy, but between October 1788 and April 1789, Short and Rutledge made a leisurely tour of Italian places Jefferson never visited: Vicenza, Venice, Rome, Naples and Florence.[118] From Short's letters in particular, Jefferson derived great vicarious pleasure and profit.

Commencing their joint travels at Milan, they visited the "slightly mad" Anglo-Virginian couple, John and Lucy Ludwell Paradise, at Alzano, the seat of their son-in-law conte di Barziza.[119] At Verona, they saw the amphitheater and admired buildings by San Micheli and Pelligrini. Of Vicenza, "the birth place of Palladio," Short wrote: "Most of the best places there were built by him or on his designs. Le Theatre Olympic is considered one of his greatest works. His own house is there also, a modest little building, in its external appearance. . . . I bought there a book offering prints of several of them." After visiting Padua, they descended the Brenta, observing on its banks "superb country houses of almost perfect architecture." [120]

Mrs. Paradise had suspected that the gentlemen's trip to Venice might have some amatory purpose and in a great scene forbade her long-suffering husband and Barziza to accompany Short and Rutledge there.[121] If there were such a purpose, Short never mentioned it to Jefferson. He wrote only that his stay in that "terraqueous town" four rainy days were sufficient for a "general view" of its "manners, usages, and amusements." A week later, he admired the "porticoes" and university at Bologna. The Roman bridge attributed to Vitruvius at Forlì, the arch honoring Augustus at Rimini, the arch to Trajan at Ancona, and the aqueduct at Spoleto provided the two Americans with an introduction to Rome before the dome of St. Peter's swam up out of the Campagna to greet them.[122]

Short and Rutledge arrived at Rome three days before a snowy Christmas. Thanks to a letter of introduction from Jefferson's friend and Lafayette's aunt, Mme de Tessé, they were afforded much hospitality by the cardinal de

Bernis, the French ambassador to the Holy See. De Bernis kept a princely establishment, as befitted both enlightened Rome in the last days of the Ancien Régime and a man who had been a protégé of Mme de Pompadour, the principal minister of Louis XV, and the friend of Casanova. Viewing the great monuments of antiquity, the ceremonial of Papal Christmas mass, and the whirl of Roman society during its Epiphany carnival,[123] Rutledge exclaimed: "Everything seems like enchantment. Wherever I go, I seem to be on fairy ground."[124] Although Short was sorely disappointed to find so little remaining of the ancient Roman capitol on the Campidoglio, he declared that he was so "stunned" by his visit to the Pantheon that for the first time he felt "the effect of the sublime." With an architectural tutor, they observed at the Vatican many of the statues Jefferson had yearned to see: the *Laocoön*, the *Apollo Belvedere, Antinous*, renamed *Meleager*, a sarcophagus and bust of Scipio Africanus, and Raphael's works. Short noted that the Vatican's works by Raphael "are some of the finest remains of his pencil, as the connoisseurs say." Sensibly, he remarked of St. Peter's basilica, "There are many things to admire in detail, but it is the whole which fills everybody with enthusiasm . . ., [a] chef d'oeuvre of modern architecture."[125]

Leaving Rome in early January, Short and Rutledge went to Naples for a stay of almost three weeks. There, Short bought for his patron a mold for making macaroni or spaghetti.[126] At Jefferson's request,[127] he satisfied himself that the laurel at Virgil's tomb was no growing shrub, but only a bough stuck into the ground by guides to fool the gullible.[128] Dutifully filling a lengthy letter with an account of his visit to Herculanaeum, Pompeii and Mount Vesuvius and of the merits of Falernian and Lachrymae Christi wine, he failed to mention the infection he suffered as the result of a Neopolitan amatory indiscretion.[129] In 1806 Short commissioned Rembrandt Peale to paint his portrait with the Greek temple of Paestum in the background,[130] but he did not in fact leave the Bay of Naples to see this great monument some eighty miles to the south.

During their second stay at Rome, Short and Rutledge went to the Villa Borghese, they saw the Pope perform the Ash Wednesday ceremony, and they visited Tivoli and other places in the Roman Campagna. Short much more enjoyed the Villa d'Este than the ruins of Hadrian's villa. Fully conscious that he had seen "a great deal of bad as well as numberless good things," he declared to Jefferson that "on the whole, I have received infinite satisfaction" from visiting Rome.[131] He did not tell him, as Shippen did later, that on one occasion he got a "headache from intemperate dancing" at a ball given at the capitol by a senator for the princess of Saxony.[132]

Professing to be thunderstruck by the realization that he would be at least a month late in returning to his tasks at the Paris embassy, Short persuaded Rutledge to abbreviate their visit to Florence and then to go posthaste to Genoa, instead of returning to Milan.[133] The two young men stayed with friends of Filippo Mazzei at Florence, Adamo and Giovanni Fabbroni. Although Short recited to Jefferson the glories of the city, its palazzi, its paintings and its statues, they did not linger. Nor did they stop at Pisa to avail themselves of their hosts' offer to present them to the grand ducal court which was in residence there.[134]

Perhaps the most important contribution that Short and Rutledge made to Jefferson's understanding of the fine arts was Short's judicious opinion that Americans could indeed profit from the study and even from the acquisition of works of art.[135] Jefferson adhered to this view before going to France, as we have seen, but in his memorandum for Shippen and Rutledge he advised that "Painting [and] Statuary [are] Too expensive for the state of wealth among us. It would be useless therefore, and preposterous, for us to make ourselves connoisseurs of those arts. They are worth seeing, but not studying." [136] It is well known that Jefferson did not follow his own advice in this and in many other instances. At almost the same time that Short wrote to him of the continuing benefits to be derived from paintings, Jefferson commissioned John Trumbull to have made copies of portraits of Francis Bacon, John Locke and Isaac Newton,[137] and he authorized Filippo Mazzei to commission copies from the Uffizi Gallery's portraits of Columbus, Amerigo Vespucci, Cortez and Magellan.[138] It is fair to conclude that Short's opinion strengthened Jefferson's reverting to his original belief that it was worthwhile for him to acquire some paintings, especially those of historical personages.

Though Short often fed back to the illustrious their own opinions, he sometimes improved their phraseology. Nowhere did Jefferson quite so well describe his and Short's preference for architecture over painting and sculpture, as when Short said, "It keeps under [control] . . . what might otherwise become a passion with me . . . a love of pictures and statues." [139]

If there be evidence of the influence of Italy's fine arts upon Thomas Jefferson, it is to be found in three places: in the houses that he built for himself at Monticello and Poplar Forest; in the capital city that he helped build for the nation; and in the university that he built for his fellow citizens' enlightenment.

It would be excessive to claim for the palazzi of Genoa, with their use of hillside basements for service functions, any influence on the way that Jefferson arranged the housekeeping rooms in the basement of Monticello. There are many prototypes for the piazzas with which he terminated the wings of the Monticello he rebuilt, without claiming for the Palazzo Marcello Durazzo any special kinship. But it is undeniable that Monticello did become more of an Italian palazzo than it had been. Besides indebtedness to Palladio's writings and to British architectural writers of the neo-Palladian and classical Roman school, French influences usually are claimed for the remodeling of the house, but Jefferson himself designated the north and south porches as piazzas, a term which he may have popularized for American usage,[140] just as he did the geographical term piedmont. Despite Jefferson's annotated derivation from Palladio of so many of the details of Monticello, that residence is nevertheless an amalgam of all that he had read and all that he had seen.

When Thomas Jefferson placed his paintings and statues at Monticello, they were unusual, if not unique, in America as to kind, variety and manner of display. And well they might be, since their collector roundly condemned "artificial canons of criticism" and set as his standard for such works of art "only ... whether it gives me pleasure, whether it is animating, interesting, [or] attaching." [141] However, one must conclude that, however personal his criteria, he was by no means immune to the trend of his times. The collection of art and antiquities enjoyed international vogue; yet the practice was especially Italian because of the archaeological excavations at Herculanaeum, Pompeii and Rome, and because Italian princes of both church and state were in a preferred position in the race for such ancient treasures. Although Jefferson had seen few of these, William Short wrote to him about many more, along with shrewd comment on the competitiveness and sources of revenue of such collectors as the Pope and Prince Borghese.[142] Jefferson's own desire to rebut Buffon's views on animal species in the New World led him to write sections of his *Notes on the State of Virginia* about the native fauna, and although he did display at Monticello at least one marble statue in the classical style, *Ariadne,* he more emphasized a collection of fossilized bones and of American Indian artifacts.[143]

Surely it is not too speculative to attribute to the universities of **Turin,** Milan and Pavia some influence on Jefferson's plans for the University of Virginia. His first designs for the latter called for a large square cortile, surrounded by arches on piers and punctuated by pavilions — suggesting a subtle kinship to Pavia's smaller, but similar courts. The derivation of the rotunda from the Pantheon at Rome is well known, but many forget that its great room originally was ringed by one-story columns in pairs, instead of the gigantic, two-story ones there between the 1890s and 1970s.[144] Because the use of columns in pairs had been introduced from Italy to France and because this was a practice that Jefferson seems to have observed more in northern Italy than in any other place that he visited, the latter's influence must have been paramount.

Jefferson hung at Monticello only one painting which was on the list of desiderata which he had compiled before going to Europe — the Biblical scene "Jeptha leading his daughter Lelia to be sacrificed." [145] He possessed about sixty portraits, or biblical or historical scenes, and no landscapes. His interest in portraits of the founders of America developed after going to Europe, and in actuality this shift in taste resulted in the acquisition of more originals and fewer copies. [146] Among the portraits other than those of the family were Mather Brown's *John Adams,* [147] Joseph Boze's *Lafayette,* [148] Joseph-Siffrede Duplessis' *Franklin* (long thought to be by Jean-Baptiste Greuze), [149] Robert Edge Pine's *Madison,* [150] Trumbull's *Thomas Paine,* [151] and Joseph Wright's *Washington.* [152]

There was no piece of statuary among Jefferson's collection that was approximated on his early want-list. Instead, he had a baker's dozen of portrait busts (seven of which were by Houdon) of such worthies as John Adams, [153] Tsar Alexander, [154] Franklin, [155] Hamilton, [156] Andrew Jackson, [157] John Paul Jones, LaFayette, [158] Madison, [159] Napoleon, [160] Turgot, and Voltaire. [161] In addition, there was his own bust by Giuseppe Ceracchi, the rival of Canova. Two original works of sculpture of considerable merit were the great multi-color marble pedestal which Mme de Tessé presented to Jefferson as a farewell gift [162] and a marble reclining statue of Ariadne. [163]

As Fiske Kimball commented almost sixty years ago, Jefferson indeed deserves to be considered "the first American connoisseur and patron of the arts." [164] And it was an Italianate décor that he gave to his mountaintop villa. At Monticello, he planted a few Lombardy poplars that he cherished as the tree of liberty. [165] Later, he was to cause double rows of poplars to be set between the president's house and the capitol at Washington. [166] From the piano nobile of Monticello, Jefferson could look past paintings and statuary through arcaded piazzas and columned porticoes upon scenes which, if they were not Elysian nor those of the Roman Campagna, were at least an arcadian Piedmont.

Notes

1. Dumas Malone, *Jefferson and His Time,* 5 vols. (Boston: Little, Brown, 1948–), 1: 53, 73-74, 78. See also Helen Cripe, *Thomas Jefferson and Music* (Charlottesville: The University Press of Virginia, 1974), pp. 6, 14, 88.

2. Malone, *Jefferson,* 1: 285. See also Charles Bellini to Jefferson, Feb. 13, 1782, *The Papers of Thomas Jefferson,* ed. by Julian P. Boyd *et al.,* 19 vols. (Princeton: Princeton University Press, 1950–), 5: 150 (hereafter cited as *Papers*).

3. Jefferson to Bellini, Sept. 30, 1785, in *Papers,* 8: 569.

4. François-Jean, marquis de Chastellux, *Travels in North America in the Years 1780, 1781 and 1782,* trans. and ed. by Howard C. Rice, Jr., 2 vols. (Chapel Hill: University of North Carolina Press, 1963), 2: 390.

5. William Short to John Hartwell Cocke, July 8, 1828. Cocke Papers, University of Virginia, Charlottesville, Va.

6. Jefferson, "Statues, Paintings, &c.," Notebook for Building Monticello, *c.* 1770-1782. Coolidge Collection of Jefferson Papers, Massachusetts Historical Society, Boston, reproduced in facsimile in Fiske Kimball, *Thomas Jefferson, Architect,* ed. with new introduction by Frederick D. Nichols (New York: Da Capo Press, 1968), pl. 79. See also E. Millicent Sowerby, *The Library of Thomas Jefferson,* 5 vols. (Washington: Government Printing Office, 1952-1959), 4: 389-399. Polymedes was a 7th century B.C. sculptor from Argos whose best known work was in the shrine of the Pythian Apollo at Delphi. Spence's work was published at London by R. Dodsley in 1749. Of the nineteen other books on art and sculpture that Jefferson sold to the Library of Congress in 1815, thirteen were printed before 1787. Though he recorded their price, he did not note the date he purchased them (Sowerby, *Library,* 4: 389-399).

7. Jefferson, "Statues, Paintings, &c" in Kimball, *Jefferson, Architect,* pl. 79. Fiske Kimball expanded this list, as does the present author, by adding to it from a somewhat later memorandum the subjects Belisarius, Prodigal Son, Susanna and Curtius and the artists Hogarth and Hayman, for which see his "Jefferson and the Arts," *Proceedings of the American Philosophical Society, 137* (July 1943), 241-243. Marie Kimball summarized this in her *Thomas Jefferson,* 3 vols. (New York: Coward-McCann, 1943-1950), 1: 154, as did Eleanor D. Berman in her *Thomas Jefferson and the Arts* (New York: Philosophical Library, 1947), p. 77. Jefferson's titles for these works are placed in quotation marks.

8. Hayman is perhaps as well known as the teacher of Thomas Gainsborough as for his own work. Emmanuel Bénézit, *Dictionnaire critique et documentaire des peintres, sculpteurs, dessinateurs et graveurs . . .,* 9 vols. (Paris: Librairie Grund, 1957), 4: 621-622.

9. There are numerous treatments of this subject, such as those by Giovanni Battista Tiepolo and Sebastiano Ricci. Massimo Pallotino, ed., *Encyclopedia of World Art,* 15 vols. (New York: McGraw-Hill, 1966), 14: pl. 61, and Bénézit, *Dictionnaire,* 7: 218. The story of Seleucus appears to be a confused reference to the 3rd century B.C. struggle between the widow of Antiochus II, Berenice, and her stepson Seleucus II.

10. Paolo della Pergola, *The Borghese Gallery*

in Rome, trans. by M. E. Stanley (Rome: Libreria della stato, 1952), p. 6. See also Richard Cocke, *Pier Francesco Mola* (Oxford: Clarendon Press, 1972), *passim.*

11. Luitpold Dussler, *Raphael: A Critical Catalogue of his Pictures, Wall Paintings and Tapestries* (London and New York: Phaidon, 1971), pp. 101, 104-106.

12. Pallotino, *Encyclopedia,* 12: pl. 377. See also Piero Torriti, "I fiamminghi a Genova," and Franco Sborgi, "Il ritratto a Genova . . ." in *La pittura a Genova e Liguria,* 2 vols. (Genova: Sagep Editrice, 1971), 2: 41-50, 63, 301-304, 316.

13. Bénézit, *Dictionnaire.*

14. Della Pergola, *Borghese Gallery,* pp. 41, 48.

15. Bénézit, *Dictionnaire,* 7: 348.

16. Bénézit, *Dictionnaire,* 7: 348. Rosa's contemporary Mola, among many others, painted a version of this subject which is in the Hermitage, Leningrad, Cocke, *Mola,* p. 47.

17. Della Pergola, *Borghese Gallery,* pp. 50, 103. See also Samuel Edwards, *Peter Paul Rubens: A Biography of a Giant* (New York: David McKay, 1973), p. 140.

18. Bénézit, *Dictionnaire,* 6: 748.

19. Joseph Fattorusso, *Florence . . .,* no. 3 in Medici Art series (Florence: Fattorusso, 1937), p. 255.

20. Fattorusso, *Florence,* p. 199. Bénézit, *Dictionnaire,* 1: 749.

21. Pallotino, *Encyclopedia,* 7: 18.

22. Pallotino, *Encyclopedia,* 7: pls. 164, 167. Fattorusso, *Florence,* p. 255.

23. Fattorusso, *Florence,* p. 255.

24. Germain Bazin, ed., *The History of World Sculpture* (Greenwich, Conn.: New York Graphic Society, 1968), p. 151. See also Pallotino, *Encyclopedia,* 7: 18.

25. Maurizio Calvesi, *Treasures of the Vatican* (Cleveland: Skira—World Publishing Co., 1962), pp. xiv, xvi, 125, 190.

26. Calvesi, *Treasures,* pp. xv, 125; Bazin, *History of World Sculpture,* p. 180.

27. Della Pergola, *Borghese Gallery,* p. 6. Pallotino, *Encyclopedia,* 7: 324.

28. Bénézit, *Dictionnaire,* 1: 45; Bazin, *History of World Sculpture,* p. 161.

29. Pallotino, *Encyclopedia,* 7: 330, 331, pl. 164.

30. Bazin, *History of World Sculpture,* p. 161 Pallotino, *Encyclopedia,* 7: 328, pls. 164, 167.

31. Kimball, *Jefferson, Architect.*

32. In chronological order these were: Bernard Mayo, *Jefferson Himself: The Personal Narrative of a Many-Sided American* (Boston: Houghton Mifflin, 1942); Marie Kimball, *Thomas Jefferson,* 3 vols. (New York: Coward-McCann, 1943-1950); and Dumas Malone, *Jefferson and His Time,* 5 vols. (Boston: Little Brown, 1948–).

33. See for example, Jefferson to Clérisseau, June 2, 1786; Jefferson to Trumbull, Oct. 13, 1786; Jefferson to Mme de Tott, Nov. 29, 1786; in *Papers,* 9: 602, 10: 460, 431, 554; John Trumbull, entry for Aug. 10, 1786 in *Autobiography,* ed. by Theodore Sizer (New Haven: Yale University Press, 1953), p. 107, and Jefferson, *Papers,* 10: 252n, 454n; and Jefferson to James Barbour, Jan. 19, 1817, *Writings of Thomas Jefferson,* ed. by Andrew A. Lipscomb and Albert E. Bergh, 20 vols. (Washington: Thomas Jefferson Memorial Association, 1903), 19: 242.

34. Helen D. Bullock, *My Head and My Heart: A Little History of Thomas Jefferson and Maria Cosway* (New York: G. P. Putnam's Sons, 1945), *passim.*

35. Jefferson to William Wirt, Nov. 12, 1816, in *Writings of Thomas Jefferson,* ed. by Paul L. Ford, 10 vols. (New York: G. P. Putnam's Sons, 1899), 10: 61.

36. Jefferson to Trumbull, Aug. 30, 1787, in *Papers,* 12: xxxiv, 69.

37. Thomas Jefferson, *Notes on the State of Virginia,* ed. by William Peden (Chapel Hill: University of North Carolina Press, 1954), p. 149.

38. Jefferson, "A Bill for the More General Diffusion of Knowledge" and "A Bill for Establishing a Public Library" in *Papers,* 2: 526-535, 544-545.

39. Benjamin H. Latrobe to Jefferson, Aug. 13, 1807, *The Journal of Latrobe, Being the Notes and Sketches of an Architect, Naturalist and Traveler in the U.S. from 1796 to 1820* (New York: D. Appleton, 1905), pp. 141-144.

40. Jefferson to Maria Cosway, Apr. 24, 1788; in *Papers,* 13: 104. See, for example, a less complete quotation and discussion by Merrill D. Peterson, *Thomas Jefferson and the New Nation: A Biography* (New York: Oxford, 1970), pp. 351-352.

41. Jefferson to Mme de Tott, Feb. 28 and Apr. 5, 1787; Mme de Tott to Jefferson, Mar. 4, 1787; in *Papers,* 11: 187-188, 198-199, 270-273.

42. James A. Bear, Jr., "The Furniture and Furnishings of Monticello," *Antiques Magazine,* 105 (July 1972), 118, 120; and *Report of the Curator to the . . . Thomas Jefferson Memorial Foundation* for 1974 (Charlottesville, 1975), pp. 12-13. See also Kimball, *Jefferson, Architect,* p. 86. See also Marie Kimball, *Thomas Jefferson,* 3: 114, 323-324; Marie Kimball, *The Furnishings of Monticello* (Charlottesville: Thomas Jefferson Memorial Foundation, 1940), pp. 7-13.

43. Jefferson to Bellini, Sept. 20, 1785; in *Papers,* 8: 568-569.

44. Jefferson to Pierre Charles L'Enfant, Apr. 10, 1791; *Writings,* ed. Lipscomb and Bergh, 7: 162.

45. [Anonymous] *Guide pour le voyage d'Italie en poste, nouvelle édition, avec les changements dans les postes, et augmentées de routes des états de terre ferme de S. M. le Roy de Sardaigne . . .* (Genoa: Gravier, 1793; xerox copy at Virginia Polytechnic Institute & State University, Blacksburg). No copy of the 1786 Turin edition which Jefferson may be presumed to have bought in that city can be found. See Sowerby, *Library of Jefferson,* 4: 128.

46. [Carlo Bianconi] *Nouva guida di Milano, per amanti delle belle arte e delle sacre e profane antichita milanesi . . .* (Milan: Nella Stamperia Sirtori, 1787; microfilm at Virginia Polytechnic Institute & State University, Blacksburg). This is probably the same edition bought by Jefferson in Milan and included in his sale to the Library of Congress in 1815. See Sowerby, *Library of Jefferson,* 4: 133.

47. [Giacomo Brusco] *Description des beautés de Génes et de ses environs, ornée de différentes vues, de tailles douce: et de la carte topographique de la ville* (Genoa: Yvres Gravier Libraire, 1781; copy at University of Virginia Library, Charlottesville). This is the same edition bought by Jefferson in Genoa and included in his sale to the Library of Congress in 1815. See Sowerby, *Library of Jefferson,* 4: 132-133.

48. Jefferson to Maria Cosway, July 1, 1787, in *Papers,* 11: 519.

49. Jefferson to Thomas Mann Randolph, Sr., Aug. 11, 1787, in *Papers,* 12: 2-22.

50. Jefferson to Jay, Oct. 23, 1786, Jay to Jefferson, July 27, 1787, in *Papers,* 10: 484-485, 11: 627-628.

51. Jefferson to Maria Cosway, July 1, 1787, in *Papers,* 11: 519. Jefferson did not charge these expenses to the government.

52. Jefferson to William Short, Mar. 15 and Apr. 12, 1787, in *Papers,* 11: 214-215, 287. See also Jefferson, entry for May 1, 1787, Account Book, p. 457, xerox copy at University of Virginia Library. James A. Bear, Jr., curator of Monticello, kindly made available to the author his transcript of the Account Book. There are minor variations between the author's and Bear's reading of entries, particularly in place names, which here are modernized. The spelling of major French and Italian cities is anglicized here; minor place names are given the national spelling of today.

53. Jefferson to Mme de Tott, Apr. 3, 1787, in *Papers,* 11: 271.

54. Jefferson to Lafayette, Apr. 11, 1787, in *Papers,* 11: 283.

55. Jefferson to Thomas Mann Randolph, Sr., Aug. 11, 1787, in *Papers,* 11: 20-22.

56. Entries for Feb. 28 and Apr. 10, 1787, in Jefferson Account Book, pp. 454, 456.

57. Jefferson to Grand and Grand to Jefferson, Feb. 28, 1787, in *Papers,* 11: 184-185.

58. De Scarnafis to the American commissioners, Feb. 2, 1785, in *Papers,* 7: 632-633. Jefferson used the French version of the minister's name, which in its Italian version was Filippo Ottone Ponte, conte di Scarnafiggi. He had been a student of Giambattista Beccaria at the University of Turin. See Antonio Pace, "Benjamin Franklin and Italy," *American Philosophical Society Memoirs,* 47 (Philadelphia: American Philosophical Society, 1958): 95 *passim.* See also Philip Mazzei, *Memoirs of the Life and Peregrinations of the Florentine, Philip Mazzei, 1730-1816,* trans. Howard Mararro (New York: Columbia University Press, 1942), p. 326.

59. Jefferson to the abbés Arnoux and Chalut, Apr. 12, 1787, in *Papers,* 11: 287-288. The abbés provided entrée to André Sasserno at Nice, who in turn gave Jefferson letters for the abbé Deleuze at Turin and conte Francisco dal Verme at Milan. Mazzei considered Arnoux and Chalut "very ignorant" (*Memoirs,* p. 293). Deleuze may be a misreading of conte Giuseppi Angelo Saluzzo of the Turin Academy of Sciences. Pace, "Franklin," p. 63.

60. Jefferson to Mazzei, Apr. 4, 1787, in *Papers,* 11: 266-267. Mazzei's opus is *Recherches Historiques et Politiques sur les États-Unis . . . par un Citoyen de Virginie* (Paris: Froulle libraire, 1787).

61. Gaudenzio Clerici to Jefferson, Mar. 5, 1787, Jefferson to Clerici, Aug. 15, 1787, and Aug. 31, 1788, Clerici to Jefferson, Jan. 20, 1789, in *Papers,* 11: 199-200, 12: 38-39, 13: 553-554, 14: 475.

62. Jefferson to Short, Apr. 7, 1787, in *Papers,* 11: 280-281.

63. Jefferson to L'Enfant, Apr. 10, 1791, *Writings,* 7: 162; Jefferson also recommended that tourists buy, in addition to the guidebooks he used, Joseph Addison's *Remarks on Several Parts of Italy* (London, 1745 and later eds.), but he did not buy until 1788 the copy of Addison's book which he sold to the Library of Congress (Sowerby, 4: 128-133). See also Jefferson, "Hints to Americans Travelling in Europe" in *Papers,* 8: 268.

64. Entry for Apr. 10, 1787, in Jefferson Account Book, p. 456. See also Jefferson to Mazzei, Apr. 4, 1787, to Short, Apr. 7, 1787, in *Papers,* 11: 266-267, 280.

65. Entries for Apr. 6-10, 1787, "Notes of a Tour into the Southern Parts of France . . . and Northern Italy, in the year, 1787" in *Papers,* 11: 429-430, 463n; entry for Apr. 13, 1787, in Jefferson Account Book, p. 456. He visited the commandant, the director of the Royal Tobacco Factory, a banker, and two merchants.

66. Jefferson to Short, Apr. 12, 1787, in *Papers,* 11: 287; entries for Apr. (14-)15, 1787, in Jefferson Account Book, p. 456; *Italie en poste,* pp. 48-49; Karl Baedeker, *Italy: Handbook for Travellers . . ., First Part: Northern Italy,* 9th remodeled ed. (Leipzig: Karl Baedeker, 1892), p. 80.

67. Jefferson to Maria Cosway, July 1, 1787, in *Papers,* 11, 520.

68. Entry for Apr. 14, 1787, "Notes of a Tour," in *Papers,* 11: 432. His description of Saorgo to Mrs. Cosway was based on this. His spelling of "Saorgio" has been modernized.

69. Jefferson to Maria Cosway, July 1, 1787, in *Papers,* 11: 520. Earlier he had begged in his famous "My Head and My Heart" letter that she paint Niagara Falls, the junction of the Potomac and the Shenandoah, the Natural Bridge of Virginia, and Monticello; Jefferson to Maria Cosway, Oct. 12, 1786, in *Papers,* 10: 445.

70. Baedeker, *Italy: Handbook,* p. 80, and the author's observations.

71. Cosway Collection, College of Santa Maria della Grazie, Lodi, Italy.

72. Entry for Apr. 15, 1787, "Notes of a Tour," in *Papers,* 11: 433; entry for Apr. 16, 1787, in Jefferson Account Book, p. 456; *Italie en poste,* pp. 48-49.

73. Entries for Apr. 15-16, 1787, "Notes of a Tour," in *Papers,* 11: 433-434; and for the same dates, Jefferson Account Book, p. 456. See also *Italie en poste,* pp. 48-49; and American [Theodore Dwight], *A Journal of a Tour in Italy in the year 1821* (New York: A. Paul, 1824), p. 466; Baedeker, *Italy: Handbook,* p. 55; and Richardson Wright, *The Story of Gardening* (New York: Dodd, Meade & Co., 1934), pp. 270-296.

74. Entries for Apr. 16-19 in Jefferson Account Book, p. 456. Quotation from entries for Apr. 17-18, "Notes of a Tour," in *Papers,* 11: 435. See also Charles Pinot-Duclos, *Voyage en Italie, ou Considerations sur l'Italie* (Paris: Buisson, 1791), p. 324. Pinot-Duclos made his trip in 1767 when he was historiographer of France and *secretaire perpetuelle* of the Académie Française. Professor Raimondo Luraghi kindly furnished the author with comments on wines in the course of conducting him to eighteenth-century places of interest at Turin.

75. Entries for Apr. 17-19 in Jefferson Account Book, p. 456; Maria Cosway to Jefferson, July 9, 1787, in *Papers,* 11: 568-569 and 464n. He visited two bankers and two or three merchants, whom he questioned concerning the potential market for American tobacco, whale oil, and fish products.

76. De Scarnafis to the American commissioners, Feb. 2, 1785, in *Papers,* 7: 632-633. See also Jefferson to C.W.F. Dumas, Dec. 9, 1787, to John Adams, July 1, 1787, in *Papers,* 12: 407, 11: 516; and Malone, *Jefferson,* 2: 40-49.

77. Entry for Apr. 17, 1787, in Jefferson Account Book, p. 456; Sowerby, 4: 128-133.

78. Pinot-Duclos, *Voyage,* p. 325.

79. Eustace, *A Classical Tour through Italy,* 8th ed., 3 vols. (London: T. Tegg, 1841), 3: 166-169. Based on travels in 1802, the book is marred by Francophobia but it accurately reflects the classicists' distaste for both the Gothic and baroque.

80. Dwight, *Journal,* p. 466. See also Seigfried Geidion, *Space, Time and Architecture: The*

Growth of a New Tradition (Cambridge: G. P. Putnam's Sons, 1941), pp. 55-61; and Richard Pommer, *Eighteenth Century Architecture in Piedmont: The Open Structure of Juvarra, Alfieri & Vittone* (New York: New York University Press, 1967), pp. 7-11. For Dwight's unflattering view of Jefferson, see Theodore Dwight, *The Character of Thomas Jefferson as Revealed in His Writings* (Boston: Weeks, Jordan & Co., 1839).

81. Pinot-Duclos, *Voyage,* p. 325; "Notes of a Tour" in *Papers,* 11: 464n.

82. Eustace, *Tour,* 3: 167-169. The academy also served as a preparatory school for civil and military service. It is thought that Jefferson became an honorary member of the academy.

83. Clerici to Jefferson, July 14, 1787, in *Papers,* 11: 585-586.

84. Entry for Apr. 18 in Jefferson Account Book, p. 456; "Notes of a Tour" in *Papers,* 11: 435; Short to Jefferson, Oct. 18, 1788, in *Papers,* 14: 27; Eustace, 3: 167-169; Baedeker, *Italy: Handbook,* p. 38. Quotation is from Pinot-Duclos, pp. 328-329. When Pinot-Duclos went to Superga, one of the carriages overturned and was dragged, but without human injury. The palazzo is now a military academy.

85. Entry for Apr. 18, 1787, in Jefferson Account Book, p. 456; Hugh Thomas, "Stupinigi," *Great Houses of Europe,* ed. by Sacheverell Sitwell (London: Spring Books, 1970), pp. 198-205; Pommer, *Architecture in Piedmont,* pp. 61-78.

86. Eustace, *Tour,* 3: 106.

87. Dwight, *Journal,* pp. 465-466; Short to Jefferson, Oct. 18, 1788, in *Papers,* 14: 27.

88. "Notes of a Tour" in *Papers,* 11: 22-24; entries for Apr. 19-20, 1787, in Jefferson Account Book, pp. 436-437.

89. Count Francesco dal Verme (1758-1832) belonged to an ancient and wealthy family of Verona and Milan. He had friends in high places—conte Ludovico di Belgioioso (1728-1801) sometime Austrian ambassador at London and his uncle by marriage Giacomo d'Aquino, principe di Caramanico, sometime Neapolitan ambassador at London. See Elizabeth Cometti, trans. and ed., *Seeing America and Its Great Men: The Journal and Letters of Count Francesco dal Verme, 1783-1784* (Charlottesville: The University Press of Virginia, 1969), pp. xi-xv, 97.

90. Entries for Apr. 23-24, "Notes of a Tour,"

in *Papers,* 11: 437, 464; dal Verme to Jefferson, Feb. 12, 1788, in *Papers,* 12: 587-588; Jefferson to dal Verme, Aug. 15, 1788, in *Papers,* 13: 42-43; and entries for Apr. 20-23, 1787, in Jefferson Account Book, p. 456. It is not known whether Jefferson acted upon his memorandum to visit a certain abbé de Regibus, or whether he meant instead to visit the brothers Reycends who were book dealers. Pace, *Franklin,* p. 12.

91. Short to Jefferson, Oct. 28, 1788, in *Papers,* 14: 41-43.

92. "Notes of a Tour" in *Papers,* 11: 437; World War II bomb damage of the area was very heavy but much has been restored. The Casa Belgioioso should not be confused with the present Gallery of Modern Art, formerly the Villa Reale and before that the Villa Belgioioso which was built by Leopold Pollak in 1790 for conte Ludovico Barbiano de Belgioioso. The latter sold it to the Cisalpine Republic for Napoleon's Eugene Beauharnais' use. Baedeker, *Italy: Handbook,* pp. 95, 96, 110; Ente Provinciale per il Turismo de Milano, *Tutta Milano* (Milan, 1969), p. 38.

93. D'Ancona, Paolo, and Leoni, Francesca. *Tiepolo in Milan: The Palazzo Clerici Frescoes,* trans. by Lucia Krasnik (Milan: Edizioni del Milione, 1956). See also Ente Provinciale Turismo, *Milano* (Milan, 1969?), p. (9); *Tutta Milano,* p. 39.

94. Marie Henri Beyle [Stendhal], *Rome, Naples and Florence,* trans. Richard N. Coe (New York: Braziller, 1960), pp. 36-38, 337.

95. Jefferson to George Wythe, Sept. 16, 1787, in *Papers,* 12: 127. See also Baedeker, *Italy: Handbook,* p. 97; Touring Club Italienne, *L'Italie en une volume,* ed. Cesar Chiodi, Les Guides Bleus series (Paris: Hachette, 1952), p. 45.

96. Marie Kimball, *Jefferson,* 3: 114.

97. "Hints to Americans Travelling in Europe" in *Papers,* 13: 272; see also *Papers,* 13: 268; Eustace, *Tour,* 3: 125, 128-129.

98. Eustace, *Tour,* 3: 130-131.

99. Jefferson to Maria Cosway, July 1, 1787, in *Papers,* 11: 519-520.

100. Entries for Apr. 23-24, 1787, Jefferson Account Book, p. 456; Eustace, 111, 107-109; Baedeker, *Italy: Handbook,* pp. 141-144; and *Italie en Poste,* p. 33 and pl. 19.

101. *Papers,* 11: 464; Pace, Franklin, pp. 96, 97, 114-115, 119 identifies Minister Resident

Spinola as Christoforo Vincenzo Spinola. Julian P. Boyd *et al.* in Jefferson's Papers identifies him as Jean-Baptiste de Spinola. It may be that the latter was in fact the person to whom Jefferson was intended to present the letter of introduction.

102. Entries for Apr. 24-28, 1787, in Jefferson Account Book, p. 456; "Notes of a Tour" in *Papers,* 11: 440-441, 464; Jefferson to Short, Feb. 28, 1789, in *Papers,* 14: 598. See also Brusco, *Gênes,* p. 11; quotation from Eustace, 3: 82-97, 102. He presented letters of introduction from Le Clerc to the bankers Bertrand, Ricard & Bramerel and from Guide to the merchant Aimé Regny.

103. Brusco, *Gênes,* pp. 51-56; John Canaday, *The Lives of the Painters,* 4 vols., New York: W. W. Norton, 1969), 4: *passim.* See also Editors of Réalités, *Great Houses of Italy* (New York: G. P. Putnam's Sons, 1968), pp. 128-131.

104. Edwards, *Rubens,* p. 106.

105. Brusco, *Gênes,* pp. 110, 111.

106. Eustace, *Tour,* 3: 82-97, 102.

107. Fiske Kimball, *Jefferson, Architect,* p. 38.

108. Pace, *Franklin,* p. 50.

109. Brusco, *Gênes,* pl. 1 *et seq.* See also *Great Houses of Italy,* pp. 124-127.

110. Jefferson to Short, Feb. 28, 1789, in *Papers,* 14: 598.

111. Benjamin H. Latrobe to Filippo Mazzei, Mar. 6, 1805 and Latrobe to Jefferson, "Report," Mar. 23, 1808, quoted in Saul K. Padover, *Thomas Jefferson and the National Capital . . . 1783-1818* (Washington: Government Printing Office, 1946), pp. 355-358, 400, 507, 510.

112. "Hints for Americans Travelling in Europe" in *Papers,* 12: 270.

113. Jefferson to Martha Jefferson, May 4, 1787, in *Papers,* 11: 348; Brusco, *Gênes,* p. 7; Pinot-Duclos, Voyage, pp. 11-18. Twenty years before, Pinot-Duclos' boat had suffered somewhat the same fate.

114. "Notes of a Tour" in *Papers,* 11: 441-443. Spanish possession of an enclave between Genoa and Nice, 1598-1713, left a residue of calculated insularity.

115. Jefferson to Lafayette, Apr. 11, 1787, in *Papers,* 11: 283.

116. Jefferson to Clerici, Aug. 15, 1787, in *Papers,* 12: 38; Malone, *Jefferson,* 2: 234-235.

117. Jefferson to Shippen, Sept. 29, 1789, in *Papers,* 13: 642.

118. Short to Jefferson, Oct. 2 nd 18, 1788, in *Papers,* 13: 655, 14: 25-28. This tour is summarized in Malone, *Jefferson,* 2: 149-150, and Edward Dumbauld, *Thomas Jefferson, American Tourist* (Norman: University of Oklahoma Press, 1946), pp. 144-147.

119. Short to Jefferson, Oct. 28 and Nov. 19, 1788, *Papers,* 14: 41-44, 272-273. Quotation is from Short to William Nelson, May 30, 1788, Short Papers, Library of Congress, Washington, D.C. See also Archibald B. Shepperson, *John Paradise & Lucy Ludwell of London and Williamsburg* (Richmond: Dietz Press, 1942), pp. 182-187, 312 *et seq.*

120. Short to Jefferson, Nov. 29, 1788, in *Papers,* 14: 310-314.

121. Shepperson, *John Paradise,* pp. 346-350.

122. Short to Jefferson, Dec. 23, 1788, in *Papers,* 14: 377-383.

123. Short to Jefferson, Dec. 31, 1788, in *Papers,* 14: 405-406. See also Sir Marcus Checke, *The Cardinal de Bernis* (New York: W. W. Norton, 1958), *passim.*

124. Rutledge to Jefferson, Dec. 31, 1788, in *Papers,* 14: 404.

125. Short to Jefferson, Dec. 23, and 31, 1788, in *Papers,* 14: 381-383, 405-406.

126. Short to Jefferson, Feb. 11, 1789, in *Papers,* 14: 540.

127. Jefferson to Short, in *Papers,* 14: 540 and Sept. 20, in *Papers,* 13: 621.

128. Short to Jefferson, Feb. 17, 1789, *Papers,* 14: 571-575.

129. Short to Rutledge, Feb. 3, 1790, Gilpin Papers, Historical Society of Pennsylvania, Philadelphia, Pa.

130. Short to Rembrandt Peale, Nov. 8, 1806, Short Papers.

131. Short to Jefferson, Feb. 25, 1789, in *Papers,* 14: 591.

132. Shippen to Jefferson, Mar. 16, 1789, in *Papers,* 14: 666.

133. Short to Jefferson, Nov. 29, 1788, Feb. 25 and Mar. 23, 1789, in *Papers,* 14: 312, 590-592, 607-608.

134. Giovanni Fabbroni to Jefferson, Mar. 25, 1789, in *Papers,* 14: 701.

135. Short to Jefferson, Dec. 23, 1787, and Feb. 25, 1789, in *Papers,* 14: 381-382, 591-592.

136. Jefferson, "Hints to Americans Travelling in Europe," enclosure to Rutledge, June 19, 1788, in *Papers,* 13: 269.

137. Jefferson to Trumbull, Jan. 12 and Feb. 15, 1789, and Trumbull to Jefferson, Mar. 10, 1789, in *Papers,* 14: 440, 561, 634. See also James A. Bear, Jr., *Report of the Curator* for 1959 (Charlottesville: Thomas Jefferson Memorial Foundation, 1957), p. 11.

138. Boyd *et al.,* note on Jefferson's copies of pictures in the Uffizi Gallery, *Papers,* 15: xxxv-xxxvi, 425.

139. Short to Jefferson, Nov. 29, 1788, in *Papers,* 14: 312.

140. Sarah N. Randolph, *The Domestic Life of Thomas Jefferson* (New York: Harper & Brothers, 1871), p. 334, designates the north and south porches as piazzi and the west and east porches as porticoes. William A. Lambeth and Warren H. Manning, *Thomas Jefferson as an Architect and a Designer of Landscapes* (Boston and New York: Houghton Mifflin Co., 1913), pl. II, designates the north and south porches as piazzi and the west and east porches as porches. Kimball, *Jefferson, Architect,* p. 59, designates the north and south porches as loggias.

141. Jefferson to Wirt, Nov. 12, 1816, *Writings,* ed. by Ford, 10: 61.

142. Short to Jefferson, Jan. 14, 1789, in *Papers,* 14: 449-451.

143. Bear, *Report of the Curator* for 1960, pp. 14-16, and for 1961, pp. 17-19.

144. Frederick D. Nichols, *Thomas Jefferson's Architectural Drawings* (Boston: Massachusetts Historical Society, 1960), pp. 8-9, pl. 27. See also Nichols, "The Rotunda," *University of Virginia Alumni News, 43* (Mar. 1953), 5-7.

145. Marie Kimball, *Jefferson,* 3: 326-327. The want list's title varies from this. He also had an oil on canvas of "Susanna and the Elders" after Coypel, instead of a copy of Rubens' treatment of this theme. He had an engraving after the 1790 painting by Frederick Rehberg instead of an oil copy after Salvator Rosa's treatment of Belisarius. Bear, *Report* for 1958, p. 8.

146. Bear, *Report* for 1957, p. 7, and for 1959, pp. 19-20.

147. Trumbull to Jefferson, Mar. 6, 1788, and Boyd *et al.,* note, *Papers,* 12: xxxvii, 514; Marie Kimball, *Jefferson,* 3: 116-117, Bear, *Report* for 1965, p. 9.

148. Short to Jefferson, Dec. 28, in *Papers,* 18: 356. Illustration in *Papers,* 5: 185. Marie Kimball, *Jefferson,* 3: 323.

149. Marie Kimball, *Jefferson,* 3: 323; Bear, *Report* for 1957, p. 6, for 1959, p. 19, and for 1965, p. 9. Valade to Jefferson, *Papers,* 12: 54.

150. Marie Kimball, *Jefferson,* 3: 327. Bear, *Report* for 1961, pp. 16-17.

151. Boyd *et al.,* "Thomas Jefferson and Thomas Paine, 1788" in *Papers,* 14: xxxvi-xxxviii, 328. Bear, *Report* for 1957, pp. 6-7.

152. Jefferson to Martha Jefferson Randolph, June 27, 1790, in *Papers,* 16: 577-578, and Boyd *et al.,* note, in *Papers,* 18: 36. Marie Kimball, *Jefferson,* 3: 323.

153. Bear, *Report* for 1959, p. 11. This was a plaster copy of the bust by John Binon, c. 1818.

154. Bear, *Report* for 1961, facing p. 12.

155. Boyd *et al.,* note, Short to Jefferson, Nov. 7, 1790, in *Papers,* 18: 10. Bear, *Report* for 1958, p. 8, and for 1961, facing p. 12.

156. Bear, *Report* for 1961, facing p. 12.

157. Bear, *Report* for 1959, p. 9.

158. Boyd *et al.,* note, Short to Jefferson, Nov. 7, 1790, in *Papers,* 18: 10: Bear, *Report* for 1958, p. 8, and for 1961, facing p. 12.

159. Bear, *Report* for 1959, p. 9.

160. Bear, *Report* for 1964, p. 10, and for 1961, facing p. 12.

161. Boyd *et al.,* note, Short to Jefferson, Nov. 7, 1790, in *Papers,* 18: 10. Bear, *Report* for 1958, p. 8, and for 1961, facing p. 12.

162. Boyd *et al.,* "The Comtesse de Tessé's Parting Gift to Jefferson, 1788" in *Papers,* 18: xxxiii-xxxiv, 37, facing 269. Bear, *Report* for 1961, facing p. 12. See also Alfred L. Bush, *The Life Portraits of Thomas Jefferson* (Charlottesville: Thomas Jefferson Memorial Foundation, 1962), pp. 27-29.

163. Bear, *Report* for 1961, facing p. 12.

164. Fiske Kimball, *Jefferson, Architect,* p. 86.

165. Concerning this conceit, see Victor Alfieri, *Memoir of the Life and Writings of Victor Alfieri,* 2 vols. (London: H. Colburn, 1810).

166. Jefferson to Thomas Munroe, Mar. 21, 1803, quoted in Saul K. Padover, *Thomas Jefferson and the National Capital* (Washington: Government Printing Office, 1946), p. 300. See also Malone, *Jefferson,* 4: 47-48.